S. MORRIS EAMES

Pragmatic
Naturalism

AN INTRODUCTION

SOUTHERN ILLINOIS UNIVERSITY PRESS
Carbondale and Edwardsville

FEFFER & SIMONS, INC.
London and Amsterdam

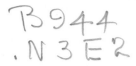
Library of Congress Cataloging in Publication Data

Eames, Samuel Morris
    Pragmatic naturalism.

    Includes bibliographical references and index.
    1. Naturalism. 2. Pragmatism. 3. Philosophy,
American—19th century. 4. Philosophy, American—20th
century. I. Title.
B944.N3E2   146   76-58441
ISBN 0-8093-0802-9
ISBN 0-8093-0803-7 pbk.

For Ivan Lee and Anne

CONTENTS

Preface

THIS WORK is intended to be a guide to the leading ideas of a movement in philosophy which has been called by the various names of "pragmatism," "instrumentalism," "experimentalism," "empirical naturalism." For reasons explained in the text I prefer to call the movement "pragmatic naturalism." This movement involves many thinkers, and I have not tried to include all the people who have made significant contributions to its development. I have limited the treatment to the four scholars who are generally regarded as the founders of the movement: Charles Sanders Peirce, William James, George Herbert Mead, and John Dewey. It is hoped that this introduction will stimulate the reader to become acquainted with the original writings of these men, and at the end of each division in the book there is a suggested order of readings of some of their most important works. The selection of the order of readings is directed by the order of topics of each section and by the experience of teaching students about this movement.

I wish to express appreciation to my former teachers at the University of Chicago, Charles Hartshorne and Charles Morris; seminars I had with these scholars afforded me the foundation upon which my later work proceeded. Various people read the manuscript at different stages of its writing and to them I am grateful for their criticisms and suggestions: Herbert W. Schneider, Lewis E. Hahn, Joe R. Burnett, Arthur W. Wirth, Charles A. Lee, Joseph S. Wu, John A. Broyer, Cho Yee To, Conrad J. Koehler, Ivan Lee Eames, Thomas M. Messer, Bruce and Marlene Jannusch, Romona

Ford, and Rudolph Vanterpool. Jo Ann Boydston and Polly V. Dunn of the Center for Dewey Studies, Southern Illinois University, gave expert aid in helping me with source materials. I am indebted to Willis Moore and David S. Clarke of the Department of Philosophy and to the Graduate School, Southern Illinois University, for generous aid and grants. I am grateful to Pamela Seats and Elaine Stonemark who typed the manuscript. My wife, Elizabeth Ramsden Eames, is so closely affiliated with my life and work that any statement of my gratitude to her would be inadequate.

S. Morris Eames

Carbondale, Illinois
September 1976

Introduction

IT IS OFTEN SAID that America came of age intellectually with the appearance of the pragmatic movement in philosophy. This philosophy originated in the late nineteenth- and early twentieth-century writings of Charles Sanders Peirce and William James. These men, each in his special way, developed the pragmatic method of thinking, thus setting the stage for later developments in this new way of philosophy. Two other thinkers, George Herbert Mead and John Dewey, made original contributions to the movement. Although scores of other thinkers made significant contributions to this philosophical approach, it is now generally agreed that Peirce, James, Mead, and Dewey are its intellectual founders and chief exponents.

Pragmatic naturalism is an American movement, but its philosophical and scientific roots go deep into the past. All of the founders were grounded in the history of philosophy, and each man selected and rejected certain ideas and methods from the philosophical and scientific heritage. What each rejected he criticized as distorting the nature of experience or as blocking the road to inquiry; what each selected from the past does not emerge as a reordering and a reclassification of traditional concepts. Their selection of historical concepts about experience and of methods of inquiry are critically analyzed and transformed in order to reflect experience more adequately and to guide human practices more intelligently.

The term "pragmatic naturalism" is chosen to designate the numerous and varied writings of Peirce, James,

Mead, and Dewey; the selection of this term is made with historical awareness, for it was James who associated the movement with the name of "pragmatism." Peirce, however, appears to be the originator of the term. Peirce did not like the way some philosophers interpreted the pragmatic method, and in his later years Peirce sought to correct any misapprehension about his use of the method by adopting the new name of "pragmaticism," a term he thought "ugly enough to be safe from kidnappers." When Dewey published his *Logic: The Theory of Inquiry* in 1938, he wrote: "The word 'Pragmatism' does not, I think, occur in the text. Perhaps the word lends itself to misconception. At all events so much misunderstanding and relatively futile controversy have gathered about the word that it seems advisable to avoid its use."[1] The term "pragmatic" has been misinterpreted to mean "practical" in a vulgar sense, in the sense of success at any cost to the moral and aesthetic aspects of experience, and of narrow and short-range consequences of an idea or action which ignores the broad and long-range consequences to the welfare of humanity.

Dewey adopts the term "naturalism" instead. The meaning of "naturalism" as used here is arrived at by a denotative method explained below under the topic, "The Fullness of Experience" (pt. 1, sec. 4). "Pragmatic" refers to a method of thinking, and is treated below in part 2. Since there are other types of naturalism, it seems justifiable to use the term "pragmatic naturalism"[2] to describe the common themes of this movement from Peirce through Dewey.

Sometimes the terms "instrumentalism" and "experimentalism" are employed to designate this philosophical movement.[3] These terms have suffered from the same kinds of misrepresentation as has the term "pragmatism." "Instrumentalism" is sometimes described in the narrow sense as synonymous with "expedience," with getting things done in an executive way, with practical concerns irrespective of moral considerations. The most extreme meaning assigned to "instrumentalism," from the moral point of view, is that of making human beings subservient or instrumental to the desires of some person with selfish or narrowly conceived purposes; for instance, instrumentalism is misrepresented to mean that human beings are instrumental to some individual's accumulation of money. In other contexts "instrumentalism" is taken to signify that "the value of knowing is instrumental to the knower."[4] None of the foregoing meanings assigned to instrumentalism are applicable to pragmatic naturalism. "Instrumentalism" as employed by the pragmatic naturalists has a technical philosophical meaning. The term does not refer to expedience in the way of getting things done or to personal factors or disposition in the experience of knowing. "Instrumentalism" refers to the role which knowledge plays in human experience, the role of mediating between an indeterminate situation (the point at which an answer to a problem is unknown) and the eventual solution of a problem (the point at which the answer to a problem becomes known). In other words, the knowing process is instrumental to solving problems, to moving from the *unknown* to the *known*; on this view, the use of "instrumentalism" is so obvious that one wonders why its philosophical meaning became clouded with so many misconceptions.

The term "experimentalism" has fared no better than the terms "pragmatism" and "instrumentalism" as a reliable name for this movement. Originally, "experimentalism" was intended to designate the experimental way of thinking, a method of thinking in which suggestions and hypotheses are entertained as possible solutions to problems. The term "experimentalism" is meant to designate the new way of inquiry which grew out of the methods of modern scientific investigators. When a person thinks hypothetically, he makes a connection in thought between the hypothesis entertained and the consequences to which that hypothesis leads. Experimental thinking is a kind of logical manipulation of meanings which make up the mind. This kind of thinking starts with simple operations like these: If I put this chemical compound with some other chemical compound, what is likely to happen? If an atomic bomb is dropped somewhere upon the earth, what is likely to happen to human life and to the environment? In modern scientific thinking the role of the hypothesis is central in the process of attaining knowledge, and pragmatic naturalists have sometimes employed the term "experimentalism" to indicate that their method of thinking grows out of the experience of the scientific investigator.

It is easy to see why critics became alarmed with the introduction of the term "experimentalism" to designate a new philosophy. The term was given meanings which were never intended by the pragmatic naturalists. For instance, medical scientists experiment with animals for humane purposes, and it is easy for critics of pragmatic naturalists to make the inference that the latter advocate experimenting with human beings in the manner of the Nazis under Hitler. Because so many misconceptions gathered around the term "experimentalism," the term gradually disappeared from the writings of the pragmatic naturalists.

Some writers describe pragmatic naturalism as a movement rather than as a systematic philosophy.[5] As a movement, pragmatic naturalism is a growth, a development over several decades. Leading ideas and methods were modified and refined as they were critically analyzed and thought through. Pragmatic naturalists were influenced by each other and by their critics and followers. Peirce and James were classmates at Harvard and their friendship continued until the end of their lives. Mead and Dewey were colleagues at the University of Michigan and later at the University of Chicago, and the influence of each upon the other is admitted by both. The development of each pragmatic naturalist's thought, of their interactions with each other and with their critics, has been studied by several scholars.[6]

The founders of pragmatic naturalism by psychological temperament and intellectual conviction are not system builders. All of them believe that intellectual activity begins with specific doubts; they do not believe, as Descartes did, that universal doubt is possible; that is, they think that it is psychologically impossible to doubt everything at once. While one is doubting some specific belief, other beliefs are taken for granted. When some specific intellectual problem occurs, it must be treated in the context of a specific situation. Thus, pragmatic naturalism is "problem oriented"; over the years, however, almost every philosophical problem known to man has been studied by one or another of the pragmatic naturalists. The leading ideas of these men can be clustered together into a philosophy which is held together by a pervasive philosophical method; thus it seems appropriate to designate their views as a distinct philosophical movement.

Whereas pragmatic naturalists are not system builders in the old metaphysical sense of that term, all of them are concerned with the problem of the unity of knowledge. Peirce thinks that philosophers should try to unify human knowledge, but this unifying procedure must be developed from the ground up, not from a priori principles, as has been done in previous metaphysical systems. James maintains that the human organism strives to balance all of its functioning parts, that the human consciousness tries to unify itself, but this unification of all life and conscious activity must proceed from empirical not speculative premises. Mead and Dewey think that philosophizing has two primary functions, those of analysis and synthesis, and here synthesis means synthesis of the conclusions of modern science. Furthermore, all of the pragmatic naturalists think that beliefs about the world, as warranted by science, and beliefs about values must be brought into a working harmony and unity.

The founders of pragmatic naturalism were dynamic,

resourceful, and creative men. A brief glimpse into their intellectual backgrounds, interests, and achievements reveals some aspects of their varied and richly complex lives. Charles Sanders Peirce (1839–1914) was the son of Benjamin Peirce, a professor of mathematics at Harvard. The leading men of science, particularly astronomers and physicists, were entertained in the Peirce home, and since Benjamin Peirce was a man of wide cultural interests, many of the foremost literary people of the day visited him. Early in his life Charles Peirce began reading philosophy under the guidance of his father, and while yet in his teens he was reading Hobbes, Kant, and other great thinkers. At eight years of age Peirce was studying chemistry, and at twelve he had his own laboratory. The experience of Peirce in the scientific laboratory during much of his life is often pointed to as the source of many of his ideas in the philosophy of science and in his philosophy generally. Peirce was graduated from Harvard in 1859 and from the Lawrence Scientific School of Harvard in 1863. He was employed by the Coast Survey, working with this group intermittently for over thirty years. Under Louis Agassiz he studied zoological classification. He began teaching as a graduate student, but for some reason which is not entirely clear, he was not asked to join the faculty at Harvard. He was made a Fellow of the American Academy of Arts and Sciences in 1877 and later became a Fellow of the National Academy of Sciences.

In 1879 Peirce was appointed lecturer on logic at the Johns Hopkins University, and he spent several years there. His courses in logic reflected his own deep interest in the subject. He taught modern formal logic, Boolean algebra, mathematical reasoning, the logic of relations, and on many of these topics he made significant contributions. One of Peirce's students at Johns Hopkins was John Dewey, who later attributed to Peirce many of the insights for his own theory of inquiry.

There are many sides to Peirce; he wrote on many topics ranging all the way from the problems of logic to those of ethics and metaphysics. One of his most notable contributions is a comprehensive and complex theory of signs and symbols. He developed new categories for his own metaphysical system, and a new vocabulary to express them. He was interested in religious ideas, particularly the idea of God as a metaphysical concept. He emphasized the importance of science in education, and perhaps his vehement insistence on the inclusion of logic in the graduate program at Johns Hopkins was one factor leading to his dismissal there in 1883.[7]

Peirce began to write on scientific and philosophical problems at an early age.[8] His published writings are in the form of articles and reviews, but a large number of his writings remained unpublished during his lifetime. Although James and Dewey publicly credited Peirce with great originality, it was not until the publication in six large volumes of the *Collected Papers of Charles Sanders Peirce* (1931–35)[9] that interest in his philosophy gained momentum. Two more volumes of his writings were subsequently published in the same series.[10]

When Peirce died in 1914, he was without funds. His widow sold some of his papers to Harvard University, and when she died in 1939, many of the remaining papers of Peirce were taken from the house and burned by the new owners of the property, a tragic loss of part of the writings of one of America's greatest philosophers. Estimation of the importance of each of the pragmatic naturalists varies with the interest and evaluation of their devoted students. Philip P. Wiener, one of the many admirers of Peirce, has said that Peirce is "the most versatile, profound, and original philosopher that the United States has ever produced."[11]

William James (1842–1910) was the son of Henry James, the elder, and the brother of Henry James, the famous novelist. Henry James, the elder, had a lasting influence upon his children. When William James's son compiled his father's letters, he inserted a note about the father of these two famous brothers: "He was not only an impressive and all-pervading presence in the early lives of his children, but always continued to be for them the most vivid and interesting personality who had crossed the horizon of their experience."[12]

The first nineteen years of William James's educational experience were haphazard; he was shifted from one private school to another. He went back and forth to Europe, studying in London, Paris, Boulogne-sur-Mer, Geneva, and Bonn, where he spent a summer studying German. He entered the Lawrence Scientific School in 1861 where he met Peirce, and this was the beginning of a long friendship. In 1864 he entered the Harvard Medical School, and in 1865 he accompanied Agassiz to Brazil on a zoological expedition. In 1867 he went to Germany to study physiology and to use the laboratories there. His health began to fail; he suffered from back trouble, his eyes bothered him, and the illness, nervous in part, troubled him off and on for the rest of his life. He returned to Cambridge in November 1868 and received his medical degree in June 1869. His scientific training was important to his intellectual development, but it should not be overlooked that he had an interest in philosophical problems which developed simultaneously with his interests in science.

In 1872 James was appointed instructor of psychology at Harvard, where he remained on the faculty for thirty-five years until he resigned in 1907. The course which he taught in physiological psychology was moved into the philosophy department in 1877 and was called "psychology." James began to attract worldwide attention for his theories in psychology; in 1890 he published a two-volume work, *The Principles of Psychology*. The work was an immediate success. James was a popular lecturer, always in demand, and from 1893 to 1899 he gave many lectures, some of which compose the volume, *The Will to Believe and Other Essays*.

He was asked to give the Gifford Lectures in Edinburgh, and the five lectures composing the first half of the series were delivered in the spring of 1901. He returned to Harvard to teach for a year, and then went back to Edinburgh to deliver the second half of the lectures in 1902 as *The Varieties of Religious Experience*, a work which Peirce praised as his best.

In 1905 James attended an International Congress of Psychology in Rome; there he delivered his famous paper on consciousness, which he read to the group in French. At the congress he received an enthusiastic response, particularly from the younger philosophers. He returned to the United States, and in 1906 delivered a series of lectures at the Lowell Institute, later repeating them at Columbia University, and these were published under the title of *Pragmatism*. In April 1908, James again went abroad where he had been asked to give the Hibbert Lectures in England; these were published as *A Pluralistic Universe*. During his lifetime James was given many national and international honors.

By 1910 James's strength was giving out; again he went to Europe, hoping that the health baths would restore his energy. He realized, however, that his life was drawing to a close, so he came back to his home in Chocorua, New Hampshire, where he died. William James is one of America's best-loved philosophers, and his biographer and student, Ralph Barton Perry, has written that "he was modern, in the sense that is applicable to all ages. Hence it is that James is a philosopher of the twentieth century as well as of the nineteenth, and that much of his thinking, as well as of the man himself, seems formed in the fashion of today. And were he alive now, he would, as always, be looking to the future."[13]

George Herbert Mead (1863–1931) was the son of a professor of theology, Hiram Mead, who taught at the Oberlin School of Theology. Mead entered Oberlin College in 1879 and graduated in 1883. According to his son and biographer,

the formative years of Mead's life were influenced by the
English historians, Thomas Babington Macaulay and
Thomas Buckle, and by the American historian, James Lath-
rop Motley. The curriculum at Oberlin was composed
chiefly of the classics, rhetoric and literature, moral philosophy, mathematics, and "a smattering of elementary
science—chemistry and botany."[14] Mead was especially interested in Wordsworth, Shelley, Carlyle, Shakespeare,
Keats, and Milton. The historians "opened the door to him
for the magnificent drama of conflicting social forces," and
the classical portion of the curriculum at Oberlin gave Mead
a broad cultural background. His biographer says: "His later
knowledge of poetry and literature was phenomenal; he also
kept up his technique in the classics for much of his technical work and read in the original Greek and Latin to a very
late period."[15]

At Oberlin, Mead met Henry Castle and his sister Hel-
en, whom Mead later married. Mead and Henry Castle became lifelong friends. During their college days they worked
through the problems of their inherited Puritan theology
and the dogmas of the church. Their dialogue concerning
religious and philosophical topics which began in college extended over a long period.

After graduation from Oberlin, Mead spent the next few
years teaching and working as a surveyor. In 1887 he entered
Harvard, studying mostly with Josiah Royce and William
James, and graduated in 1888. During the year and the fol-
lowing summer, Mead was the tutor of James's children.
From 1888 to 1891 he spent some time studying in Berlin
and Leipzig. John Dewey employed Mead at the University
of Michigan, and later Mead went to the University of
Chicago when Dewey became head of the Department of
Philosophy, Psychology, and Pedagogy in 1894.

At Chicago, Mead developed the original and creative
social psychology and the philosophical outlook for which
he became famous. In addition to the many articles pub-

lished during his lifetime, the more important sources of Mead's work appear in the form of notes taken by students in his classes and published posthumously. Two of these significant works are *Mind, Self, and Society* (1934) and *The Philosophy of the Act* (1938). Another work, *Movements of Thought in the Nineteenth Century* (1936), is an edited compilation of notes taken by students. In 1930 Mead was accorded the highest honor his philosophical colleagues in the United States could bestow upon him when he was elected to give the Carus Lectures. Mead had planned to revise these lectures for publication in a book, but he died before this was accomplished. The lectures were edited and published later under the title he suggested, *The Philosophy of the Present* (1932).[16]

Mead's influence primarily was upon the students who attended his classes at the University of Chicago. He had an impact upon a whole generation of sociologists and philosophers, and since the publication of his lectures in books, his importance has continued to grow. Not the least among those influenced by Mead were his colleagues; one of these with whom he had a long association and friendship was John Dewey, who expressed in generous terms his indebtedness to Mead whom he regarded as "a seminal mind of the very first order."[17]

John Dewey (1859–1952), a native of Vermont, graduated from the University of Vermont in 1879. His philosophical interests were not awakened until he took a course in physiology in which a text written by Thomas H. Huxley was used. Dewey says that the course gave him "a sense of interdependence and interrelated unity that gave form to intellectual stirrings that had been previously inchoate."[18] After his graduation Dewey taught in the public schools of Pennsylvania and Vermont and spent some time reading philosophy under the guidance of his former university professor, H. A. P. Torrey. During his first year after graduation from college, Dewey wrote an article and sent it to William T. Harris, leader of a group of St. Louis Hegelians and editor of the *Journal of Speculative Philosophy*. Harris encouraged Dewey to make philosophy a career, and in 1882 he entered Johns Hopkins University to do graduate work. At Johns Hopkins, Dewey studied psychology with G. Stanley Hall, who had been to Germany to study with Wilhelm Wundt. He studied logic with Charles Peirce, but at the time was not impressed with Peirce's emphasis upon mathematical logic. At Johns Hopkins, Dewey met George Sylvester Morris, the Hegelian scholar, who was teaching there on a year's leave of absence from the University of Michigan. Morris and Dewey became friends, and when Dewey graduated, Morris employed him at Michigan.

Dewey's career at Michigan began in 1884 and lasted until 1894, with one year away at the University of Minnesota in 1888–89. Morris died in 1889, and Dewey returned to Michigan as professor and chairman of the department. During the Michigan years Dewey worked out many of the germinal ideas of his philosophy. In 1887 he published a text, *Psychology*, which was revised in 1889, and again in 1891.[19] Several other books were published during the Michigan years. While at Michigan, Dewey employed James H. Tufts, a recent Yale graduate, and when Tufts left for Germany to continue his studies, Dewey then employed George Herbert Mead.

A turning point in Dewey's life came in 1894 when he was asked to become head of the Department of Philosophy, Psychology, and Pedagogy at the University of Chicago. His appointment contained an agreement that he could initiate a laboratory school in education, a venture which was especially exciting to Dewey, for it gave him opportunity to test some of his philosophical ideas in educational practice. Tufts had already joined the Chicago faculty when Dewey arrived; Mead went to Chicago with Dewey. This combination of men, along with Addison W. Moore and Edward Scribner Ames, became the nucleus of "The Chicago

School" in philosophy. William James was so impressed with the work done at Chicago that he referred to it as a "real school" with "real thought."[20]

Dewey left Chicago in 1904 to join the faculty at Columbia University in New York City. At Columbia he exerted a powerful influence, and his students carried his ideas into many parts of the world. Dewey himself traveled abroad at various times in his career to give lectures and to advise on matters of education. In 1919 he gave a series of lectures in Japan, published as *Reconstruction in Philosophy*. During the years 1919–21, he gave many lectures in China. He traveled to countries in Europe, and visited Russia, Turkey, and Mexico. He was honored by giving the Carus Lectures in 1922, published as *Experience and Nature* (1925); and by giving the Gifford Lectures in 1929, published as *The Quest for Certainty* (1929). Dewey retired from active teaching in 1930, but in the following decade some of his most important books and articles were written. During his lifetime he wrote 40 books and almost 700 articles which were published in 140 journals.[21]

Attempts have been made to interpret the pragmatic naturalists against the background of the frontier life of America and to maintain that their philosophical ideas stem from these pioneer social and economic origins. Emphasis upon the "practical" by Peirce, James, and Dewey, allusions to "making nature over" by James, encouragement of innovation and invention by Mead and Dewey, and a commitment to a certain view of individualism by all of them are said to be reflections of the frontier social and economic life in their intellectual outlooks. Whereas it is true that the foregoing terms are frequent in the writings of these men, the meanings of the terms have special philosophical significations. "Practical" is used in a special philosophical context in which an empirical and experimental test is given to ideas and hypotheses; the observational consequences of hypotheses are their "practical effects." "Making nature over" is used in the context of an evolutionary view of nature, where making life over, or adaptation, is one of the most important means of human adjustment and survival. Innovation and invention refer to the creativity of new ideas in scientific, social, and philosophical subject matters and methods. The concern of all the pragmatic naturalists for the fate of the individual in a growing corporate society stems from the liberal philosophical influence inherited from European and American thinkers of the last two centuries. The terminologies adopted were attempts to break away from the traditional and to draft new terms with which to describe the scientific and philosophical revolutions of contemporary times.

In the case of Dewey, who lived the longest, who wrote the most, and who engaged in more intellectual controversies, some of the interpretations of the origins of his thought are so extreme that they are absurd. For instance, some claim that Dewey's thought is an expression of Vermont culture, of Yankee folkways, and that his philosophy is founded upon social conditions which emphasize independence and initiative.[22] This kind of sociology of knowledge ignores the intellectual influences which were operating on the American scene during Dewey's lifetime, influences which flowed from European and sometimes Oriental sources, and which were an important part of American intellectual culture.

Unfortunate terminology used by James and Dewey causes others to interpret their philosophies as stemming from the emphasis upon industrial accomplishment and the commercial values which accompany this social and economic way of life. When James said that one must bring out of each word its "practical cash-value," he opened the way for a host of misinterpretations of his views. Dewey also was subjected to this kind of unfortunate interpretation. An example of the kind of criticism stemming from the assumption that pragmatic naturalism is an expression of an industrial society is found in Bertrand Russell who writes: "Dr. Dewey has an outlook which, where it is distinctive, is in harmony with the age of industrialism and collective enterprise."[23] This interpretation of his thought is rejected by Dewey, and he replied to Russell: "Mr. Russell's confirmed habit of connecting the pragmatic theory of knowing with obnoxious aspects of American industrialism, instead of with the experimental method of attaining knowledge, is much as if I were to link his philosophy to the interests of English landed aristocracy instead of with dominant interest in mathematics."[24]

William James once made an observation about one of the theories held by pragmatic naturalists which might be applied to the entire movement. James wrote concerning the history of a theory's career: "First, you know, a new theory is attacked as absurd; then it is admitted to be true, but obvious and insignificant; finally it is seen to be so important that its adversaries claim that they themselves discovered it."[25] Perhaps this statement oversimplifies the current intellectual situation concerning pragmatic naturalism, but at least three dominant trends appear to be taking place. First, some contemporary scholars approach the work of the pragmatic naturalists in a new light; they claim that James and Mead, particularly, have affinities with existential philosophy and phenomenology.[26] Second, there is renewed interest in pragmatic naturalism as a historical movement, and attempts are being made to probe the depths of the movement as a whole and of the contributions of each of its founders in particular.[27] Both Peirce and Dewey have had learned societies named in their honor.[28] The Charles S. Peirce Society and the John Dewey Society are engaged in scholarly undertakings which go beyond historical interests; creative work on the growing edge of contemporary intellectual life is encouraged and supported. There has been established the Center for Dewey Studies at Southern Illinois University, Carbondale. Third, since the pragmatic naturalists are problem oriented, much of the discussion of contemporary philosophical problems draws upon their insights and suggestions.[29] "Pragmatic naturalism" or "pragmatism" may be regarded as names for this historical movement in philosophy; the specific problems which the founders treated, however, persist in contemporary philosophical discussion; in this respect the analyses and ideas put forth by the pragmatic naturalists have an abiding and relevant value.

The creative ideas of the founders of pragmatic naturalism have had significant impact upon all phases of contemporary life, both in America and abroad. A full account of the influence of these men upon philosophers, natural scientists, social scientists, logicians, psychologists, political theorists, moralists, artists, theologians, and educators would take many volumes to describe in detail. Students of intellectual history are currently at work recording and analyzing various aspects of this movement as the ideas of the original thinkers express themselves through myriad patterns in contemporary life and thought.

The present work is intended to be an exposition of the leading ideas of the pragmatic naturalists on the topics treated. An exposition obviously involves a selection and an interpretation of the ideas taken to be representative of each thinker's mature thought, as well as the selection and interpretation of the leading ideas of the movement as a whole. The leading ideas of these pragmatic naturalists are grouped around the broad topics of "Nature and Human Life," "Knowledge," "Value," and "Education," with subdivisions of selected problems. Each philosopher has his special interests, however, and not all of the pragmatic naturalists write to the same extent on the topics selected. For instance, Dewey and Peirce are concerned especially with problems of logic and methodology; James and Mead are concerned especially with problems of psychology and social psychology; and none of the others are as dedicated to the problems of education as is Dewey. In the treatment which follows, the primary contributions of each man to a special topic are emphasized. The common bonds which unite the pragmatic naturalists, however diverse their inquiries, are a general philosophical method and a general philosophical outlook.

Suggested Order of Readings

1. Mead, "The Philosophies of Royce, James and Dewey in Their American Setting," *International Journal of Ethics* 40 (1929–30): 211–31. Reprinted in *George Herbert Mead: Selected Writings*, ed. Andrew J. Reck (Indianapolis: Bobbs-Merrill Company, 1964), pp. 371–91.
2. Dewey, *Philosophy and Civilization* (New York: Minton, Balch & Company, 1931). "The Development of American Pragmatism," pp. 13–35.

PART I

NATURE AND HUMAN LIFE

1. The Influence of Darwin

Charles Darwin's theory of the evolution of natural species had a profound influence upon the pragmatic naturalists. They are concerned with the implications of evolutionary theory for a general view of nature and of human life, for a new theory of knowledge, and for a general theory of value.

The Darwinian revolutionary outlook can be understood best, perhaps, by contrasting some of its features with conceptions of nature and human life which preceded it. At least from the time of Aristotle many people believed that "nature does nothing in vain" and that the species or forms of nature do not change. Although the development of modern science from the time of Galileo had changed much of the knowledge of nature on which these assumptions were based, the views of antiquity and of medieval times persisted. The assumption that natural species are changeless affects not only the general picture of nature but also the kind of knowledge which is possible of natural forms. Before the advent of experimental science the primary logical methods applied to the study of nature were definition and classification. The work of the natural scientist, on this view, consists primarily in classifying all the species of nature in a hierarchical order and in formulating definitions of their "essences," that is, of the universal, necessary, and determinate characteristics of these unchanging forms. Thus, if the forms or species of nature are thought to be unchanging, and if the classifications and definitions of these forms are complete, and believed to be correct, then knowledge built upon these forms is absolute and certain. Once the essences or definitions of the forms are correctly formulated, then the work of the natural scientist is over. The definitions and classifications of all substances from the highest being to the lowest were worked out in elaborate schemes in medieval times. Some medieval thinkers thought that their understanding of nature was complete, and they regretted that future generations would have nothing to learn from observing and studying nature.

Most ancient and medieval philosophers believed, however, that inquiry could be extended beyond the work of the natural scientists. The higher subject matters of learning were believed to be contemplation of God, sometimes conceived as the First Cause and the Last End or Final Purpose of all things in nature. All nature was believed to be moving toward some divine goal or final end. While it was rather common on the Aristotelian scheme of knowledge to think of mathematics and physics as fixed in their subject matters, thus giving inquirers some emotional comfort in the permanence of this kind of knowledge, the real challenge, it was thought, is that of answering two fundamental questions which have always in some way or another challenged the curiosity and imagination of human beings. The ultimate questions, on this view, are: Where did all life, all forms of nature, all natural physical things come from? To what end or purpose are all the creations in nature, including human beings, moving? Failure to give some rational answer to these primary questions, it was held, means a failure of the intellectual enterprise. Interest in a First Cause and a Final End of all creation was said to be a rational speculation, yet the solution of these problems was considered to be on a higher level than the study of natural forms or of the practical affairs of human life. It was often admitted that this kind of intellectual activity "bakes no bread," that is, it is not practical in the sense of controlling nature and of creating a more secure life within nature.

The problem of what is permanent and what is changing in nature has been perplexing from the early inception of the critical method of philosophical and scientific inquiry. Ancient and medieval thinkers observed that change takes place in the individual during its lifetime. For instance, a specific individual living in space and time grows to a mature form and gradually loses this form in death. The growth toward maturity of an individual within a species was often called "generation"; the disintegration of the form of the individual was called "decay." For example, particular horses are born, grow to maturity, and begin gradually to decay until death destroys the particularized form they embody. Thus, it was held that particular individuals within natural species are changing; the important point, however, for the ancient and medieval thinkers was that the form or species does not change; each species is fixed, unchanging and permanent.

While others entertained ideas of evolution before Darwin, it is his place in the history of science to bring previous hypotheses together and to present them in a generalized theory of nature. There are parts of the Darwinian theory which the pragmatic naturalists do not accept without qualification, and they think that intelligence plays a far greater role in human survival in an evolutionary world than Darwin allows. Two central parts of Darwin's theory, however, have had significant impact upon the pragmatic naturalists' conception of nature and of human life. The first of these conceptions is that the forms or species of nature are changing; this is a denial that there are absolutely unchanging forms in nature. Some species may become extinct, as have the dinosaurs; others, as those now living in our present world, may survive.

The second idea of Darwin's of importance for a conception of nature concerns the survival of the various species. Survival of some species takes place by production of millions of progeny, and not all these reproductions survive.

One species survives by consuming other species; mutations occur, environmental conditions change, and some species become extinct. These facts throw doubt upon the view that "nature does nothing in vain," and upon those views of nature which are called "teleological," that is, views which state that each natural species has a purpose or that nature as a whole has a purpose. Darwin's conception of nature points up the precarious existence of all natural forms, including human life. The belief in a changeless nature, in fixed and permanent forms, was shattered by this new conception of nature. Intellectual responses to Darwin's views of nature have varied; some try to harmonize the view of changing forms and species with a belief in a general direction or purpose of all evolutionary change; others deny that there is any purpose or goal involved in the changing species of nature.

All of the pragmatic naturalists were deeply influenced by the idea of evolution in developing their ideas of nature and of human life. Peirce was among the first to show that the older conceptions of science cannot deal adequately with novelties and emergents which occur in an evolutionary world. He holds that the laws of nature themselves have evolved. Peirce thinks that we live in a universe in which chance is real, and he calls this theory of chance *tychism*. Peirce's cosmology, or vision of the world, is one in which the laws of nature are treated as habits of behavior, habits which change and modify through time. The world may be settling down to some regularity, but, as of now, it is far from having an absolute order.[1] The idea of evolution weaves its way into James's thought in two significant ways: he is impressed with the fact that the evolutionary view of nature and human life accounts for the spontaneity and the creativity in human beings; secondly, he is concerned with the adjustment of human beings in an evolving world.[2] Dewey sees the idea of evolution affecting all of nature and human involvement in it. He writes: "Doubtless

the greatest dissolvent in contemporary thought of old questions, the greatest precipitant of new methods, new inten-
tions, new problems, is the one effected by the scientific
revolution that found its climax in the 'Origin of Species.' "[3]

The idea of evolution affected not only the conception
of nature, but also theories of knowledge and of value. What
happens to our beliefs which were thought to be settled and
permanent if the forms of nature upon which those beliefs
are built are changing? Changing species of nature obviously
implies a changing knowledge of them. A description which
is accurate at an early stage of development of a species will
no longer apply to its present form. The description of a
horse, for instance, must change from time to time with the
evolving form of that species through its history. Thus, the
time element becomes important in understanding developmental forms of nature and of human life. Knowledge
regarded as permanent and unchanging because the objects
upon which it is built are regarded as permanent and unchanging no longer fits this new conception of nature. The
experience of knowing needs a new description and analysis,
and, as will be shown later, the concept of truth needs to be
reconstructed in order to be adequate in an evolving world.

The entire field of values also needs reconstruction because of the new conceptions of nature and human life. Ends
and purposes in nature and human experience have long
been associated with values, with what humans seek, with
what makes life worth living. What is the purpose of human
life? What should human beings seek as the ultimate good?
Pre-Darwinian views supplied answers to these questions.
When the ultimate goals of human life, goals which were
thought to possess an ultimate and absolute character, are
questioned because they rest upon inadequate conceptions
of nature and human existence, then we are thrown into intellectual confusion. When a Final or Absolute Good which
was thought to be secure has lost its underpinning, then
where shall we look for goals of living which have meaning-

fulness and produce intellectual and emotional satisfaction?

The disruption in human knowledge and values brought about by the Darwinian conception of nature becomes a primary concern of the pragmatic naturalists. The status and function of human beings in a changing world, where their own species is undergoing change, is a serious problem to which all philosophers and scientists must turn. Human beings are living in an unstable, precarious world, and they must gather all the resources they can muster to survive. We can no longer rest in complacency, secure in our beliefs that nature does nothing in vain and that all the world is moving toward some far-off divine event. No longer can we make inquiries with the view that we are seeking knowledge for the sake of knowledge or for the sake of some intellectual adornment. To rest in a pre-Darwinian intellectual complacency is a sure way of inviting disaster. We must find new ways of dealing with our own existence; we must find new ways of understanding and controlling nature. Knowledge in all fields of natural studies is more important than ever for practical purposes; these practical purposes now take on an ultimate sense, for we are faced with the alternatives of continued existence or of becoming extinct. Our understanding of values, of what is ultimately important, is more vital than ever. Knowledge can no longer be regarded as a luxury; it is a necessity. If human beings are to live and to live well, they must understand the kind of world in which they exist and the kinds of values appropriate to that existence.

2. Accommodation, Adaptation, Adjustment

William James sees the problem of human life in a world of changing forms and species to be one of "adjust or die." For the pragmatic naturalists, adjustment is composed of two processes, radically different in the attitudes and responses they involve. On the one hand, there are many situations in human experience which cannot be changed. We must *accommodate* to them. When we cannot change weather conditions, we accept this situation and accommodate to it. When death comes, whether because of some unplanned cause or because of past mistakes, this process of nature cannot be changed; we must accept it. Trying to escape from the disruptions of life over which we have no control avails nothing, and no amount of wailing and gnashing of the teeth will change some of the distressful situations we must live through and endure. Situations demanding accommodation require a stoical attitude and the acceptance of the hard facts of experience.

On the other hand, there are situations in which some aspects of human experience and nature can be changed; in these situations resignation and the arts of acceptance are not the appropriate attitudes. For instance, we can divert rivers to irrigate the land, and we need not accommodate to the merciless effects of drought. We can control the rivers, and we need not suffer the devastating consequences of floods. Of over two hundred known diseases, we can control all except a few. The process of controlling nature and life is called *adaptation*. Adaptation is the process of manipulating pliable natural processes, of "making life over," and of directing activity to meet human needs. This process of adaptation in pragmatic naturalism is related to the Renaissance writings of Francis Bacon, whose most popular aphorism is "knowledge is power." By this is meant that human beings should turn their energies to understanding and controlling natural processes. The parts of nature which yield to being made over can be turned in the direction of human good.

In contemporary discussion there is a confusion of the terms "accommodation," "adaptation," and "adjustment." Sometimes these terms are taken to be synonymous, but for the pragmatic naturalists each of these terms has a different meaning, and these meanings must be clearly discriminated. Dewey writes: "There are conditions we meet that cannot be changed. If they are particular and limited, we modify our own particular attitudes in accordance with them. Thus we accommodate ourselves to changes in weather, to alterations in income when we have no other recourse."[4] Since most of our accommodations are particular and limited, they do not affect our whole lives; that is, specific situations require specific accommodations. A small loss of money, the departure of a friend, a rain that delays a golf game are instances requiring minor accommodations. Death of a loved one, catastrophic destruction in a war, contracting an incurable disease require deeper and more extensive accommodations. Pessimism usually accompanies situations in which we can do nothing but submit. In most cases, however, there are parts of our lives which are harmonious and adapted; over these parts we have some measure of control, and a partial unity of the self results. It may become the case, however, that we find so many distressing conditions of life flooding upon us that our entire attitude is one of resignation and despair; accommodation is uppermost; the entire self is passive, and a general pessimism results.

There are other situations in which a more active part of the self is free to operate. Again, these situations are particular; that is, they are specific situations in which we feel that we can do something about changing our lives and parts of the world about us. As Dewey says: "We re-act against conditions and endeavor to change them to meet our wants and demands. . . . Instead of accommodating ourselves to conditions, we modify conditions so that they will be accommodated to our wants and purposes. This process may be called adaptation."[5] Conditions we can change are those about which we are optimistic. According to Dewey, the two processes of accommodation and adaptation make up what is called by the more general name, "adjustment."[6] Hence, the pragmatic naturalist is pessimistic about some situations, those which cannot be changed and to which one must accommodate; there is optimism about other situations, those which can be changed and molded to meet human needs.

Often it is said that the pragmatic naturalists place too much emphasis upon adaptation, upon the ability of human beings to change the world and to direct and shape their own destinies. They have been accused of being overly romantic. Furthermore, when the pragmatic naturalists emphasize adaptation, the active process of human adjustment and a process which calls for the employment of human intelligence, they have been accused of having a naïve faith in the progressive development of human life. These criticisms neglect what all pragmatic naturalists have held from the beginning—that there is a precarious aspect to human existence and that human beings survive in a world which is not completely organized and balanced. In a world of change and instability there is no basis for an absolute, fixed mode of life, but neither is there a basis for complete resignation. Although they have been charged with romanticism and a naïve faith in human progress, pragmatic naturalists contend that it is not they but other philosophers who have neglected to take account of the disharmonious, the unbalanced, the unstable, and the conflicting parts of experience. Again, pragmatic naturalists escape the criticism of being overly romantic because they take account of each specific problematic situation in terms of the strictest of disciplines, that is, the discipline of scientific inquiry, and because they pay careful attention to the solution of each problem as it is encountered. For the pragmatic naturalists there is no shortcut to the achievement of harmony, balance, and order in human experience. Harmony is the result of an arduous process of thought and action.

Accommodation and adaptation are the two principal processes of adjustment, but the difficult task is that of determining in a given situation whether one should accommodate or whether one should try to change or modify elements by adapting them. When does one submit to conditions and when does one try to make them over? This is often a crucial matter to decide, and the pragmatic naturalists hold that one ought not to submit to conditions until one has taken care to see that a change or adaptation cannot be made. This is why, as will be shown later in more detail, the ability to state a problem is very important. The careful and cautious statement of a problem reveals what kind of a problem is present, whether it is one calling for accommodation or one calling for adaptation.

A philosophy of experience which points up the precarious, the unstable, the unbalanced, the conflicting situations through which human beings must live is not new. Since the dawn of experience, human beings have felt and known the uncertainties of life.[7] The pragmatic naturalists' analysis of how humans respond to troublesome situations, however, differs from some other accounts. The unstable and distressing situations of life are real, and they are not explained away by dissolving them into an Absolute in which all evils are reconciled. Emotional comfort is not attained by recourse to a realm of abstract concepts, permanent and unchanging, which are projected beyond the troublesome affairs of natural existence. Pragmatic naturalists hold that human beings should use all their capacities and the resources of nature to make life as secure as possible here and now. They are aware that the quest for certainty, for security, for serenity in the midst of a world of vicissitudes has long been the direction of human efforts. In situations of trouble and instability human beings have sought either to accommodate or to adapt in terms of the descriptions of these processes given above. The specific methods adopted have been many. Sometimes human beings have used sacrifices, ceremonial rites, and magical forms in trying to change the world and make it conform to their needs. Some peoples have tried to control the disasters of experience with contrite hearts or with attitudes of religious resignation, a resignation which places all responsibility for the human plight in the hands of a supernatural God. Alongside these ways of coping with the precarious and the unstable, have grown methods of active and practical control. For instance, human beings built homes as fortresses against the storms of nature; they harnessed the fire and the water and the wind to serve the interests of survival and the enhancement of life.

Since the term "adjustment" appears in contemporary intellectual circles with so many ambiguities and often has come into disrepute through a misinterpretation of its meaning in the context of the "life-adjustment" views of some psychologists and educators, a fuller explication of its meaning may be needed. Too often the term "life-adjustment" has meant social conformity or accommodation in the sense described above. The individual accepts whatever social habits are current in his group associations. Many people are made to conform, to accept conditions as they are, to accommodate, because there is no other recourse open to them. Parents often make it impossible for their children to do anything but conform to adult behavior patterns. Teachers often set rules and norms of behavior in their classrooms by authoritarian methods. Some employers are literally "bosses" who impose upon their workers certain conformist behaviors. Politicians have been known to ostracize, penalize, and even put to death those who do not conform to a particular political code. These instances of conformity are in no way akin to what the pragmatic naturalists mean by adjustment. The individual who conforms to what parental, educational, industrial, political or other social groups happen to impose upon human life may be the most maladjusted of humans. Of course, there may be instances where the individual cannot change the social habits of a group without committing suicide. Conditions then become so crucial that it is a matter of the individual deciding between life and death. The decision to accommodate may be only temporary; that is, the individual accepts the conditions which force accommodation until he can change those conditions and adapt them to a better way of life.

On the pragmatic naturalist's view of adjustment, sometimes the term "integration" is used as a synonym. James thinks that integration involves the following conditions: 1) An individual's impulses are consistent with each other; 2) what one chooses or wills follows without difficulty the guidance of intelligence; 3) the passions are not excessive; and 4) life has a minimum of regrets. A condition of integration or adjustment is a rare achievement. Where is the person whose loves, fears, angers, ambitions, sympathies, detachments, curiosities, and cautions are so evenly balanced that there are no conflicts among these impulses? And where is the person who always acts intelligently, who has no conflicting habits, and who always desires what intelligence judges to be true and good? Most people, if not all, have regrets and repentances which they would rather not experience. Integration or adjustment as an accomplishment never lasts indefinitely; the unstable, the precarious, and the disharmonious are ever-present realities. Integration or adjustment viewed from this broad and abstract way is the goal of all life; for the pragmatic naturalists integration as described above is the goal of their educational philosophy.

Pragmatic naturalists are generally agreed upon the description of the desired state of adjustment, but some of them disagree with some of the means put forth by James for its accomplishment. James appears to think that an individual should lay claim upon anything which may aid one in coming to peace with the world. If there are ideas which cannot be verified directly by scientific method, yet make some difference in human conduct, and if these ideas appear to lead to a more integrated and unified personality, then James sees no reason for not adopting them. He writes: *"If theological ideas prove to have a value for concrete life, they will be true, for pragmatism, in the sense of being good for so much. For how much more they are true, will depend entirely on their relations to the other truths that also have to be acknowledged."*[8] Thus, if religious ideas can help one to live, then these ideas have value. If a belief is emotionally satisfying, and even if such a belief cannot be verified by scientific method, then James believes that such a belief has value for an individual in effecting adjustment. James was interpreted, correctly or incorrectly, as saying that if ideas adopted by an individual "work" or are successful in helping to achieve the integration of the total personality, then such ideas are true and good for that person; thus, James appears to make some beliefs a species of the good. The wide humanistic meaning which James gives to the means of human adjustment brought upon him a deluge of criticism. When he attempted to widen the range of beliefs to which the term "truth" applies, he met resistance from the intellectual establishment. He appears to say that any belief which helps an individual adjust is true. James is concerned with the psychological and emotional consequences of beliefs upon an individual's life; this is a dimension of experience which he thinks has been neglected by philosophers and scientists. The crux of the problem, as James sees it, is that some beliefs which are scientifically unverified produce emotional responses in human beings. The emotional responses to such beliefs are important elements to some people at least in effecting their total adjustment.

Other pragmatists are critical of some of the means which James adopts in attempting to bring about human adjustment or an integrated life. Dewey and Mead think that means and ends cannot be divorced from each other; quality of means adopted affects the quality of the ends or consequences produced. One cannot arbitrarily adopt any belief, even though it is emotionally satisfying, if that belief is unverified. Furthermore, some truths are emotionally disagreeable to those who entertain them. For instance, a person who has incurable cancer surely does not take emotional satisfaction in learning of that truth. Dewey and Mead do not interpret truth in terms of good. Dewey and Mead hold that integration is a fusion and union in one individual of knowing, creating, and doing. When an individual inquires and finds the truth, when one creates something and finds aesthetic fulfillment, when one seeks and finds moral worth, and when one harmonizes these activities into the unity of one life, then adjustment results. Adjustment is intellectual, aesthetic, and moral harmony; it is the supreme fulfillment of human life in nature.

---

3. Emergence
and Non-reductionism

Darwinian revolution brought with it the concept of emergence. New forms or species emerge out of old ones. What was *Eohippus* has become horse, and this species is undergoing change and may pass away or become something very different. Where nature is ongoing, that is, where new forms have survival value and do not pass into extinction, these new forms make new demands upon other parts of nature. For instance, the development of lungs in animals involves the new function of breathing, and breathing is a complex affair involving the lungs and the air. The emergence of mammals upon the evolutionary scene brought forth many activities and functions which made new demands upon the environment.

The concept of emergence means that there is a line of continuity linking the lower, less complex forms of nature with the higher and more complex forms. An example of this line of continuity is the growth of a seed into a plant. The seed emerges into a plant, and the various qualities of the plant function differently from the qualities of a seed. The process of the seed becoming a plant is called *development* or *growth;* that is, new structures emerging in the plant mean new transactions with the environment. Much has been written as to whether or not the emergence of new characteristics and functions from the conditions which foreshadow them is one of mutation or of gradual increment. For the pragmatic naturalist, theories about the process should not overshadow the fact that development occurs; on any theory of how development comes about, the important point is that there is not a complete break between the preceding or antecedent forms and functions and the emerging forms and functions. In other words, the ties between the older forms and the new ones are intimate, no absolute discreteness or sharp demarcation separates the old and the new.

Forms and functions of rocks, plants, animals, and man are characteristically different. Human life, for instance, has physical characteristics, and a complete description of human beings must take account of the physical particles, the chemical elements, which make up the body. The peculiar organization of these physical elements brings about functions which we call "organic"; that is, human beings breathe, reproduce by sexual union, and the like. The physical and biological conditions are the foreshadowings of emergence of psychological and mental functions. One of the most important emergents in humans is the occurrence of speech. There was a time when some psychologists thought they could reduce speech processes to the movement of the voice box. The pragmatic naturalists criticize this view on the grounds that the more complex functions of speech and language are explained in terms of physical and organic conditions which foreshadow the emergence of speech. Whereas it is true that the occurrence of the voice box is a biological condition which makes the emergence of speech possible, it is a mistake to reduce complex speech functions to their preconditions.

Determining whether a specific problem occurs on a physical, organic, psychological, or social level is not always easy. For instance, if a child is doing poorly in reading skills, what procedure is used to locate and define the cause or causes? The child could be suffering from poor eyesight, or the type in the books could be too small for the normal functioning of the child's eyes at a certain stage of physiological development. The child could have psychological problems, or the classroom situation or the family environment could have social elements which disturb the emotional life of the child. Furthermore, the child's problem could be the result of a combination of several causal factors operating simultaneously. The problem of the child's poor reading performance can be determined only by a careful analysis of the kind of situation which is present. If we accuse the child of deliberate negligence, we do him or her an injustice if some physiological condition, such as poor eyesight, is the cause. Children are often the victims of the adult's inaccurate analysis of the level on which behavior occurs; praise and blame are used too often as if the level of a child's performance reflects the child's intention or effort. A correct analysis of the levels on which forms and functions of behavior appear is important for the solution of any problem.

Emergence and novelty are conceptions with which contemporary philosophers have been greatly concerned. Some thinkers hold that emergence, or what Mead calls "emergent evolution," can be explained by the reduction of complex objects to their "elements"; complex objects are said to be "nothing but" an aggregation of their simple components. Mead shows what problems appear when complex objects are analyzed in terms of their simple ingredients: "When we analyze the object as such into physical particles . . . we have lost the character of the object" as an object. "If we break up water into oxygen and hydrogen, it loses the character which belongs to it in a combination of the two. We cannot carry the water character over into the elements. If one wants to quench his thirst or put out fire, water is there to act under those particular conditions, but it is not water from the point of view of the atoms and their relationship to one another. It is of interest to see that, in the doctrine of emergence as the result of the combination of elements with one another every complex as such, in so far as it is a resultant, at any time does bring with it something that was not there before."[9] The attempt to explain the more complex functions of nature and human life in terms of the simpler conditions which foreshadow them or precede them is called *reductionism.*

William James shows the consequences of reductionism when complex religious phenomena are considered as "nothing but" physiological conditions. He calls this approach "medical materialism," and he writes: "Medical materialism seems indeed a good appellation for the too simpleminded system of thought which we are considering. Medical materialism finishes up Saint Paul by calling his vision on the road to Damascus a discharging lesion of the occipital cortex, he being an epileptic. It snuffs out Saint Teresa as an hysteric, Saint Francis of Assisi as an hereditary degenerate. George Fox's discontent with the shams of his age, and his pining for spiritual veracity, it treats as a symptom of a disordered colon. Carlyle's organ-tones of misery it accounts for by a gastroduodenal catarrh."[10] James thinks that the complexities of religious experience cannot be explained by a method of reductionism.

One of the most crucial points on which Dewey has been frequently misunderstood is his contention that logical functions of inquiry develop out of biological preconditions. Dewey shows that logical processes grow out of, but are not reducible to, the preconditions of organic responses of the organism. The organism responds; its responses are a kind of crude classification of its life. The amoeba, for instance, pushes out into its immediate environment or conditions of its life. If this simple organism finds parts of its environment unfriendly, then it recoils and rejects those parts; if it finds other parts of its environment friendly, then it selects those parts. On this very simple level of organic life, there is emerging in the responses of the organism a kind of logic; that is, the processes of selections are affirmations and the processes of rejections are negations. Thus, organisms make discriminatory responses, and, in a crude way, they are classifying and defining. These crude beginnings are not on the level of a more complex and highly developed logic, a logic concerned with abstract symbols and their implications.

By relating the more complex and sophisticated logical operations to the organic conditions out of which they emerge, Dewey cuts the ground from under theories which attribute the origin of logical forms to the structure of the human mind (as in Kant) or to some transcendental reality (as in Hegel). Dewey argues for a "naturalistic" logic, a logic in which complex logical operations are emergents or developments out of the less complex and simple responses of organic life. Dewey is not maintaining that there is or can be a reduction of logical operations of the more complex and sophisticated kind to biological functions. To criticize his naturalistic logic as a biological logic of the reductionist type misses the point of how emergence functions in his philosophy.[11]

Transformation is the key concept in explaining how complex forms and functions develop out of simpler forms and functions. The development of emergent qualities from the seed into the plant involves a process of changing forms and their interactions, but it is a change which involves a continuity. In order to understand the development of the plant in its growth dimensions, it is necessary to chart its history, and history means that transformations take place through time. "Things in process," or things changing and being transformed through time, is the way of all nature.

There is another kind of reductionism which the pragmatic naturalists reject. One explanatory technique frequently adopted is that of analyzing complex forms and functions by reducing them to their historical origins. The explanation of emergent and transformed qualities and functions in terms of their origins is called *the genetic fallacy*. For instance, the plant is said to be "nothing more" than its original state, which was a seed. This explanation of the plant's emergent qualities and their interactions ignores the transformations the plant has undergone in its developmental history. When the explanatory technique of reduction to origins is carried over into studies of organic, social, and cultural life, then descriptions of any process become distorted. Take, for instance, the explanation of the emergent complexities of the human species. Emergent life-functions are reduced by this method to the genetic state or origin, which is the embryo, and the many transformations a human organism goes through in its development are ignored. The more complex social and cultural organizations of human life, such as family, political, and economic systems, are explained by a description of how each originated. American democracy has undergone many transformations since the founding fathers wrote the Mayflower Compact. To claim that the complex forms of democracy which have developed since the early seventeenth century are "nothing more" than their original forms is to commit the genetic fallacy.

---

4. The Fullness of Experience

Much of traditional philosophizing has a history of postulating the separation of what is called "experience" from what is called "nature"; experience is taken to be something subjective, and nature is taken to be something objective. Thus, some confusion may occur if the references to these terms in the preceding pages are taken to mean that the inherited separation of experience and nature is accepted by pragmatic naturalists. Pragmatic naturalists reject the dualism of experience and nature; for them experience and nature are correlative. "Nature" is a word for all that is, has been, and may be experienced. "Experience" is not a solipsistic term; "experience" does not refer to an individual's experience alone; it includes the experience and reports of other people, living and dead, mature and immature, normal and abnormal. The circularity of experience and nature is admitted; but the circularity is a wide one which includes all that is felt and known in present experience, which includes continuously reconstructed pasts, and which includes potentialities arising out of present experience.

When nature and experience are viewed in this full and broad sense, it is difficult to find a starting place for any account of the main features. Perhaps the best starting place is with James's notion of "pure experiences." "Pure experiences" are feelings without known contents, existential "thats" which are not yet "whats," existences without essences. Experience is a stream, a flow, according to James, and it is punctuated with pulsations which come to us with no credentials. In James's words, the primal state of life is a "blooming, buzzing confusion." A child enters the world without knowledge of colors, shapes, sizes, relations, ideas, or anything else. As Peirce describes them, a child's responses are gross, general, wholesale. As a child experiences "bumpings," to use Peirce's term, or feels shocks and pulsations in his life, he comes to discriminate objects. Out of the gross contexts of random activities a child begins to construct his world; it is not his private world, to be sure, but a world which adults share with him. He learns to symbolize objects and to communicate meanings.

When it is said that a child's first feeling-states in the continuity of experience are "pure thats" which are not as yet known, this means that each pulsation is *neutral*. The neutrality of a bare given feeling is called *neutral monism*. In this context, monism refers to the notion that all "thats" given in experience are on the same level of existence, and neutral means that experience as yet has not disclosed whether the given feeling is psychical or physical, that is, whether the feeling refers to psychical events or to physical bodies.

Some feelings are perceptions which eventuate in sensations; other feelings eventuate in concepts. Some perceptual feelings are found to be more dependable than others; they are rather constant in their appearances and functions in the stream of experience, and human beings have come to designate these pulsations as objects of a physical world. Thus some feelings come to have references beyond their own immediate existences to physical objects; in this sense James is a realist. In the ongoing of experience concepts occur, and these are regarded as shorthand transcriptions of certain aspects of the flow of experience. Concepts are intellectual formulations generated out of the stream of experience; they are more or less abstract, more or less static. The development of logic and mathematics is made possible by those concepts which eventuate in abstractions. Concepts are useful for understanding and manipulating other parts of experience; their primary function is the management of all the particularities found in the flow of experience. Since early Greek philosophy, the notion has been prevalent that the realm of sensory perceptions is to be set over against the realm of concepts and rational forms, thus creating a dualism. Pragmatic naturalists reject this dualism; they think of sensory perceptions and concepts as having a connection in their genesis; both arise from the stream of experience. In the past, sensory experiences have been taken to be unrelated with one another; thus it has been held that some higher faculty, such as a mind, had to be brought in to relate sensory perceptions to one another. Philosophers who are rationalists (emphasizing conceptual forms) and philosophers who are empiricists (emphasizing sensory perceptions) have agreed generally that "relations" are not given in direct experience. The pragmatic naturalists reject the traditional philosophies, both rationalistic and empiricist, on the notion of relations. James shows that relations belong in the stream of experience as much as anything else; that is, relations are immediately felt or "given." He says: "Every examiner of the sensible life *in concreto* must see that relations of every sort, of time, space, difference, likeness, change, rate, cause, or what not, are just as integral members of the sensational flux as terms are, and that conjunctive relations are just as true members of the flux as disjunctive relations are."[12] The notion that relations are immediately felt and given in experience James calls *radical empiricism*. Radical empiricism also differs from views held by many contemporary logical empiricists who trace their heritage on the nature of sensations and relations back to David Hume.

In the pragmatic naturalists' view of the fullness of experience, the *real* includes both the *actual* and the *ideal*.

That the actual, the existent, the fact felt and known is a part of experience has long been accepted by philosophers. Even when the actual is regarded as a shadowy counterfeit of a postulated real world of concepts, there has never been a denial that such facts are in experience. On the other hand, the reality of what James calls the "unseen" and what Dewey calls the "ideal" has been regarded by some philosophers as figments of the human imagination. For pragmatic naturalists, however, the ideal is real because potentialities exist in nature. We have seen that the seed has the potentiality of becoming the plant. In human experience projected ideals and goals give life a direction. The projected but unactualized college education which one seeks, for instance, is an ideal which governs behavior; this ideal draws a cluster of diverse activities to itself, and it determines the selections and rejections one makes on the path to that ideal. A student carries such an ideal or goal in the mind, yet the goal or ideal is not wholly or exclusively a private affair. The ideal of a college education not yet actualized is forged out of the college environment of teachers, courses, textbooks, classrooms, and numerous other aspects of the situation in which the ideal functions. An ideal of this kind is integral with the funded experience of other people from their pasts and presents; it is a present potentiality; it is a promise, and when actualized becomes a fulfillment. Ideals which are integral to actual situations are real, and whereas they may lay hold upon the energies residing in a single individual, they are parts of a social existence.

The fullness of experience envelops the generic traits of existence, traits of stability and instability, order and disorder, harmony and disharmony, continuity and discontinuity. In much of previous philosophy some of these traits have been emphasized more than others. The desire for something absolutely certain has been so strong in some that they erect a world of perfect and abstract ideas, which are unchanging and permanent, above the world of sensory

perception which seems to be constantly shifting and changing. A philosopher such as Leibniz may try to reconcile the
stable and the unstable, the harmonious and the disharmonious parts of experience, by constructing a world of
synthesis and unity. Evil and falsehood and ugliness are reconciled to good and truth and beauty by ignoring the former, or by minimizing their actualities, or by making them
in all of their manifestations a part of a preestablished harmony. Thus, the certainty of order and harmony is saved by
a manipulation of thought; emotional comfort is attained by
an apparent intellectual security. A philosopher like Descartes, not able to find emotional peace in the world of religion or the world of physics, is able to find security in the
unchanging and permanent axioms of mathematics. Even
the philosophers who start with sensory perceptions seem to
find emotional comfort in a supposed permanent and unchanging world of "brute facts." Dewey contends that many
philosophers have ignored, glossed over, explained away, the
precarious and the unstable. The tragic and defeating elements in experience drive James to affirm the reality of evil
in the world. Because these elements have long been ignored
or explained away, Dewey puts stress upon the perplexities,
the obscurities, and the conflicting situations of human life
as integral parts of experience. Dewey once wrote that when
philosophers thought of experience as containing the tragic
and the precarious as well as the harmonious and the sub-
lime, the disorderly as well as the orderly, and when these
aspects are accepted as belonging to the fullness of experience, then the term "experience" will no longer be needed.

Human beings have been able to survive because they
have built up a stock of beliefs which they found significant
and useful. Beliefs usually fall into two kinds, common
sense and scientific. Common sense is usually designated as
a kind of "practical sense" or good judgment. Commonsense
meanings have emerged as accidental discoveries of what is
later found to be scientifically true. For instance, experience

reveals that fire burns, that water quenches thirst, that air is necessary for breathing. There are degrees of critical-mindedness in the prescientific understanding of experience, and Peirce calls this stage of human intellectual development "critical common-sensism." Common sense or "sense in common" has grown in a random and more or less uncontrolled way, and it lacks the methods of controlled investigation which afford science its precision and dependability. Nevertheless, common sense has produced some discriminations and classifications in experience which are the touchstones of science. Common sense has discriminated, even though vaguely, parts of experience such as sensations and concepts, mental events and physical things, and from these vague notions philosophy and science have grown.

Common sense has produced beliefs, however, which are not the result of critical method. Among these beliefs are found superstitions, magical formulae, and "fortune-telling" practices. Among the practices are found the occult, ceremonies to control evil spirits, and ceremonies to court favors of the gods. The stock of human beliefs contains uncritical acceptance of heroes as authorities on almost everything, of customs which maim human life, of traditions which bind the individual's freedom and which, in some cases, have required people to sacrifice their children or have demanded that an individual commit suicide. Thus, commonsense beliefs are a mixture of the useful and the useless, the practical and the impractical.

When experience is taken in a broad and full sense, then the starting place for a comprehensive philosophy must be by employment of a *denotative method*.[13] Experience is anything and everything which can be pointed to or denoted. Experience includes feelings, sensations, concepts, psychical events, physical things, relations, actualities and ideals, harmonies and disharmonies, common sense and science. Experience includes memories and imaginations, pasts and projected futures, present awareness, illusions and hallucinations; it includes truths and falsehoods, objects of beauty and ugliness, goods and evils; it includes language and events; it includes "death, war, and taxes." In other words, experience includes all that is, has been, and has potentiality of becoming. For pragmatic naturalists, experience is ultimate reality.

According to Dewey, much of past philosophizing has been the result of *selective emphasis* or *bias*. Some philosophers have selected that part of experience which appeals to them and have made it supreme and ultimate. For instance, the rationalists are partial to conceptual forms, to the abstract, to the purity of intellectual operations. They tend to raise rational forms to a status and prominence from which all other parts of experience are pale and remote. On the other hand, traditional empiricists select sensory experiences as the "most real" in experience, and they tend to use these as the vantage points from which all the other aspects of experience are viewed. The factual, the sensory, the sense-datum (or any other name by which this aspect of experience is called) becomes the base from which the criteria of truth statements are formulated. Other philosophers have emphasized the "mental," or the "psychical," and some have gone so far as to declare that these functions are the result of a mind-substance. Still other thinkers have selected the physical aspects of experience, and have gone so far as to declare that the physical objects have a material substance as their base. A common habit of philosophers has been the treatment of functional activities as if they were antecedent realities, and Dewey calls this practice "the philosophical fallacy." Any philosophy which selects and hypostatizes certain aspects of experience, which makes these hypostatized entities into ultimate criteria by which the rest of experience is judged, is a philosophy of prejudice and bias, according to Dewey. From his point of view of the fullness of experience, philosophy becomes "a critique of prejudices."

On the other hand, critics claim that the pragmatic

naturalists' view of experience is so broad and comprehensive that it becomes unwieldy. It can be claimed that, since experience is made to include anything and everything, one does not know where to take hold of such a conglomeration in order to make sense out of it. The critics of pragmatic naturalism can say that at least the opposing positions have some vantage point from which to view other parts of experience, even if that vantage point is a product of selection and bias. This is an important criticism, and one of which the pragmatic naturalists are aware. The way out of this difficulty is found by the adoption of a method, a method of inquiry or intelligence, by which the grossness and wholeness of experience can be managed. A fuller treatment of this crucial point will be considered under the topic "The Importance of Method" (pt. 2, sec. 8).

The implications of the pragmatic naturalists' view of the fullness of experience have never been fully realized. They claim that all past philosophies have selected for emphasis aspects of experience which are in fact significant; these biased selections, however, have been put in the wrong contexts. Thus, on the one hand, past philosophizing has contributed enormously to the understanding of experience; on the other hand, the special emphases have been overstressed, and this has led to distortion. Because they take experience in its fullest meaning, pragmatic naturalists have suffered from serious misunderstandings of their views. For instance, when pragmatic naturalists are analyzing an aspect of experience which they think important in an overall view, but an aspect which has connotations of the inherited biased accounts, it is easy to misread what they are saying. Thus, when the importance of the function of ideas is selected for analysis, it is easy to read pragmatic naturalists as disguised idealists; when the significance of physical objects in a full view of experience is shown, some see pragmatic naturalism as another name for materialism. Some critics think that the pragmatic naturalists' analysis and use of concepts is another form of traditional rationalism; other critics feel that the context which shows the importance of sensory experience is another form of traditional empiricism. In order to correct these biased accounts of pragmatic naturalism, it is necessary to grasp their view of the fullness of experience to which all the special emphases are relevant.

5. Immediacy, Transaction, and Continuity

For the pragmatic naturalists there are leading ideas or categories which have important functions in the analysis, description, and understanding of experience.[14] These categories have been debated often, and what follows is an interpretation.[15]

The primary existential state of life in nature is *immediate feeling*. Dewey writes: "The existential starting point is immediate qualities. Even meanings taken not as meanings but as existential are grounded in immediate qualities, in sentiencies, or 'feelings,' of organic activities and receptivities."[16] These feeling-states are simply "had"; they are not cognized or known. Even on the subconscious level, however, these feeling qualities have a powerful effect in organic behavior, for they guide organisms into similar kinds of responses or into new experiences. At later stages of human development, where more complex activities and knowing-states emerge, these organic feelings are never absent.

Sometimes in the history of philosophy it has been held that the human species encounters immediately ready-made sensations and ready-made concepts. Dewey denies this.

Humans are not born with any antecedently structured sensations and concepts, for these aspects of experience grow out of human feelings and responses as they become demarcated and symbolized. Dewey makes this clear when he says: "Immediately, every perceptual awareness may be termed indifferently emotion, sensation, thought, desire: not that it *is* immediately any one of these things, or all of them combined, but that when it is taken in some *reference*, to conditions or to consequences or to both, it has, in that contextual reference, the distinctive properties of emotion, sensation, thought or desire."[17] Thus, the primal feeling-state of the organism is undifferentiated. On this level of experience there are no sensations (no colors or shapes or sizes); there are no concepts (no definitions or classifications or forms); there are no emotions (no fears or loves or angers); there are no desires (no prizings or likings or enjoyments). Furthermore, since these primal feeling-states are existences, they can only be pointed to or denoted; they cannot be described or defined.

Immediate feeling is always present in the organism as long as it is alive; feeling pervades its whole life, its living through time. Feeling is present at every conjunction in experience and at every disjunction. Immediate feeling is present when a perplexity occurs; a *felt* perplexity exists; there is a dumb feeling that life is not going well or that something is blocking the forward movement of the organism. Even when humans reach the level of the knowing process, immediate feeling lies at the base of this experience; feeling pervades the whole process of inquiry. Feeling marks the beginning of an historical continuity and feeling marks its close.

Immediate feeling is what Dewey calls the noncognitive or the precognitive aspect of experience. At the same time, immediate feeling is not cut discretely from the higher and more complex functions of the cognitive (knowing) aspects of experience which emerge from it. To place the noncognitive in one compartment and the cognitive in another results in a radical dualism of feeling and knowing and creates problems of the relations between them. For Dewey there is no sharp line between the noncognitive and the cognitive; on the contrary, there is a line of continuity between them.

A second leading principle important for the understanding of experience is the principle of *connections* or *interactions*, or what Dewey calls in his later writings, *transactions*. Connections in experience are existential involvements; they belong to immediate experience, to the perceptual flow which contains them. Dewey says that "the actual operative presence of *connections* (which when formulated are *relational*) in the subject-matter of direct experience is an intrinsic part of my idea of experience."[18] It should be noted that this passage contains a very important distinction between connections and relations. Connections are "given" or felt in primary experience; hence they are noncognitive. Relations, on the other hand, are formulated, symbolized, and thus are known. Since there is no sharp demarcation between connections and relations but a line of continuous process, it has been customary to use "connections" and "relations" synonymously. If this is done, confusion of many important points in pragmatic naturalism will result.

The use of the principle of connections and relations is one of the primary means by which the pragmatic naturalist comes to an understanding of experience and nature. For instance, the principle of connections and relations runs through the account of chemistry, for chemical elements cannot be understood apart from their interactions. This principle is used for an explanation in physics, for the atom itself is a connection of its interacting parts. When the principle is moved over into the field of psychology, then it is seen that the organism is integrally connected with its environment. A biological process like breathing is a transaction of the lungs and the air. The principle of connections and relations is basic to the understanding of the pragmatic naturalist's value theory, for desires cannot be understood apart from some object prized or loved.

By starting with connections found in the perceptual flow of experience and by formulating these into a principle of relations, the pragmatic naturalist cuts the ground from under all dichotomies, all dualisms, from the time of Descartes thought to be important disjunctions in experience. It should be noted, however, that connections and relations are not to be assumed where they are not felt and cannot be observed and verified; to assume so might lead to an erroneous account of some specific experience, for there might be a projection into that experience of a connection in place of an actual disjunction.

A third principle of pragmatic naturalism is called the principle of *continuity*. Dewey calls this principle *the naturalistic postulate*.[19] This postulate is not arbitrary; it functions in experience and it is tested in experience. The naturalistic postulate means that there is a line of continuity from the less complex to the more complex forms and functions of life. Where there is continuity, there are no breaks in a process, and there is not need for an intuitive leap from one emerging function to another. What is important is that a new development, a transformation takes place.

The principle of continuity becomes a means by which many things in experience and nature can be understood. Continuity and discontinuity make up what Dewey calls "generic traits of existence." The principle of continuity is found in the history of natural things, of thing-in-process, things which have beginnings and termini. Knowledge situations involve a continuum of inquiry from a felt problem to be investigated to the final judgmental close. The aesthetic experience has a continuity from its inception to its consummation or fulfillment. The principle of continuity lies at the base of any constructed history, whether it be the history of an individual's life, the life of a nation, or the life of the geological world.

Peirce develops similar categories of experience, but it is not clear if his meanings are the same as those of the other pragmatic naturalists. In the first place, Peirce adopts strange and unusual names for these categories. And his attempt to strike out on a new path using a new terminology makes understanding of his meanings difficult. For instance, Peirce uses the terms Firstness, Secondness, and Thirdness. At times Peirce says that Firstness means "feeling"; he says that Secondness means "bumpings" or "reaction"; and Thirdness means "continuity." If these meanings are selected from his various uses, then it appears that Peirce and Dewey are in agreement on the basic categories or leading principles of experience. What complicates the matter, however, is that Peirce uses many names for what Firstness, Secondness, and Thirdness are supposed to designate.[20] Furthermore, he revised these principles at various stages of his thinking.[21] The similarities with and differences from the categories of the other pragmatic naturalists must be left to future inquiry to determine. If inquiry is confined to understanding Peirce, however, it is necessary to come to some understanding of his use of these categories, for they are basic to his general way of philosophizing.

Categories and principles similar to those found in Dewey and Peirce are also found in James and Mead, and in a few instances each has made his use and statement of these explicit. Even when such principles are not made explicit, they are implicit in their thinking and must be grasped in order to understand their ideas on every issue.

James uses the term "pure experience," a term which contains some ambiguity when taken in various contexts of his writings; but in one place he makes it clear that it is the name which he gives to "the immediate flux of life."[22] It is a pure *that* which is not yet any "definite *what*." In other words, it is a feeling-state which is undifferentiated, for he says: "Pure experience in this state is but another name for feeling or sensation." It has already been pointed out above that James holds that relations (connections) are given in direct experience, and in this sense he is a radical empiricist. James sometimes uses the term "relations" where Dewey uses "connections" to designate an uncognized relation, and in order to preserve the distinction between connections and relations, James's terminology is amended here. As far as the principle of continuity is concerned, James included a lecture by the title of "The Continuity of Experience" in his Hibbert lectures. The perceptual flux of life is like a continuous stream, and "the tiniest feeling that we can possibly have comes with an earlier and a later part and with a sense of their continuous procession."[23] Continuity and discontinuity are basic traits of experience; they are generic traits of existence.

Mead likewise uses the principles of feeling, interaction, and continuity, but with less emphasis upon the category of feeling. However, he does say: "The lowest form of consciousness that we ascribe to living things is feeling. In general we do not judge that living forms without central nervous systems possess feeling, though there is a difference of opinion on this."[24] Thus feeling is a basic principle. However, Mead is more concerned with the principle of interrelations, and the use of this principle runs throughout his treatment of social psychology; in fact, it is impossible to understand his writings without constant awareness that he is using this principle. Only one instance of his use of it will be cited, but it suffices to show the importance of the principle. Mead writes: "And since organism and environment determine each other and are mutually dependent for their existence, it follows that the life-process, to be adequately understood, must be considered in terms of their interrelations."[25] Thus, organism and environment are inseparable, except in abstraction, and the interrelations actually occurring are the empirical means which Mead adopts in the study of human behavior.

Mead also speaks of the ongoing of the organism, of its process, and this, of course, is an affair of its continuity. More subtle and more difficult to grasp is Mead's use of the idea of continuity in the nature of an act. He says: "It is the enduring character of the experience that contains in it the continuity of nature, that contains in it just that connection which Hume denied. There is something that continues. If there is something that continues, that which is there at the present time is responsible for what is going to be there in the future."[26] In some of Mead's more technical discussions he shows how the present act contains within it a movement in time, a continuity which includes within it its past and its future.

The leading ideas of feeling, transaction, and continuity become pivotal in understanding how the pragmatic naturalists think about experience and nature, how they analyze problems, and how they approach even the simplest of natural events. Failure to understand the use by the pragmatic naturalists of the categories of immediacy, transaction, and continuity results in many distortions of their ideas.

6. A Pluralistic Universe

During the latter half of the nineteenth century, one of the most prevailing philosophies on the continent of Europe and in Great Britain was known as the philosophy of the Absolute. There are various versions of this way of looking at nature and life, and William James appears to have taken a critical view of all of them. One version of the philosophic issue was taken to be the conflict between monism and pluralism, or what philosophers have most often posed as the problem of the One and the Many. In James's simple and direct way of putting the matter, it is the problem of the "all-form" and the "each-form."[27] By this he means that monism holds that there is one form which envelops all others, that the world is already organized in to a unified whole. James claim that it is impossible to find one form which can be related empirically to all other forms in nature and life. In some philosophers' abstract vision of things, and in their attempt to view the parts from the standpoint of the whole, they might dream of this monistic kind of unity, but it is only a dream. The world is pregnant with discontinuities, and the continuities we do encounter in experience and nature are so diverse that no certain and absolute unity can contain them. Not able to find an empirically verifiable interrelatedness of all things, a universe in which every part is internally related to every other part, James affirmed his belief in a pluralistic universe. The disjunctions found in experience and nature are too insistent and too real to be explained away by some kind of abstract manipulation.

There have been other ways of trying to bring all that exists in the world into some kind of monistic scheme or unity. For centuries there have been attempts to relate all causal lines running through nature to one all-inclusive First Cause. The pragmatic naturalist finds that such schemes go beyond an empirical justification, thus they belong to a kind of extraempirical or speculative mataphysics. That there are specific and particular causal processes running through nature there is no doubt. For instance, under certain conditions typhoid germs cause typhoid fever. In another instance, when water is heated to 212 degrees Fahrenheit under certain conditions, it boils. The typhoid fever and the boiling water are two different causal processes. What is the observable evidence which supports the claim that these two causal processes, different as they are in so many respects, are really the result of one single causal process which brings both of them about? To claim that they are united by some means, but one does not know how, is to make a leap of faith or at least a leap into speculation. As pragmatic naturalists see the world existing in its present state, it is a world in which there is both continuity and discontinuity, and both of these processes are real.

This view gives us a world that is loosely hanging together; in fact, some parts of the world do not fit in with other parts at all. In this respect, it is not a perfectly ordered universe, nor is it the best of all possible worlds as pictured by Leibniz. It is a kind of multiverse which contains some processes which are compatible with each other, but it contains other processes which are in conflict. The extreme visionary in philosophy might turn his eyes away from the anxieties, frustrations, disorders, and disharmonies which are ever present, and he might imagine a world existing above and beyond this world in some transcendental or supernatural realm where God is in his heaven and all's well with the world. When we turn toward the actualities of the natural world and our existence in it, we find that the disruptions are real. There is enough order, harmony, and continuity, however, to make life possible and bearable, and in many instances there are enough of the sustaining conditions to make living in the world delightful. Human beings struggle to bring order out of disorder, harmony out of disharmony. What cannot be adapted, of course, must be accommodated to and accepted. Pragmatic naturalists stress the difficulties in finding and preserving the harmonies of experience; in this respect they attempt to give a realistic description to the human existential situation.

Pragmatic naturalists are not averse to the use of vision in developing a scientific and philosophical view of nature and experience, but any vision of the whole must be tied closely to the observable. A vision of the whole is built up from the many experiences humans undergo from the experiences of individuals and groups, both past and present. Human experience is social. The perspective of each individual and the vision one entertains of the world depend upon how far-reaching are one's interactions, those directly undergone and those which become a part of the expanding self through the power and function of symbols. All of the pragmatic naturalists make use of the term "perspective," for they see that it is natural for each individual to build out of one's particular experiences a vision of a whole, and this vision of the whole is a perspective.

The limits which caution puts upon the vision of the whole are found in a realistic appraisal of the continuities and processes of life which are external to each other's ongoing. The continuities of life must be based upon observations, not upon a logical manipulation of abstractions which give a false view of unity. It is true that each continuity or process has its own internal organization, but continuities are plural, and some processes are external to others. A simple example should make this clear. Suppose an individual walks from home to office. This experience involves an interaction and a continuity of organism and environment. It involves getting dressed, eating breakfast, going out the door of the house, taking a particular street, turning at particular junctions, and finally arriving at the office. This is one experience in which various interacting parts in the situation are strung along "next to next," so to speak. The whole experience is open to observation. As an experience, having a beginning, a continuity, and an end, it may have little to do with other histories or continuities in other parts of the world, unless it can be shown empirically to have an intimate connection. There may be other people in other parts of the world walking to their offices, but it is unlikely that they have anything to do with *this* individual walking from home to office; their relations are external to each other.

One version of the problem of whether we live in a world which is already unified in some way or whether we live in a world which is loosely hanging together centers around the problem of internal and external relations. The monistic view of experience and nature holds that all processes and interactions are somehow internally related; thus what affects one affects every other throughout the whole system. Pragmatic naturalists do not think that this view can be empirically justified. What they observe in experience is a multitude of processes, some of which are related, some of which are not. They hold that it takes manipulation of abstract conceptions too far removed from the facts of experience to construct a completely unified and monistic world. Internal relations exist, but they exist in observable ways in the continuities of nature, and they exist among a mass of continuities which are external to each other. Continuities and discontinuities are generic traits of nature and experience; thus we live in a "pluralistic universe."

7. Human Life in Nature

Pragmatic naturalists conceive of humans as a part of nature. Although they share many organic processes with other animals in their life in nature, humans emerge above the animals in certain forms and functions. For instance, humans can construct symbols and languages, they can speak and write, and by these means they can preserve their past experiences, construct new meanings, and entertain goals and ideals. Humans can make plans and by proper selection of the means to the ends carry them through. They can write poetry and novels, compose music and painting, and otherwise engage in aesthetic experiences. They can construct explanatory hypotheses about the world and all that is in it, of electrons, protons, and neutrons, and solar systems far away. They can dream dreams, concoct fantasies, erect heavens above the earth which entice their activities to far-off destinies, and they can imagine hells which stimulate fears of everlasting torture. The emergent functions of symbolic behavior make it possible for humans to transcend parts of their immediate undergoing and experiencing and to know that death and all that it entails is a part of organic life.

There is little wonder that, with the tremendous number of functions which humans can perform, many thinkers throughout history have thought of themselves as rather special creations. Creatures endowed with powers to function in multitudinous ways and to effect the many transformations in themselves and their environment, it has been thought, could have had their origin only in some source which transcends all nature and human life. Theories abound which hold to some version of this link of humans with a supernatural or transcendental realm, and various metaphysical and speculative constructions have been constructed which set them off as uniquely different from the rest of nature.

Human evolutionary ties with other parts of nature, and with other animals in particular, are too obvious to overlook. A naturalistic view brings this kinship of human life and nature to the fore. In organic structures and functions, humans have affinities with other animals; for instance, some animals have lungs and breathing and sexual organs for reproduction. The key to understanding human life in nature is the principle of continuity in which the lower processes of organic life are tied to the higher processes and functions. In former times it was popular to say that a human being is a creature who is a little lower than the angels; the naturalistic philosopher holds that a human being, while sharing affinities with other parts of nature, is a little higher than the animals.

Pragmatic naturalists inherited a view of human beings which maintains that each possesses a soul, or mind substance, or consciousness; usually these terms are thought to designate an entity which exists outside the natural processes. The history of pragmatic naturalism could be written as a purging and a withering away of this traditional concept of human beings. James and Dewey started out with an interest in physiology and physiological psychology, and Mead's studies with James and others were always immersed in the organic view of human life. Dewey made an observation about James's classic work on *The Principles of Psychology*, an observation which could be applied to himself as well; he claims that James moves more and more within this work toward the view that human beings are organisms.[28]

The starting place of the pragmatic naturalists in their views of human life is with an organism living *by means of* an environment. From this organic base emerge the many complex and complicated processes of perceiving, remembering, imagining, symbolizing, thinking, valuing, and judging. The emergence of new organs in the human body, new differentiations in natural forms, makes possible new interactions or transactions in an environment. These new forms and functions make new demands upon the environment, and the development of organism and environment as a balance of energies expands. The relation of organism and environment is a functional affair, and it is only in abstraction that one can talk about environment and organism as things apart. This relation is not one in which a discrete entity (called the organism) and another discrete entity (called the environment) are viewed as separate and self-inclosed and then are brought together in some kind of interaction with each other. Interaction never means for the pragmatic naturalist the action and reaction between two separate entities, and that is why some would rather use the term "transaction" to describe the balance of energies which can be separated only in abstraction. The primal organic condition of human life is an organization of energy with a forward movement or *impulsion*.[29] The organism meets obstacles and is blocked in its forward movement; imbalances in the living process develop, such as hunger and thirst. Under certain conditions, the organism may set up resistances and withdrawals; in other instances it may plunge forward to its own destruction and death. What is important to its living is a balance of energies, and this balance is so intricate and delicate that it demands precision in the functioning of all its sustaining parts. In describing the processes which operate in the organism's development, the pragmatic naturalists make a distinction between *excitation-reaction* and *stimulus-response*. Behavioristic psychologists have emphasized a formula for the unit of behavior which is most frequently called "the reflex arc" concept. This is composed primarily of a sensory stimulus and a motor discharge. As this concept was first put forth, Dewey analyzed its meaning in a very famous essay, "The Reflex Arc Concept in Psychology," and he claimed that "the reflex arc is not a comprehensive, or organic unity, but a patchwork of disjointed parts, a mechanical conjunction of unallied processes."[30] For this reason, among many others, the pragmatic naturalists make a distinction between excitation-reaction and stimulus-response. Peirce, as well as Dewey, sees that an excitation can play upon the organism in such a way that no total response followed. But if a sensory excitation entering the organism's field of transaction moves through its nervous system, through the ganglia, to effect a movement of the whole organism, then this activity is much more complex and complicated, much more unified in its forward movement, than simple and compounded excitations-reactions can produce. Stimulus-response involves the movement of the whole organism.

Dewey gives an example of the distinction between excitation-reaction and stimulus-response when he tells of an animal with the organic need of hunger lying in a forest. A whiff or scent of possible prey excites the animal's organ of smell; the animal sniffs, and this is a reaction. If, however, the animal is lured by the excitation to be aroused, to stalk its prey, to search for it, and finally to consume it, then there is a response. While pursuing its prey, the animal may encounter other excitations, but these are ignored. The original excitation has now moved through the total organism, and it will not be deterred in its seriated movements toward its prey, unless, of course, something very powerful restrains its movement. The animal comes to its prey and consumes it, and the balance of its energies is restored. Stimulus-response is the whole activity from the time of the first excitation which became a stimulus to the consummation of the seriated activity. The movement of the animal from beginning to end is one unified activity. Thus, the stimulus cannot be cut or separated from the response; both are abstractions from one complete and whole experience—the earlier phase by abstraction may be called the "stimulus" and the latter phase by another abstraction may be called the "response."[31] The primary criticism made by pragmatic naturalists of behavioristic psychology rests upon the interpretation of the reflex arc. For this reason, among many others, pragmatic naturalists prefer to call their psychology *behavioral* rather than *behavioristic*.

In human evolutionary development there have emerged certain organs and functions of the organism which have expanded its life in its environment. Many of these new forms and functions have significant and far-reaching implications. For instance, the human organism is equipped with distance receptors, such as the eye, and it is from this physiological

base that an individual learns that there is a time span between its location in space and movement toward the object
which is perceived. This organic functioning becomes the
base from which imagination emerges, and imagination is
one of the processes which makes possible the formation of
goals, purposes, and ideals. After the organism has undergone a stimulus-response experience which involves the
whole organism, there is a "trace" of this sequence left in
the nervous system. This trace becomes the physiological
basis for the development of memory. Furthermore, sensory
experience is not simply a passive recording of sensory excitations or impressions, as some philosophers have held. If
sensory experience were only passive, the organism would
die. Sensory experiences are linked with enticements, with
warnings, with threats, with promises of fulfillments.

A baby during its earliest days is a bundle of energy, an
energetic process not yet wholly differentiated into its eventual functions. The baby moves its arms and legs, but has
not learned to use its hands in grasping objects and has not
learned to use its legs in walking. The baby's activities are
composed of random movements. As the baby develops, it
moves around more, grasps objects, and its activities multi-
ply. Most of these activities have now become named by
adults as certain kinds of impulses, but it should be noted
that an activity denoted and named as an impulse in one
culture may not be designated and named the same in
another culture. In our culture a child may perform the activity of what we call "grabbing food from the table"; in
some groups of our culture the adult friends may restrain
this activity, may teach the child about the consequences of
this kind of activity to itself and others. Thus, the activity of
grabbing food is called an "impulse," an activity which
takes on meaning because the adults around the child teach
it the meaning of the activity in terms of the consequences
to which the activity leads.

Thus, random activities of a child take on the meanings

of impulses. Although there is a common cluster of activities associated with each impulse, these impulses vary from culture to culture and from individual to individual within a culture. Responses and activities of certain kinds are named "fears," but these are *specific* fears of *specific* objects, depending upon how each activity is conditioned by the organism's surroundings. An object which one individual fears, another may love. Fear, love, anger, rivalry, suspicion, hatred, loyalty, affection, competition, and a host of others have come to be designated and named in general ways for certain specific activities. On this view of human nature, it can be seen that new impulsive activities can emerge as a certain kind of activity is encouraged or discouraged by the culture in which the activity takes place. Again, some of the old impulsive activities arising from a different context and no longer functioning in organic and cultural life may die out. This is why the pragmatic naturalists claim that there is not a ready-made and antecedent stock of impulsive activities native to human beings. Their position does not mitigate the importance of understanding impulsive activities in analyzing human behavior; the position allows taking account of the fact that some cultures are warlike and some are peaceful, that some are competitive and some are cooperative. Much depends upon how the random activity of children is first given meaning and encouraged or restrained in each culture.

The impulsion or forward movement of the organism thus differentiates its activities into clusters of impulsive activities which sustain, protect, and enhance its life. Clusters of impulsive activities gather around the satisfaction of an organic need, such as hunger; in more primitive times, these activities involved pursuing, hunting, killing. These activities are integrated with memories and anticipations growing out of previous and similar kinds of experiences. All of these elements function together in the fulfillment of a need; that is, all the impulsive activities, the memories, the perceptions, the anticipations, give rise to a habit. Habits are generalized responses to recurring similar needs; they are outcomes of the stimulus-response sequences in an individual's life.

In the example given above of the animal whose hunger need involved a seriated activity from stimulus through response, it was noted that, in the course of its movement, the animal ignored certain irrelevant excitations which crossed its path. The animal's habit of pursuing only certain kinds of prey has evolved over a long period of evolutionary adaptation and accommodation. On a primitive and even on a more commonsense level, humans tend to operate in the same way. Only certain kinds of objects are classified as food, and, of course, this varies among different cultures, and even among individuals within a culture. In other words, there are only certain *classes of stimuli* which an organism will admit into its responsive life. In the development of habitual behavior the classification of certain stimuli to fulfill certain needs may be extremely narrow or broad, depending upon how these have been experienced, designated, and named. Narrow classifications, such as admission of only certain objects designated as food, result in a rigid, inflexible habit. On the other hand, if the habit has been formed so that the classifications of stimuli are broad or lacking in discrimination, then the habit is sloppy and ineffective, perhaps even disastrous to the organism.

A logically flexible habit is one which admits stimuli which are scientifically determined and which produces an adaptable, intelligent response. An example of a narrowly formed habit is one in which a person knows only one way to start a fire. Let us say that the stimulus-response sequence he has learned from his culture is that of striking a match. Without a match he is lost when a need for a fire occurs. But this same person may formulate a flexible, adaptable habit, one that is scientifically determined. By this is meant that he understands that the starting of fires is by means of friction and a combustible material. Thus, striking a match, rubbing two sticks together, or striking flint rocks together are all ways, or instances, of starting a fire. These examples are not different means of starting a fire; they are instances of a generalized means to a generalized end. In this sense, there is only one means to the end of starting a fire, and that is the use of friction. This example demonstrates how means-ends are so intimately related in an experience that they can be separated only in abstraction. When one learns generalized means to generalized ends, then habit formation is flexible and adaptive.

The point has been made that human activities designated as impulses and habits are given meaning in the group or culture in which an individual is born. Meanings could not be assigned to these activities, however, without the employment and function of symbols and language. The emergence of symbolic behavior makes possible new dimensions in human life. Symbols release us from immediate existential stimulus-response sequences in behavior and allow us to inject indirect activities into a situation instead of plunging forward into a direct action which is continuous with a line of activity moving through the organism. Stopping to think is a way of instituting one line of activity, a symbolic one, for the ongoing rush of direct action. A more detailed analysis of symbolic activity, of signs, meaning, and symbols, will be given later, but it suffices to point out here that symbolic behavior gives rise to the forms of reason. The interpenetration of the functions of impulse, habit, and intelligence is the basis for man's development of a life of reason.

A brief look at some alternative views of reason and intelligence will set in contrast the view of the pragmatic naturalists. So powerful and significant has been the role of reason or intelligence in human life that some have thought that the real source of these functions must lie outside nature and human experience. Some philosophers have imagined that the forms of reason must be found in some transcendental realm, abstract and permanent and unchanging. Others have thought that these forms are embedded in nature, yet outside human experience, and discovered by humans because they have the faculties to recognize them. Still others have thought that the forms of reason are somehow innately connected with the structure of the human mind and that human beings are endowed with these forms by some superrational being whose intellect contains the eternal forms of reason.

The pragmatic naturalists claim that reason and intelligence emerge from the life of human beings in nature. The naturalization of intelligence means that symbolic behavior and forms of thinking have developed in the course of human history. The forms of reason do not descend upon humans from a transcendental realm, nor are they embedded in the heart of nature, nor are they born innately dormant in the faculties of the human mind. The so-called forms of reason, of concept formation, of classification, definition, and discrimination, and so forth, have their foreshadowing in human organic responses to various problems. The forms of reason have been transformed in their use, and new forms have emerged, such as hypothetical thinking and the sophisticated methods of modern science.

At this point it is important to understand the ties which intelligence has with impulse and habit, for the pragmatic naturalists claim that there is a continuity of these functions. In the past it has been commonplace to set the forms of reason and intelligence in sharp contrast to impulse, and to claim that impulse has no place in the function of reason. In fact, it was thought that if feelings and impulses enter into the function of rational activity in any way, this dilutes the purity of reason and throws off the determination of the inquirer to move toward objective conclusions. The rejection of impulse and habit in the function of intelligence confuses purely personal factors, such as wishes, prejudices, and irrelevant individual concerns, with the function of human impulses and habits taken in a broader and generic sense. The pragmatic naturalist agrees that purely personal factors have no place in the function of intelligence, but he holds that to eliminate the genuine human functions of impulse and habit is to distort the nature of intelligent inquiry. Some thinkers have been so insistent that impulse and feeling be eliminated from intelligent activity that they have set up a hard and fast line of demarcation between the two, thus making a dualism of impulse and reason. Pragmatic naturalists claim that making a continuity between reason and impulse is rejected by many philosophers who have been historically oriented to a different sentiment of rationality. Entire philosophical movements have been built upon an avowed dualism of impulse and reason, that is, of the noncognitive and the cognitive.

When impulse is divorced from rational forms and when only certain of those forms are held as acceptable ones, then new developments in inquiry are blocked and thwarted in their progress. In the past, narrow views of reason have hemmed in the development of science until exploratory impulse burst their confines and struck out on new paths of inquiry. Progress in methods of reason and intelligence is made not by subduing most impulsive activities while exalting another, such as detachment, but by the proper balance and use of a working harmony of them. In a significant passage, Dewey writes: "The conclusion is not that the emotional, passionate phase of action can be or should be eliminated in behalf of a bloodless reason. More 'passions,' not fewer, is the answer. To check the influence of hate there must be sympathy, while to rationalize sympathy there are needed emotions of curiosity, caution, respect for the freedom of others—dispositions which evoke objects which balance those called up by sympathy, and prevent its degeneration into maudlin sentiment and meddling interference. Rationality, once more, is not a force to evoke against impulse and habit. It is the attainment of a working harmony among diverse desires."³²

The idea of rational activity as a harmony of the impulses may seem strange to those who have been oriented to the view that the intrusion of any kind of impulse into the rational process is the major source of irrationality. One conjures up pictures of the shouting, arm-swinging activities of someone with a violent temper as an example of irrationality; this kind of extravagant bodily gyrations may be contrasted with the soft-speaking, motionless bodily activities of the other extreme, for the latter has been associated in some respects with the behavior of a calm and detached rational being. Neither of these kinds of impulsive activities, which are purely personal factors, is what the pragmatic naturalist has in mind when he describes the life of reason as a balance of impulses.

The traditional notion of reason has emphasized the impulse of detachment and has usually been sceptical of the impulse of involvement and absorption in immediate problems and their subject matters. Little imagination is required to show that the attitude of detachment, when it becomes extravagant, may breed indifference and unconcern with the immediate, pulsating flux of the present. When the impulse of detachment is carried to the extreme, philosophers erect forms, abstract and empty, far above and transcendent of the momentary and the living. They view these structures as eternal and nontemporal. On the other hand, immersion in the momentary and the throbbing present can become so extravagant that what is immediate absorbs all attention. For instance, sympathy is needed to understand the problems of the disadvantaged groups or the customs and aspirations of peoples of other nations. Sympathy for other peoples, however, can become so extravagant that it jeopardizes the process of inquiry and understanding; thus detachment is needed to see a problem in a wider perspective and to raise questions concerning the causes and conditions of events. Reason is a balance of the impulses of detachment and attachment, a balance which experience shows is not easy to accomplish.

A story is told of the ancient Greeks that they surveyed all the existing and known gods and built a temple so that they could view in panoramic fashion this part of the world's culture. Fearful that they might leave out some god and that their survey would not be complete, they built an altar to "an unknown god." This impulse toward generality, toward universality, played an important part in the Greek view of reason. Impulsive revolts against the abstract universals led other thinkers to emphasize the particular and the individual, the specific items of experience in the pulsating present. The danger of the latter impulse carried to the extreme is excessive parochialism, a narrowness of point of view, and in the process of inquiry this procedure often results in universalizing a particular existence. The impulse to center attention upon a particular object and the impulse to survey as many of the same kinds of objects as possible must achieve a balance if an effective method of inquiry is to be developed.

It has been commonplace to claim that human rational activity is primarily, if not wholly, a function of intellect and that the rest of the organism is dormant in the process of inquiry. Actual scientific practice refutes this view. Dewey shows that science is born "of impulses at first slight and flickering: impulses to handle, move about, to hunt, to uncover, to mix things separated and divide things combined, to talk and to listen. Method is their effectual organization into continuous dispositions of inquiry, development and testing."[33] The implications of this view of reason for educational theory and practice are revolutionary, and these will be treated later.

Starting with the view of a human being as an organism and showing how its life involves physical, physiological,

psychological, and symbolic functions, the pragmatic
naturalists go on to affirm that there emerges a social self. A
social self means a human has a complex of functions, of
interactions and transactions, which are related in the continuity of one life. A life involves feelings, impulses, habits,
symbolic behavior, intelligence; it involves physical, organic, psychological and cultural transactions with the environment, human and nonhuman. Thus, a human life is as
wide or as narrow as are the interactions or transactions.

One of the most comprehensive theories of how the social self emerges is found in the writings of Mead. Human
beings interact with one another and with other parts of nature; thus interaction is a precondition for the emergence of
the self. One of the human ties with the lower forms of organisms can be found in the gestures which animals use in
their interactions with each other. For instance, when an
animal scents danger, it moves away from the stimulus; its
behavior indicates to other animals the object which
threatens. A baby's cries may indicate to its parents that
something is perplexing its organism. Animals and babies do
not know that their acts are significant; there is no idea
which accompanies the gestures they make. A child learns
that its gestures are significant when it is able to indicate to
itself the nature of the object. But how does the child learn
this? It learns to indicate objects with an idea attached to the
process by learning "the meaning as it is for the other to
whom he is pointing it out." In this emerging process the
child learns to "take the role of another." Mead says: "In-
sofar then as the individual takes the attitude of another towards himself, and in some sense arouses in himself the
tendency to action, which his conduct calls out in the other
individual, he will have indicated to himself the meaning of
the gesture."[34] "Taking the role of another" involves more
complexities. Mead shows that: "We must indicate to ourselves not only the object but also the readiness to respond
in certain ways to the object, and this indication must be

made in the attitude or role of the other individual to whom it is pointed out or to whom it may be pointed out."[35]

Thus, the self is social; the self is a life with all its interactions and its continuity through time. Precarious conditions threaten the self's existence; harmonious conditions sustain its life and make possible its enhancement. Within this context of existence, care and attention must be given to the physical interactions (the body), to the primary groups (such as the family), which are parts of the self. Care and attention must be given to the community in which a self is sustained, to the conditions in which food, shelter, clothing, health, education, and other activities are made possible. An individual's life or social self includes relations to a political public, relations which are immediate and direct, and relations which are remote and indirect. When one of these functioning parts of the social whole gets out of harmony, an individual's life is affected. This is why there is a constant struggle to keep life in balance, and this balance is not a condition which can be brought about in isolation from the sustaining conditions of an individual life and its social functions.

Some traditional concepts of human life have been put forth by philosophers who view a human being as an atomic, discrete unit, a separate soul or self, a mental or spiritual substance, completely divorced from a life in nature and the transactions involved. Once this kind of dichotomy is made, then problems arise of how the mind interacts with the body, of how the mind knows objects thought to be cut off from itself, of how the separate, discrete mind can share with another separate, discrete mind. Such problems have plagued philosophers for centuries, primarily because a sharp line was drawn dividing natural processes into two irreconcilable functions, thus setting up the condition of unsolvable problems. Terms like "subject" and "object" come in to confuse the problem; the problem of the meaning of "subjectivity" is heightened. The function of consciousness as an emergent in human life is transformed into an entity, into a substance which is thought to be vital to the notion of personal identity and the basis for individuality. According to the pragmatic naturalists, the act of transforming a function into an entity is one of the greatest errors in the history of philosophy.

For pragmatic naturalists the social organism is a center of activity. Events are centered in an organism, and this is the functional meaning of subjectivity. Feelings exist in the organism, it is true, but they are not *known* as private affairs. To be known, each feeling must be connected or related to some other feeling or event, even if it be a toothache with all its throbbing pain. An event, the occurrence of some qualitative feeling-state, is understood by connecting that occurrence with something which lies outside it, either as an antecedent or as a consequence or both. A feeling of a toothache is thus connected with an exposed nerve, a cavity, or some other condition which gives the toothache an objective meaning, even though one part of the process is felt by an individual organism as a pain. If observable conditions were not present, then the science of dentistry could never have developed, and no objectivity about toothaches could have been achieved, for the dentist does not have to feel the patient's toothache in order to *know* what causes a toothache or what it leads to. Thus, many of the supposed problems of subjectivity can be dismissed if such a view of the meaning of events in terms of their conditions and consequences is adopted.

The emerging mental functions in human life are not cut off from other aspects of the developing self. The self is a complex of many activities, and among these is the mental. Mead and Dewey build their views of human mental life upon the insights of James. James shows that there are certain functions carried on by the self which can be designated as functions of what he calls the "I"; other functions are those of the "Me." Mead develops a theory of these functions of the "I" and the "Me" which goes beyond James, and which is significant in current social psychology. Mead says that "the 'I' gives the sense of freedom, of initiative." On the other hand, "the 'me' represents a definite organization of the community there in our own attitudes, and calling for a response."[36] The function of the "I" which roams over the potentialities of the present, which proposes new ventures, which acts in initiation of new hypotheses is that part of the self which is free. The function of the "Me" is that of organizing and reorganizing new acts, of incorporating new elements of the ongoing life into the self.

Pragmatic naturalists hold that there is a commonality of human nature, that all human beings have certain functional characteristics in common, but this view of the common characteristics of human beings does not rule out the occurrence of individuality. Every organism is a *unique* occurrence in space and time. The generalized habits of a group do not exist in the abstract; they find their instances in individuals which express them. Whereas there are commonalities in human beings, such as general impulses, habits, and intelligence, there are also deviations within the general modes of behavior. The energetic impulsions of humans, especially in early life, resist rigid grooving, defy the group's habits and customs. The impulse to experiment is a natural activity of a child's life. This energetic impulsion of the human organism is a source of creative innovation, provided it is properly understood and guided by the agent himself and by those other humans who are parts of its life. On the other hand, if the energetic impulsion of a child is not properly understood and guided, it may result in organic explosions, in resentments, in rebellion without purpose. When energetic impulsions are guided into creative channels by the agent himself and others who interact with him, then new acts create new habits, new ways of doing things, new customs. Creativity always breaks the bounds of rigid habits, of stifling customs, of outmoded thought patterns.

Energetic impulsion is a condition of innovation and change; but innovation in itself is not always creative; it may be destructive and suicidal. When an individual brings forth new and innovative ways of life, which in the long run result in the increase of meaning and value in human experience, then the activity may be judged creative.

Suggested Order of Readings

1. Dewey, *The Influence of Darwin on Philosophy and Other Essays in Contemporary Thought* (1910; reprint ed., New York: Peter Smith, 1951). "The Influence of Darwinism on Philosophy," pp. 1–19.
2. Peirce, *Collected Papers of Charles Sanders Peirce,* vol. 6, ed. Charles Hartshorne and Paul Weiss (Cambridge: Harvard University Press, 1931–35). "Evolutionary Love," pars. 287–317.
3. Dewey, *Experience and Nature,* 2d ed. (London: George Allen & Unwin, 1929). Chapter 1.
4. James, *The Writings of William James: A Comprehensive Edition,* edited with an Introduction by John J. McDermott (New York: Modern Library, 1968). "The Types of Philosophic Thinking," pp. 482–96.
5. Peirce, *Collected Papers,* vol. 5. "The Universal Categories," pars. 41–65.
6. James, *The Writings of William James.* "The Continuity of Experience," pp. 292–301.
7. Dewey, *The Early Works of John Dewey, 1882–1898,* vol. 6, ed. Jo Ann Boydston (Carbondale and Edwardsville: Southern Illinois University Press, 1972). "The Reflex Arc Concept in Psychology," pp. 96–109.
8. Mead, *Mind, Self, and Society,* edited with an Introduction by Charles W. Morris (Chicago: University of Chicago Press, 1934). Pt. 3, "The Self," pp. 135–226.

PART 2

KNOWLEDGE

8. The Importance of Method

Pragmatic naturalists use the term experience in the fullest and most comprehensive sense. The word denotes feelings, transactions, and continuities; it refers to physical bodies and ideas and relations; it refers to sensations, concepts, desires, and emotions; it refers to actualities and ideals. Other philosophers confronting such an array of items have usually selected some one aspect of experience as primary and ultimate; this procedure allows them to use a simple criterion against which all the rest of experience is judged. The traditional empiricists, for instance, bring all other parts of experience to the court of sensations for the ultimate test of certainty and reliability. The traditional rationalists select pure abstract concepts for a measuring rod to be applied to the rest of experience. Materialists who emphasize the physical and idealists who select some notion of the mental have elevated their particular selections into what is ultimate and real. Thus, each of the philosophical critics can say that the pragmatic naturalist makes experience to mean everything and anything, that this view of experience is so inclusive and comprehensive that there is nothing by which one part of experience can be measured, tested, and certified by any other. These are significant criticisms, and they must be met if the pragmatic naturalist is to defend the fullness of experience as his starting place.

The answer to these criticisms of competing philosophies is found in the nature of experience itself. Primary experience possesses some generic traits, and one of these is the occurrence of discontinuities. In the movement of the organism through space-time, it encounters difficulties and perplexities; questions are asked and problems are posed. How shall these irritations be removed? How shall the discontinuities be bridged and overcome so that life can proceed? In the course of the organism's impulsion through time, its forward thrust, its responses at first are of the trial and error sort. The organism explores its environment; it searches and finds some way out of the perplexity it faces; if it does not find a way out, it dies.

In trying to overcome its organic irritation and uneasiness, the organism finds that certain means which are accidentally discovered lead to certain ends. These relationships of means to ends are so intergral to each other that they cannot be separated. On the lower levels of stimulus-response sequences, where they have become automatic over the long years of evolutionary development, these sequences result in efficiencies which are difficult to match on more complex levels of deliberate control. When symbolic behavior emerges from these organic foreshadowings, then humans can transcend certain parts of their experience and can reflect upon what happens to themselves in the course of living. They become aware of the relationships which sustain them on the nonreflective level. They note that these relationships involve various parts of experience which have become differentiated into physical objects, sensations, concepts, and intellectual operations. The philosophers who single out one aspect of these interacting processes put forth a partial truth about experience, but they give biased accounts because they put the selected parts of experience in the wrong context. The occurrence of discontinuities, the appearance of the perplexing and the problematic, and the emerging awareness of how these can be overcome by the use of relations of means and ends which have actually been successful allow human beings to assimilate all relevant objects, sensations, concepts and ideas to the process of problem solving. This approach provides for an unbiased treatment of the various elements of experience which other philosphers have selected as ultimate and more real than any of the rest.

In overcoming some discontinuities of experience human beings find that certain methods are more successful than others. They study these means-ends continuities, symbolize them, and recognizing their great usefulness in the solutions of problems, evolve a method from experience which is the greatest single means of controlling other parts of experience. This method is the method of *intelligence*.

Intelligence is a method of solving problems, of establishing continuities in experience and nature where disjunctions have occurred. When intelligence is defined functionally, the problem-solving behavior of other animals may be termed "intelligent." This meaning of intelligence is consistent with the idea of the continuity of other forms of animal life with the forms of higher and more complex organisms such as humans. The method of intelligence in human life becomes more sophisticated, however, because they are able to construct and to use a language. This makes the use of intelligence subject to deliberate choice and to deliberate correction in case of errors detected in its use.

Mention has been made of the generic traits of existence, some of which are the disjunctions which occur in the perceptual flow of experience. Disjunctions are not limited to those found in human experience; disjunctions occur in other parts of nature. This generic trait is not manufactured and imposed upon nature; disjunctions, disruptions actually occur. Disjunctions exist; they are "there" in nature and in experience. They must be dealt with realistically to reestablish the equilibrium or there is disintegration. These disjunctions are "situational" in character; they involve such disruptions as an exploding volcano, a receding ice age, explosions on the sun, imbalances in animal life in which some have become extinct. Examples of problematic situations need not be as dramatic as those just cited; they occur all through nature in less spectacular ways, applying to such events as the decline of whooping cranes and the increase of buffalo herds.

In order to understand the role which intelligence can play in the healing of the disjunctions of experience, perhaps it is best to start with a disjunction which is an intimate fact of individual and social experience. Charles Peirce analyzed this condition of situational perplexities in terms of doubt and belief. He writes: "Doubt is an uneasy and dissatisfied state from which we struggle to free ourselves and pass into the state of belief; while the latter is a calm and satisfactory state which we do not wish to avoid, or to change to a belief in anything else."[1] It is the irritation of doubt which stimulates us to inquire, to search, to act. This condition is analogous to the condition in the nervous system in which the continued irritation of a nerve results in a habitual neural response.

Peirce offers a description of the attempts to hold on to beliefs, of our methods of making beliefs secure. He contrasts three other methods of "fixing" belief with the method of science. One of the oldest methods of trying to achieve a serenity of belief and to alleviate the uneasiness of doubt is the method of *tenacity*. A casual look at the history of human intellectual life reveals how some have tried to hold on to their beliefs by repeating them over and over. This is most obvious with a belief which is given the meaning of a creed. Evidence may present itself which is contrary to the creed, but usually such evidence is ignored or deliberately suppressed, and there is an attempt to seal off the belief from any disturbance which will create uneasiness with the belief, and especially if that uneasiness is likely to develop into a doubt.

There is another means by which human beings try to make beliefs secure. Peirce says: "Let the will of the state act, then, instead of that of the individual. Let an institution be created which shall have for its object to keep correct doctrines before the attention of the people, to reiterate them perpetually, and to teach them to the young; having at the same time power to prevent contrary doctrines from being taught, advocated, or expressed. Let all possible causes of a change of mind be removed from men's apprehensions. Let them be kept ignorant, lest they should learn of some reason to think otherwise than they do. Let their passions be enlisted, so that they may regard private and unusual opinions with hatred and horror. Then, let all men who reject the established belief be terrified into silence. Let the people turn out and tar-and-feather such men, or let inquisitions be made into the manner of thinking of suspected persons, and when they are found guilty of forbidden beliefs, let them be subjected to some signal punishment. When complete agreement could not otherwise be reached, a general massacre of all who have not thought in a certain way has proved a very effective means of settling opinion in a country. If the power to do this be wanting, let a list of opinions be drawn up, to which no man of the least independence of thought can assent, and let the faithful be required to accept all these propositions, in order to segregate them as radically as possible from the influence of the rest of the world."[2] This method is what Peirce calls the method of *authority*.

The method of authority in establishing beliefs has a long history in human affairs, and dogmatists and dictators of belief in ages past are familiar topics in contemporary discussion of free inquiry. Socrates was made to drink the hemlock poison because he was disturbing to the established beliefs of Athens; Bruno was burned at the stake for his radical ideas; Galileo and a long list of others suffered because their ideas ran counter to the authoritatively accepted beliefs. We do not have to move out of the twentieth century, however, to witness the method of authority in establishing beliefs and the brutal consequences which accompany it. For example, the Nazi Germans tried to control the thoughts of their citizen-subjects from the cradle to the grave, and they put in concentration camps or liquidated millions who protested. In modern times practically every country in the world has seen the abundance of self-styled dogmatists who would determine authoritatively the beliefs of others.

Peirce shows that no institution can "regulate opinions on every subject." Institutional authority as the source of beliefs can regulate only the most important beliefs, for beliefs are natural to human beings, and new beliefs often arise spontaneously from problematic situations and from minimal contacts with the rest of the world where it is found that beliefs are different. Human beings living under the cloak of institutional protection of their beliefs eventually develop a wider social experience; they see that they have been conditioned to believe what they believe, and thus doubt creeps in to their established beliefs. As long as a man "can put two and two together," says Peirce, he will come to see that every belief brought about by the method of authority "seems to be determined by the caprice either of themselves or of those who originated the popular opinions."[3]

There is another widespread method of establishing belief which is more subtle and seemingly more rational than those methods of tenacity and authority. Some people have held that their opinions are grounded in the very heart of nature or are so natural that everyone agrees upon them; these beliefs are usually not founded upon fact or, at least, they have very little reference to fact. These beliefs are taken a priori; that is, they are supposed to exist prior to a determination by fact. Peirce calls this method the *a priori method*. He thinks that it has been prevalent to a great extent in the great metaphysical and speculative systems of philosophy. Opinions take the form of self-evident truths, the so-called truths we most often take for granted. As examples of this kind of establishment of belief, one may cite the commonly uttered statements such as "every man is selfish" and "all men are created equal." These beliefs, which are seemingly founded on reason and not on personal whim, are often never challenged and become the premises from which a whole array of consequences in thought and action is drawn. Once it is pointed out that a belief which one has taken for granted really does not rest upon empirical evidence, one may admit a glimmer of doubt concerning this belief. When this is done, the belief begins to lose its hold upon the mind. A real doubt occurs, and the belief "ceases in some degree to be a belief."

After analyzing the three methods of establishing or fixing beliefs summarized above, Peirce goes on to show that one of the most successful methods developed in recent years is that of science. Science is a method which yields that "the ultimate conclusion of every man shall be the same, or would be the same if inquiry were sufficiently persisted in." Science is a method of inquiry. It is a method which moves from doubt to belief, but its procedures are not vulnerable to the criticisms directed to the other methods of establishing a belief, for science is open, self-critical, and self-corrective. Science is an objective method, not dependent upon the caprice of one individual or a group of individuals. The phrase "if inquiry were sufficiently persisted in" is important, for it is the acceptance of the comprehensive and precise methods of scientific inquiry which produces agreement in belief. For instance, the objective method of scientific inquiry has resulted in an agreement in belief by all those who "persist in" inquiry that the chemical composition of water is H_2O.

Dewey and Mead, as well as James, were deeply influenced by Peirce's description of the method of scientific inquiry. Dewey and Mead elaborated many of the general and specific features of the method. According to Dewey, all inquiry begins with an "indeterminate situation." The terminology of Peirce has been changed slightly, but the meaning is the same. Situations become doubtful, that is, qualities in their functional relations with each other become disordered. A situation is *"confused"* when "its outcome cannot be anticipated." A situation is *obscure* when "its course of movement permits of final consequences that cannot be clearly made out." A situation is *conflicting* when "it tends to evoke discordant responses."[4] An indeterminate situation becomes a problematic situation when inquiry enters. Mead describes the process in terms of human behavior; he says: "A problem can be most generally described as the checking or inhibition of some more or less habitual form of conduct, way of thinking, or feeling. We meet an obstacle in overt action, or an exception to an accepted rule or manner of thought, or some object that calls out opposing emotions."[5]

The most detailed discussion of the various stages of inquiry is given by Dewey in a chapter on "The Pattern of Inquiry" in *Logic: The Theory of Inquiry* (1938).[6] The suggestion of this pattern is found in his early writings, and it takes on definite form in *How We Think*, published in 1910.[7] He reformulated it in various later writings and reworded it in a slightly different manner in the revised version of *How We Think* of 1933.[8] A detailed account of the pattern occurs in Mead under the title of "Fragments on the Process of Reflection."[9] These accounts of Dewey and Mead are too complex and detailed to be reviewed here. The following is a summarized version of the various steps in the pattern of inquiry, with some of the more important qualifications given for each of them:

1. *Awareness of a felt perplexity, a problem occurring in primary or immediate experience.* An indeterminate situation occurs; disordered qualities of the situation are present. The shock of a disjunction is felt. These kinds of situations may occur as physical, physiological, psychological, social, or intellectual.

2. *Location and definition of the problem.* Observations are made concerning what kind of problem is present. This procedure is sometimes called diagnosis of the problem. For example, a physician may need to determine if the observa-

tions he makes constitute a case of measles or a case of smallpox. The kind of problem presented guides the inquirer to the selection of the hypothesis which will be applied for its solution. This stage is important, for a problem accurately stated is half solved.

3. *Entertainment of suggestions, hypotheses, ideas for the solution of the problem.* Suggestions are embryonic ideas, at first vague and not completely clear. An idea in this context means "a plan of action" or an hypothesis. Several hypotheses are considered.

4. *Reasoning out the consequences of each hypothesis.* This kind of reasoning takes the form: if this hypothesis is adopted, where will it lead? If some other hypothesis is adopted, what will be its consequences? What hypothesis seems likely to lead to the solution of the problem? This kind of experimental thinking is carried on in the imagination and it involves the same kind of logical conditions as are carried out in a scientific laboratory.

5. *Finally, the selected hypothesis for the solution of the problem is tested in direct action.* This kind of testing is subject to verification. Verification is not confined to one or two cases, however, for there is always the possibility that the hypothesis chosen to solve the problem is not properly grounded. Verification of the hypothesis takes place in recurring kinds of situations over a long period of time.

Pragmatic naturalists believe that the foregoing pattern of inquiry can be used in attacking any kind of problem in human experience. The pattern takes on specific variations in the scientific laboratory where test tubes, microscopes, and highly controlled conditions are possible. The *general* features of the pattern, however, can be applied to common-sense problems, to moral and political problems; whenever criticism and reflection enter into aesthetic experience, its main features are present.

A few examples will show the relevance of some of the stages of inquiry. Let us say that we are accustomed to sunlight during its normal hours, but something goes wrong. Darkness appears. The location and definition of the problem may occur anywhere along a line of continuity in the process of seeing. It may be that an eclipse is occurring; it may be that a dark cloud is obscuring the view; it may be that a dust storm is gathering; it may be that something in our organism blocks the neural passages to the brain; or it may be any number of other conditions are operating to disrupt the process of seeing. The problem, when located and defined, may occur at any juncture along this line of continuity in the process of seeing. The problem may be located at the end farthest from the organism of this continuous line in the eclipse, or it may be found in the conditions of the human organism. When the problematic situation is viewed in this way, it becomes obvious how inappropriate it is to designate the process of inquiry as "subjective" or "objective" in the traditional meanings of these terms.

The observation of Mars when its movements did not accord with Ptolemaic theory produced a doubtful situation which was noted by Copernicus. This situation of doubt concerning the behavior of Mars is open to any inquirer. The range of doubts, of problems, of perplexities runs through all the fields of knowledge. Unsettled situations are natural in the sense that the broad and full view of experience and nature as hitherto explained always contains within it some discrepancies and confusions.

A word must be added here concerning a doubtful situation which marks off a genuine problem from a doubtful situation which is manufactured by the imagination. Peirce warned about this latter kind of pseudo problem. He writes: "Some philosophers have imagined that to start an inquiry it was only necessary to utter a question whether orally or by setting it down upon paper, and have even recommended us to begin our studies with questioning everything! But the mere putting of a proposition into the interrogative form does not stimulate the mind to any struggle after belief.

There must be a real and living doubt, and without this all discussion is idle."[10] Dewey also warned against manufactured states of personal doubt which do not belong to a doubtful situation. He says: "Personal states of doubt that are not evoked by and are not relative to some existential situation are pathological; when they are extreme they constitute the mania of doubting."[11]

In the course of working through genuine problematic situations, some perplexities, doubts, confusions are settled. The inquiry is successful in solving the problem, and the final judgment which eventuates from the methodological process is judged true. Sometimes the pragmatic naturalists are criticized for placing too much confidence in intelligence as a method of inquiry and as the method by which human problems are solved. The answer to this criticism is found in experience itself. One can ask: How does the method of intelligence compare with the other methods of impulse or caprice, of blind habit, of uncritical custom, or of dogmatic authority in solving problems? From what has been said about tenacity and authority, about a priori methods of establishing beliefs, the answer seems obvious that intelligence as a method of solving problems has proven itself the most successful.

The inference must not be made that the method of intelligence is final and complete. The method has had a history; its procedures began in a vague and groping way. It arose because of the disjunctions in experience and the attempt to overcome these. Its features were not given ready-made; they evolved over the years of grappling with problematic situations. Symbolic formulations and operational procedures have been refined in use. Some of the more widely recognized features of the method of intelligence will be discussed under the topic of "Logical Procedures."

9. Signs, Symbols, and Meanings

Contemporary philosophy has shown a growing interest in the philosophy of language, in the role of signs, meanings, and symbols in human behavior. Much of the groundwork in theory and in terminology for the study of language was put forth by Peirce and Mead. Peirce worked out an elaborate and complex theory of signs, and his views continue to be a stimulus to discussion about this topic. Mead's theories of symbolic behavior have had a significant impact upon philosophers and social scientists who share his approach to language. Dewey acknowledged his debt to Peirce and Mead; he built upon their insights, and he worked out his own statement of the nature of signs, meanings, and symbols.

Because of the complexity of the symbolic process, it is not easy to find a starting place for exposition and analysis. The various functional parts of the contextual whole of the symbolic situation are so intertwined that abstraction of one part for description and analysis is likely to distort the picture of the whole, even to give the part selected an oversimplified function when viewed from its place in the larger context. This is a difficulty, however, which attends any analysis of a philosophy of context and process, and these cautions should be kept in view.

The starting place of this account of the pragmatic naturalists' theories of the various functional aspects of the symbolic situation will begin with the nature and function of *signs*. At the outset, we meet a difficulty, for the term "sign" has many connotations, and present theory has not settled the matter.[12] As a preliminary and simplified starting place, we will say that *a sign is a quality taken to be connected with another quality*.[13] In commonsense experience, we often use expressions like "smoke means fire" and "dark clouds mean rain." Here we mean that the greyish-black-spiraling qualities which we call "smoke" are connected with the yellowish-glowing qualities which we call "fire." Somehow in natural occurrences, the qualities of smoke are connected with the qualities of fire. Again, if we saw dark-cloud qualities appearing in the sky, we would likely say that these cloud qualities are connected with rain (qualities of wetness, and so forth). From commonsense experience we have come to understand the connection of cloud qualities with rain qualities. If one observed a funnel-shaped cloud appearing in the sky, surely he would infer that this "shape quality" of a cloud is a *sign* of a tornado, and tornadoes have qualities all their own. If one expands his observation of sign connections in his experience, it should be obvious how tremendous is the role which qualities take as signs have in our lives. A baby's cry (sound quality) may be a sign to the mother of the baby's hunger. A rash appearing on the body is a sign of some disease. When we see our lawns turn yellow and brittle (color qualities and tactual qualities), we take these to be signs of lack of moisture (the qualities of dryness).

After we have had experience of the connection of smoke with fire, if we were to see smoke qualities in a distance, we could *infer* that there is a fire, even though the fire is not presently observed. If someone asks us what evidence we have that there is a fire, we could reply that the smoke qualities which we see are *evidence* of the fire qualities which we have experienced to be connected with them. Thus, inference and evidence are built upon the experiences of quality connections. Qualities, such as colors, shapes, sizes, movements, along with smells, tastes, hard, smooth, and so on, play an important role in both common sense and science. In fact, scientists in every field of subject matter must learn how to read the signs, the meanings and connections of the qualities they encounter.

Attention is called to the word "taken" when it is said that a quality of an object is taken to be a sign of some other quality in another object. In the cases mentioned above, it is assumed that these qualities taken as signs of their connections with other qualities actually occur in existence. That is, smoke is actually connected with fire, or there is a kind of *existential involvement* of smoke qualities with fire qualities. We have learned of their connections in commonsense experience, and we have further verified their connections by scientific test. There are instances, however, when we "take" a quality to be a sign of some other quality when, in fact, the connections of these qualities are not found in existence. One need only survey the countless superstitions and magical notions in the history of man's beliefs to be aware of this. For instance, some people have believed that a certain shape-quality of a man's head is the sign that he is a criminal. Sailors have thought that if they saw a rainbow in the evening, this is a sign of a fair day on the morrow. These examples show that man can "take" certain qualities as signs of other qualities when these connections are not borne out by natural existence; we have "made" meanings out of these qualities because we have connected them with each other. The fact that human beings can "make" meanings by connecting qualities with each other which have no basis in existence shows how we can construct fantasies and how we can create meanings of poetry and literature which need have little basis in existence. This dimension of the symbolic life allows the building up of meanings which are a delight to the imagination. In the practice of science, however, qualities taken as signs must actually have an involvement in existence with other qualities as a basis for truth.

Scientists seek for dependable signs, and when direct experience does not yield these, then the scientist invents elaborate instruments to aid in detecting the qualities which lie below the surface of the commonsense object. For instance, reading the needle of a barometer is a different dimension of sign interpretation from observing dark clouds as the approach of rain. Weather prediction now rests upon the sign connections of a falling or rising barometer with certain atmospheric conditions. A barometer needle falling to a very low point is a sign that a tornado is imminent, although the funnel-shaped cloud has not yet appeared on the horizon. The use of a thermometer in detecting whether or not a person has a fever is more dependable as a sign than feeling the body for unusual warmth. When the mercury in the thermometer rises over 98.6 degrees Fahrenheit, it is a sign of fever.

Thus far we have been speaking as if one can interpret signs without the use of language, and this is highly doubtful. What has been intended in the foregoing explanation of sign connections is to make vivid the connections of qualities with each other, which is a very important dimension of meaningful experience. It is unlikely, however, that quality connections can be detected without the aid of symbols to mark off and discriminate a quality of any kind, and especially if it is related to another quality. At least one point seems clear: Human beings cannot know that a quality is a sign without the use of a symbol. We would respond to the appearance of a quality as an animal responds to it, the quality would function as an excitation for a reaction only.

A symbol is a quality or cluster of qualities taken to *represent* objects as sign connections. This statement may seem strange until it is realized that symbols, such as words, are simply *visual marks* on paper (color and shape qualities) or *sounds* which are uttered. The marks or scratches on paper have a shape, a size, a configuration, and these are taken to stand for objects. In English, we have adopted the shape and combination of the letters "smoke" to represent or stand for the actual greyish-black-spiraling qualities which we have seen in existence. In another language, the shape and combination of the letters for the greyish-black-spiraling qualities of the object we call "smoke" may be different, as any student of foreign language knows. This fact points up the arbitrariness of language; that is, for some reason or another, which has been lost in history, those of us who use the English word agreed upon using "smoke" as a symbol for the object these marks represent. Shakespeare's famous line, "A rose by any other name would smell as sweet," makes us aware of this distinction between the object's qualities taken as signs—like the sweet-smelling quality—and the name or symbol ("rose" in English), arbitrarily adopted to represent this sweet-smelling object.

Caution must be used at this point concerning the statement about the arbitrariness of symbols. In common usage we do not know why particular symbols were first chosen; thus, we could have called that sweet-smelling object ("rose" in English) by another name. The adoption of a symbol in use and for communication, however, is not arbitrary. Two or more people must respond to the use of a symbol in such a way that the symbol represents for both of them the same object. Let us say that two people are sitting by a fireplace, and one asks the other to take the poker and stir the fire. If the other person responds to the symbols used by taking the poker and stirring the fire, we say that communication has taken place. Of course, each must understand what the symbol "poker" in English refers to, what "fire" stands for, and what "stir" means in terms of an activity. This is why it is maintained by students of language that symbols and language have a social origin.

Thus far description of the use of symbols has been presented as if a symbol is singular, isolated from other symbols. Singling out an individual symbol has been done for analysis, but this breaks up the contextual whole in which individual symbols operate. Symbols operate in contexts and usually they operate in conjunction with other

symbols, as in a sentence, a paragraph, or a universe of discourse. If one were to simply utter "smoke," "clouds,"
"chair," "boy," and so on, it is likely that associates would
think one mentally deranged. We speak or write in sen-
tences, thus individual words are combined with other
words to make sense. There is much truth in the description
that "a sentence is a complete act of thought." Instead of
simply uttering "chair," if we said, "Some chairs are com-
fortable," and our listener knew what the words referred to
and had some knowledge of the fuller context in which the
sentence is uttered, then it is likely that communication
would take place.

The question may be raised, however, concerning the
utterance of individual words in special contexts, where
those contexts are well enough known that communication
takes place. Take the occasion in which a fire breaks out in a
crowded theater and someone yells "Fire!" Or, take the case
of someone swimming who calls out "Help!" These individual symbols operate in special contexts in which communication is possible because in our culture we fill in the
context which is taken for granted.

The foregoing discussion points up the fact that individual symbols are related to each other in constellations of
meanings, or symbol-sets, or what we call "language." Thus,
symbols are *implicated* with one another, and implication
here has a wide designation indicating all the ways that
symbols are related to each other. Logical symbols, for instance, are a special set of symbols with special rules for
their specified implications with each other. Symbols used
in chemistry are a special set of symbols, like the use of H_2O
for water, and so on. Poetry and literature use symbols with
different purposes and in different contexts from those of
logic or chemistry. Once it is grasped that the emergence of
symbols in human life allows expanded meanings with
many different uses, it is easy to see how very significant is
this dimension of experience.

In summation, the foregoing account of signs and symbols reveals three kinds of relations: 1) qualities are *connected* with other qualities as signs; 2) symbols are *related* to objects in a reference function; 3) symbols are implicated with each other in symbol-sets or constellations of meanings which we call a language.

The account thus far of the symbolic dimension of experience is a simplified introduction to this study. Symbolic experience is very complex, and a brief look at some of the points made by Peirce and Mead will show this.

Peirce adopts the word "semiotic" as a general term covering the entire field of the study of signs and symbols. He appears to group his classification of signs around his three categories of experience explained earlier. If we keep to the synonyms used previously for these categories, we can indicate briefly some aspects of his general theory. The category of Firstness (feelings or qualities) contains what Peirce at one place calls "qualisigns," such as a feeling of red. The category of Secondness (interactions) has signs corresponding to it called "indexical signs," which mean the relation of a sign to what it represents, for instance, a weathercock. The category of Thirdness (continuity) has signs associated with it called "symbols," for example, words such as "man." These examples are given as an indication of a possible starting place for understanding Peirce's complex theory. If one were to delve deeper into his theory, it would be found that Peirce has a classification of signs of sixty-six different kinds.[14]

Peirce says in one place that "a sign . . . is something which stands to somebody for something in some respect or capacity."[15] This statement is another expression of the pragmatic analysis of meaning discussed above. Peirce gave the special name of *representamem* for the relation of a sign (symbol) to the object it represents. Heretofore it was explained that symbols enter into communication when the symbols used call out similar responses of the users; that is, symbols are meaningful only when there is conjoint behavior. Peirce adopts a new term for this dimension of the meaningful relations of symbols in conjoint behavior which he calls the *interpretant* of a sign or symbol. The use of a symbol or sign in communication sets up another sign in the persons using the sign or symbol, and this is its meaning in a social situation of discourse.

Mead's theory of signs and symbols also reveals how complex is this dimension of experience. Again, a simple element will be selected out of the more complex description of behavior as an example. Mead is famous for his description of the nature of gesture in behavior, animal as well as human. He analyzes in some detail how animals respond to each other in certain situations. A certain activity in one animal calls out another activity in the other animal, and this is a simple kind of *gesture*.[16] These interacting forms of activities become complex even on the animal level, and this is noted if one observes two dogs in a fight. Each dog's growling, snarling, striking, biting, and other postural activities become gestures to the other animal; the second animal, in turn, responds with its own forms of activity and its gestures. Such gestures are not on the level of gestures which have an "idea" behind them, or to put the matter another way, the animals do not "know" that these activities are gestures. As far as we know, the gestures of animals are simply stimulus-response sequences which bring forth other stimulus-response sequences. On the human level, when an idea accompanies a gesture and the communicant *knows* that this is the case, then the gesture is a *significant symbol*.[17] But significant symbols do not arise unless the user of the gesture takes the role of his communicant, so that the symbol becomes a meaning for both of them. Seeing that the other responds to the symbol in the same way as does the user is the primal condition of symbolic behavior. "Taking the role of the other" becomes an important aspect of all symbolic behavior.

Modern philosophers of language face a challenge in trying to bring all the various functions of language into some classificatory scheme so that the subject matter can be managed. Much of our language and the symbols which compose it have grown up in our culture without any reason for any symbol being adopted for various objects. Humans faced various kinds of problems and invented symbols for coping with them. When different kinds of problems arose, symbols used in the past context evidently were transferred into the new settings. Thus, we have a symbol which means one thing in one context and means something else in another. For instance, take the example of how the word "cold" in English is used. In one situation the symbol "cold" means temperature, as when we say, "It is cold outside today." In another situation the symbol "cold" refers to a disease, and here the symbol refers to a condition in the context of health. It is not necessary to expand such examples to illustrate how confusing is our language in common use. Dewey referred to the ambiguity of meanings of the symbols in common use as constituting "the babel of communication."

Scientific usage of symbols tries to overcome the ambiguity of symbols found in common use. Science attempts to attain precision of meaning, so that there is no question as to what the symbol stands for or in what context it functions. Thus, when a symbol is adopted in physics or chemistry, that symbol has a reason for its function in the constellation of meanings. This is why scientists prefer to use special symbols, such as those used in chemistry, to eliminate ambiguity and vagueness and to foster accurateness and precision.

The richness of language is found, however, in all the meanings which language makes possible. It was pointed out before that human beings construct meanings by "taking" certain qualities as signs of other qualities, even when the qualities, in fact, are not connected. Thus we can imagine relations of meanings, can construct pictures, can assign meanings to signs and symbols. The poet, the novelist, the painter, the musician each has a kind of language which is different from scientific language and from the language of common use. The painter, for instance, puts meanings into colors, lines, forms, which make up his own medium. The novelist and the poet can build up pictures in the imagination purely for their own and others' enjoyment. The musician works with sounds, rhythms, melodies which arouse emotional meanings in himself and in others.

The foregoing treatment of signs, symbols, and language indicates the complexity of the symbolic dimension of experience. Philosophers of language and linguists have made significant progress in this field, and the field itself has become a department of specialized study. Pragmatic naturalists were among the first to make studies of the problems of signs and symbols; Peirce and Mead made lasting contributions to the field. The elementary treatment given this subject here indicates how important are signs, symbols, and language in determining *how* we know and *what* we know.

10. Antecedents and Consequences

In 1878 Charles Peirce published an article entitled "How To Make Our Ideas Clear."[18] This essay has had a profound influence on the entire development of pragmatic naturalism. In the first part of this essay, Peirce criticizes the method of Descartes for the attainment of clear ideas, a method which had dominated many philosophers' minds for over two hundred years. According to Peirce's analysis, Descartes thought that the goal of the knowing process is the attainment of clear and distinct ideas, ideas so clear that no reasonable man could doubt them. The clear idea, it was held, is present to the mind, but in order to sustain itself as clear, the idea must undergo the test of dialectical examination. If, in the process of this kind of analysis, the idea stands the test and remains clear, then the idea is distinct.

According to Peirce, Descartes added the requirement of distinctness to that of clearness, perhaps because he saw that humans hold many ideas, each claimed as clear, but that some of these ideas are in conflict with each other. The test of dialectical examination is carried out by examining one's own self-consciousness by the method of introspection. Peirce thinks that there is an ambiguity in Descartes' account, that Descartes failed to provide for the distinction between ideas "*seeming* clear and really being so." Furthermore, the apparent clearness of an idea is often the result of being familiar with it, and familiarity is not a reliable basis for real clarity.

Peirce claims that the Cartesian method belongs to philosophies of the past, and he proposes that "it is now time to formulate the method of attaining to a more perfect clearness of thought, such as we see and admire in the thinkers of our own time."[19] Peirce sets out to demonstrate this new method of clarifying ideas, a method which he holds to be integral to the procedures of science. The new method of clarification may be applied, as Peirce applies it, to the meaning of "hard." When we say that an object is hard, we determine that meaning by bringing the object into an interaction with another object. We see which object will scratch the other, and the object which produces the scratch is the harder. For instance, we determine that a diamond is hard because nothing will produce scratches on it, but the diamond will produce scratches on other things. Thus, this kind of experimentation with the interactions of objects will bring to light what sensible (that is, observable) effects the interactions will produce, and this method elicits the meanings of the qualities of the object. Let us by further experimentation see what other observable effects a hard object will produce, and if we continue to do this, all the conceivable effects associated with "hard" will constitute its meaning.

Experimental determination of the meaning of a quality is not new to scientists who work with the interactions of various liquids, solids, and gases in the laboratory. In the history of chemistry, chemists have learned to determine the meaning of an acid by applying it to blue litmus paper. If any substance has qualities which turn blue litmus paper red, then it is an acid. Turning blue litmus paper red is one of the sensible effects produced by acids, and this consequence helps to determine and make clear the meaning of acid.

Peirce formulates these operations in a rule or maxim, and the maxim is stated: "Consider what effects, that might conceivably have practical bearings, we conceive the object of our conception to have. Then, our conception of these effects is the whole of our conception of the object."[20] The language in which Peirce casts this rule or maxim may sound strange; furthermore, the term "practical bearings" came to be misinterpreted. What Peirce intends by "practical" is the sensible or observable as determined by active inquiry. Because of the ambiguity of the word "practical," his meaning sometimes has been taken in the vulgar sense of "expedient." Perhaps if Peirce had used the term "empirical bearings" the statement of his maxim would not have encountered this difficulty. At any rate, Peirce wrote many years later that he was disappointed in the various interpretations which had been given his maxim.

It is interesting to compare the statement of the pragmatic maxim as James states it with the original Peircian account. In James's language it is formulated: "To attain perfect clearness in our thoughts of an object, then, we need only consider what conceivable effects of a practical kind the object may involve—what sensations we are to expect from it, and what reactions we must prepare."[21] James's application of the pragmatic method is perhaps not what Peirce had in mind, for James applies the method to the influence of ideas upon human conduct. James admits that he resurrected Peirce's maxim after its having lain dormant for twenty years and applied it to religion. James quotes with approval a letter from a man of science who wrote: "All realities influence our practice, and that influence is their meaning for us."[22] Whereas it is true that scientific beliefs or any other kinds of beliefs influence our behavior, this dimension hardly seems what Peirce had in mind when he formulated his maxim. Thus, it appears that James expanded the meaning of Peirce's original maxim from its context in conceptual and scientific matters to include the context of the effects which beliefs have upon human conduct.

In James's hands the pragmatic method centers primarily on psychological matters concerning beliefs and their consequences. He was fond of saying, "What difference would it practically make to any one if this notion rather than that notion were true?" When James applies this method to religious problems, the interpretation seems to take another turn. In this field one might ask: What difference does it make to my conduct if I believe or do not believe in God? In this case, it may not be possible to prove that God is a reality, but the *idea* of God has consequences to human conduct whether it is observably true or not. James adopts Peirce's notion that a belief is a habit of behavior, and when this view of habit is coupled with the pragmatic method as James understood it, there arises James's philosophy of belief and the role that belief plays in human behavior.

In James's hands the pragmatic method is applied to a wider range of experience, including a host of metaphysical concepts. Philosophical ideas, concepts, and principles have consequences, and James says that these consequences are concrete, factual. Ideas produce effects in terms of action and power. In a significant passage he tells what the pragmatic method means in his interpretation. It is: *"The attitude of looking away from first things, principles, 'categories,' supposed necessities; and of looking towards last things, fruits, consequences, facts."*[23] An idea has potency in what it leads to, in what it produces in the way of conduct in our lives. There is no doubt about the significant dimension of the role of ideas in our lives, whether these ideas (beliefs) be true, or false, or mythical. The beliefs about devils, ghosts, goblins, witches, and mythical characters have influenced large numbers of people throughout history. False ideas have had powerful consequences to human life. True ideas, those founded on scientific method (such as the idea that typhoid germs produce typhoid fever), also have had their effects upon human conduct. Whether James misunderstood or misinterpreted Peirce's maxim, there is little doubt of the significance of the analysis James puts forth concerning beliefs and their consequences to human life.

The emphasis upon consequences led many critics to claim that Peirce and James were not interested in the antecedent conditions of an idea or event. Sometimes it is held that they repudiated the past. This criticism does not hold; perhaps it is understandable that this inference is made from their writings, since both men repeatedly emphasize the consequences of a concept. The antecedent conditions for the emergence of a concept are of utmost concern to both of them, and both hold that concepts arise from percepts and that concepts are not reducible to the prior conditions from which they arise. This procedure of reducing emerging concepts to their prior conditions is rejected, for it would result in the kind of reductionism explained earlier. Once a concept has emerged, its meaning is found in the further consequences to which the concept leads, and it is not a matter of tracing back the emergence of the concept to the original percepts out of which.it arose.

Dewey had the advantage of working over both Peirce's

and James's versions of the pragmatic maxim. For Dewey, analyzing, describing, and explaining the occurrence of any event is based upon the procedure of looking at the event in two directions: 1) the conditions which brought about the event and 2) the conditions or consequences which flow from the event. Dewey claims that this procedure is the heart of science. He writes: "The knowledge of the relations between changes which enable us to connect things as antecedents and consequences *is* science."[24] This way of looking at nature and experience permeates all of Dewey's writings, and it is important to note that his analysis and explanation of all events, whether they be events of far-reaching consequences or simple events such as sugar sweetening coffee, are based upon it.

As an example of how Dewey approaches an event, let us return to his treatment of the occurrence of a quality. Dewey says that an event is the occurrence of a quality with meaning. In the section on "Signs, Symbols, and Meanings" it was pointed out that the occurrence of any quality has meaning only in relation to some other quality. It does not matter what quality we consider for an example, but let us return to the example of the occurrence of a funnel-shaped cloud in the sky. The conditions which bring this quality about are water vapor, wind currents, air pressures, and so forth; thus the funnel-shaped cloud is a sign of the conditions which brought about its occurrence. But there are consequences which flow from the occurrence of the funnel-shaped cloud, these being the destructive winds of a tornado, and one side of its meaning is in terms of these. When this procedure of looking at the antecedent conditions of an event and the consequent conditions flowing from it is observed as the approach of the scientist, the justification of Dewey's claim that this method *is* science is evident.

So pervasive is Dewey's use of this method of analysis in dealing with any subject matter that unless one is aware of how he approaches the explanation of things and their qualities, one is likely to miss the point in much of what he writes. For instance, on Dewey's view, it is not enough for a student of philosophy to know that Plato and Aristotle emphasized the importance of Forms in their philosophies. How did the notion of Forms arise in Greek experience? What are the antecedent conditions for its occurrence? What have been the consequences of erecting Forms into an eternal realm or into a static species in subsequent thought? The antecedent conditions which produce concepts or ideas may vary according to circumstance. In some cases concepts come about because of social and economic conditions, as Dewey thinks that the class divisions in Greek culture split the connection of the theoretical and the practical. Sometimes the conditions of the practical arts, the arts of making things, foreshadow the abstraction of the forms from these arts and their intellectualization into a separate realm. Some concepts emerge from prior intellectual conditions. It is not always easy to determine the antecedent conditions for the occurrence of a concept or idea, and there are those who do not agree with Dewey's selection of the specific antecedents which he claims have brought about certain ideas in the past. His selection of the forms in the practical arts of Greece as the antecedents of philosophical ideas may be disputed. Nevertheless, he attempts to explain this part of Greek thought in terms of what conditions brought the forms into focus, what conditions gave them status on an abstract level, and what consequences this intellectual condition created in later intellectual history.[25]

The foregoing treatment of antecedents and consequences rests, for the most part but perhaps not exclusively, upon a certain view of causality. The usual way in which antecedents and consequent conditions enter into our knowledge is through a sequential linkage which is logically determined and is stated in terms of cause and effect. The cause and effect relation is a powerful means by which nature and experience are understood. To discriminate sequential linkages, to know what conditions are related to other conditions is not an easy task, primarily because experience is so intertwined and complex. There are many theories of the nature and meaning of causality, and these run from the extreme view that a causal sequence is an atomistic line sequentially and regularly leading from one event to another to the organic view which relates one part of a process to another in an integrated continuum.

The pragmatic naturalists came upon the philosophic scene in the late nineteenth century when there was a lively debate over whether all nature should be viewed mechanistically or teleologically. The development of physics in the seventeenth and eighteenth centuries seemed to support what was called "mechanistic determinism." Using the concepts of early nineteenth-century science, some scientists and philosophers believed that everything can be explained in terms of matter in motion; they held that the laws of mechanics finally would unlock the secrets of nature, including those of the complicated behavior of animals and humans. Along with these notions went a belief in determinism, that is, a belief that if we have complete knowledge of the position, direction, and velocity of all atoms of matter as we do of the laws of mechanics, we can predict exactly what events will occur.

Another view of cause followed from Aristotle's analysis of causes, a view which treats one meaning of cause as final or teleological. By final is meant "end" or "purpose," and a teleological view of causes maintains that causes are purposive or end-directed. Variants of this view occur in religious thought where divine purpose is taken as directing the course of nature as a whole. In humans purposes are taken to be efficacious, and this endows them with moral responsibility. A different kind of teleological concept of cause is involved in the position of "vitalism," such as Henri Bergson's *élan vital*, in which the living part of nature is taken to be characterized by nonmechanical causal force.

Some nineteenth- and twentieth-century philosophers of the idealist type, in making mind the basic category of metaphysical and epistemological explanation, saw mind-like or purposive relations as characteristic of all nature.

To both of these views of cause—cause as mechanistically determined and cause as purposive—the pragmatic naturalists have had serious objections. As Dewey reads the history of philosophy on this point, both views are the result of one-sided interpretations of nature and humans. To Peirce the chief difficulty in previous views of cause is that the real element of chance was overlooked. Peirce's tychism is an interpretation of natural laws as similar to habits, the gradual growth of regularities in the occurrence of events which permit of statistical formulations.[26] Such mathematical formulae, however, must not be interpreted as referring to perfect regularities or uniformities, or as exhaustive of all aspects of experience. Closer scrutiny by improved scientific techniques reveals less, not more uniformity. Better scientific formulations result in more complete statements of "margins of error." Nature is not through and through determined or uniform or even rational. The areas of partial uniformity are surrounded by a sea of the uncomprehended, the erratic, the "bumpings" (Secondness) and the "feelings" (Firstness) which have not been touched by the growth of continuities or laws (Thirdness).

To James both the mechanistic and the teleological views of cause of previous philosophies are objectionable because they are part of the "folio edition" of philosophies which are complete and systematic and, thus, unsuitable to a universe which is strung along, pluralistic, open, and still in the process of being made. Hence, any monistic view of cause must be inadequate in this world. His objections to mechanistic determinism and absolute idealism, however, did not hinder him from welcoming Bergson's creative evolution. James saw in Bergson's philosophy the world still in process, and producing new things. Causes acting forward to the future are of more interest than causes referring ret-rospectively, or to a determination from the past. This ex-plains why James looked to the consequences of present events more than to the conditions which produced the present events.

For Dewey there are connections in nature, and these give us a basis for the development of sign significances; and these connections afford us the basis for the verification of our symbolic formulations. When symbolic formulations are developed into generalizations, these are termed "causal laws."[27] The connections and transactions in experience can be described as in themselves neither mechanistic nor pur-posive. These terms refer rather to the context of inquiry for which the causal explanation is required. That is, causal explanations are continuities constructed in inquiry to solve the problems arising from the discontinuities met in ex-perience. These causal explanations may be part of physical, biological, psychological, sociological, philosophical, or commonsense problem solving. If the inquiry is part of physics, the causal law may be stated in mechanistic terms, for there are mechanisms in nature. If the inquiry is part of biology, causes may be stated in terms of organic develop-ment. If the inquiry is part of psychology, causes may be stated in terms of such conditions as motives and purposes. There are various levels of interaction in an evolutionary world, and part of the problem of locating cause-and-effect relationships is that of determining through inquiry at which level a particular causal law pertains. This is a way of avoiding any reductionist or genetic fallacy in the treatment of cause.

The concept of cause and effect is an effective intellec-tual tool in the explanation of human behavior. Mead relates cause-effect relationships and means-ends relationships in the following way: "In the relationship of cause and effect there is the relation of the responses to each other in the sense of dependence, involving the adjustment of the steps to be taken with reference to the thing to be carried out. The arrangement which may appear at one time in terms of means and end appears at another time in terms of cause and effect. We have here a relationship of dependence of one response on another, a necessary relation that lies inside a larger system. It depends upon what we are going to do whether we select this means or another one, one causal series or another."[28] In the human being there emerges a consciousness of causal relations; it is then possible to select from the various causal continuities and adapt them consciously as means to ends.

The ability to adapt cause-effect continuities in experience as means to ends is an important emergent in human beings, for, as far as we know, few animals are able to perform this function. Pragmatic naturalists make a distinction between "causes of" and "reasons for" the occurrence of an event.[29] In ordinary speech these terms may be used synonymously, but the term "reasons for" is used by pragmatic naturalists in a distinctive sense; it means that an event occurs because there has been a deliberate plan of action on the part of some individual or group of individuals to bring it about. We frequently say that someone did something "on purpose"; by this we mean that he deliberately set out to execute certain means to the end he had in view. It is not always easy to determine if human activity and what it produces should be explained on the basis of unconscious cause and effect relationships or on the grounds of conscious, purposive behavior. Let us say that a child yells when it is hurt. The excitation-reaction sequence is easily understood, and there are "causes of" the child's yell. But let the situation be different; let the child wish to attract attention to himself. In this case the yell becomes a means to an end; the yell is executed "on purpose," and there are "reasons for" its being adopted. Again, we sometimes speak of an event being "accidental," as, for example, we would describe a child's problem of having locked himself in a room. Here, we do not mean that there are no causes of what happened; we mean that the child was not locked in the room on purpose. In fact, parents may spend a great deal of effort explaining to a child the cause and effect sequences which result in his being locked in a room "accidentally." As will be shown later in the treatment of moral behavior, the distinction between "causes of" and "reasons for" certain actions is highly important, for usually praise and blame are assigned only to those actions which are done on purpose.

Peirce and James do not claim originality for the invention of the pragmatic maxim or the pragmatic method in science and philosophy. Analyzing and explaining events in terms of their antecedents and consequences, Peirce claims, was done by others long before his day. Among those who saw the usefulness of this method in certain activities was Kant, who used the term "pragmatic" in much the same sense when he formulated his hypothetical imperatives, the rules of skill and the counsels of prudence. If you want to be able to acquire a certain skill, says Kant, then you must fulfill certain antecedent prerequisites for its performance. If you want to be happy, then cultivate certain conditions which will lead to happiness. James writes: "There is absolutely nothing new in the pragmatic method. Socrates was adept at it. Aristotle used it methodically. Locke, Berkeley, and Hume made momentous contributions to truth by its means."[30] These men used only fragments of the method, however, and it was not until the time of Peirce and James that the method became generalized. In James's words, pragmatism "has no dogmas and no doctrines save its method." To him it is a way of explaining art, religion, science, and metaphysics.

Thus, the pragmatic naturalists have a method of analysis and explanation of events, concepts, principles in terms of looking into the antecedent conditions which bring these about and in terms of looking to the consequences to which they lead. This method gives meaning to nature and experience. On the side of looking to the consequences of an event or an idea for its meaning, Peirce claims that the notion can be traced back to ancient times and that one of its earliest and most significant formulations is: "Ye may know them by their fruits."[31]

11. Logical Theory

The history of modern logic shows the many contributions of Peirce.[32] Peirce was far ahead of others in his day, at least in America, and it is only recently that he has become recognized as an original thinker on this subject. When Peirce went to Johns Hopkins in 1879, logic was not yet a major course in the universities in America. His courses at Johns Hopkins covered subject matters which have now become standard in many of our universities. These were courses dealing with formal logic, Boolean algebra, the logic of relations, theory of probability, mathematical reasoning, induction, and scientific reasoning.[33] Dewey was a student in some of Peirce's courses. It was not until later, however, that Peirce's influence made itself felt upon Dewey in his own development in this field.

Peirce thinks that logic went into an eclipse from the end of the Middle Ages until the middle of the nineteenth century. Science progressed, to be sure, but Peirce explains this advance on the grounds that scientific investigators were motivated by the search for truth and not by the role played by formal procedures. The result was an antiquated logic inherited from the past; in the meantime a host of new methods of inquiry had grown up with the advance of experimental science. Peirce came to the study of logic by the route of the scientific laboratory, and when he encountered this discrepancy in the development of methods of thinking, he made a survey of the development of logic up to and including his own age. In his theory of logic he attempts to preserve, improve, extend, and integrate the best of two worlds—formal methods on the one hand, and laboratory procedures on the other.

Dewey seems to have come to his interest in logical methods by the way of his readings in biological science. During his undergraduate days the reading of Huxley awakened him to the importance of scientific procedures, and in Dewey's first writings, he shows awareness of the problem of the relation of formal methods to actual scientific procedures. When Dewey began teaching at the University of Michigan, he taught courses in logic, but it was a logic in the philosophical tradition, a tradition which projected the formal methods of the past into the present situation. Dewey saw that the historical development of formal methods and of actual scientific procedures resulted in a dualism of the worst kind, and at first he thought that some kind of Hegelian approach might cure the ills which had befallen logic and its relation with other methods. As his career developed, he relinquished most of his early Hegelian ideas on the subject, but the problem of the relation of formal methods to other scientific methods is always present in his writings. When he wrote his major work on logic in 1938, he was still trying to bring formal logic and other scientific procedures into a working harmony.

What are regarded as Peirce's most significant contributions to the field of logic will depend, perhaps, upon the interests of those who read him. His writings on the subject are voluminous, and here only a brief selection of his ideas on logic can be discussed. We have already seen that Peirce believes that scientific inquiry is a method which can mediate between a doubt occurring at one end of an experiential spectrum and the establishment of a belief at the other. This procedure directs scientific inquiry in the direction of truth as a goal. A doubt occurs; a procedural means involving the cooperation of conceptual formulations and existential operations in the attainment of the settlement of the doubt or a belief is adopted. One important aspect of the inquiry which intervenes between the doubt which creates the problem and the settlement of the doubt is the selection of a *hypothesis* for its solution.

Peirce was among the first to claim that the role of the hypothesis is central to scientific thinking. All logicians are aware of the two methods of inference which are called "induction" and "deduction." To these Peirce adds a third, hypothetical thinking, or what he calls "abduction." At one place he writes that "every single item of scientific theory which stands established today has been due to Abduction."[34] On the function of the three types of inference in inquiry, he says: "Abduction is the process of forming an explanatory hypothesis. It is the only logical operation which introduces any new idea; for induction does nothing but determine a value, and deduction merely evolves the necessary consequences of a pure hypothesis."[35] Again he writes: "Deduction proves that something *must* be; Induction shows that something *actually is* operative; Abduction merely suggests that something *may be*."[36]

Hypothetical thinking, however, did not wait for Peirce and others to write about it before it was actually used, and Peirce shows that this kind of thinking goes back to the very beginning of human cognitive life. In the development of the formulation of scientific procedures, however, Peirce's theory concerning the function of the hypothesis in scientific and commonsense inquiries was among the first. Sometimes it is said that Francis Bacon is the father of modern science, but this statement must be qualified in many ways, for Bacon was more a popularizer and enthusiast of the promise of scientific investigations of nature than a significant pioneer in its methods. For instance, Bacon noted all the objects which had heat, made long lists of these occurrences, but all he was able to uncover by inductive method was that there is some connection of heat with motion. Peirce seizes upon the hypothetical type of inference to show that it is a powerful method in extending man's knowledge. One may gather fact after fact, arrange them this way and that, but if one does not have a hypothesis to explain what the facts mean in terms of new discoveries, then the enterprise leads nowhere.

When he says that modern science is experimental, Peirce intends this term to carry the meanings of hypothetical inference. While this kind of reasoning is integral to the laboratory experiment, it is by no means confined to the manipulation of test tubes. Abduction is a way of thinking; it is entertaining hypotheses and determining logically what consequences flow from them by deducing new facts. This is the way the human mind pushes out into the world of the unknown, and it is in this sense that Peirce says that we move from what we know to what we do not know. Since hypothetical thinking is a reach into the unknown, its performance involves a risk, a risk of error as well as a risk of finding the truth. It may also involve the risk of disaster, as noted by the number of scientists who have lost their lives in experimentation. In the contemporary problem of atomic testing, hypotheses are tested in which the risks concerning the effects of atomic fallout on the health and even the survival of the human race and on the rest of nature are not entirely known. Experimental thinking always puts the status quo of any situation in jeopardy, says Dewey, and no one is absolutely sure where the venture will come out.

Peirce's writings on various elements of logic are interesting both because of his insights and because of his suggestions. Even the proposals he made which went astray are fascinating to read. He developed what he called a "critical common-sensism," which starts with experience of human beings in common, and he shows how some of these beliefs seem indubitable. Take, for instance, the belief that fire burns, that if one puts his hand on a hot stove, then he will be burned. No matter how involved become the sophisticated theories about heat in modern science, there is always a relationship between theories of molecular motion and the commonsensical notion that a hot stove will burn your hand. Ordinary experience and ordinary language which reports it are thus connected with the sophisticated theories and precise language of science.

Peirce worked out some interesting theories about syllogistic reasoning, which in his day had become mechanical and uninteresting. In his first studies in logic, he worked within the confines of the subject-predicate logic, a logic familiar to beginning students in the forms of such propositions as "All men are mortal" or "All S is P." Here "men" is the subject class and "mortal" is the predicate. The form of the subject-predicate logic runs into difficulties when relations other than inclusion and exclusion are considered, for it is impossible to fit some kinds of relations into the subject-predicate mold and make sense out of them. About 1866, Augustus De Morgan sent Peirce his essay "On the Logic of Relations, etc." Peirce later wrote of this essay that he came to see it "as De Morgan had already seen, a brilliant and astonishing illumination of every corner and every vista of logic."[37]

The problem of relations became one of Peirce's chief interests. He saw that there are cases which create difficulty when they are pushed into the logic of classes as treated in the subject-predicate logic. He writes: "The fact that A presents B with a gift C, is a triple relation, and as such cannot possibly be resolved into any combination of dual relations."[38] The relation given here is what is called a triadic relation (or a triad). Monadic relations are made up of single characters like "white" and "large." (For example, "All whales are large.") A dyadic relation (or dyad) is a fact involving two subjects so joined that their meaning is determined by the union of the two. (For example, "John is

Mary's brother.") Peirce goes on to treat these problems of relations in detail and with much qualification (such as dyad being genuine or degenerate), but an expanded treatment of this part of his theory carries us beyond our present purpose. The fact remains, however, that Peirce developed De Morgan's theory of relations further, and his own calculus of relations, which was built upon the work of such men as Boole and Schröder, is perhaps his most important contribution to this field. When A. N. Whitehead and Bertrand Russell wrote *Principia Mathematica* in the first part of this century, many of their ideas on relations were built upon the work of Peirce.

Peirce developed a theory of probability which merits some consideration because it has affinities with some latter-day formulations of the problem. In one of his most significant passages he writes: "Probability applies to the question whether a specified kind of event will occur when certain predetermined conditions are fulfilled: and it is the ratio of the number of times in the long run in which that specified result would follow upon the fulfillment of those conditions to the total number of times in which those conditions were fulfilled in the course of experience."[39] Peirce limits this view of probability to the real course of events and claims that it cannot be applied to possibilities, for "they are not capable of being counted." By the use of careful definitions of the concepts and terms used in calculating probabilities in the real world, one could arrive at some meaningful ratios.

James and Mead appear to have had little interest in the field of logic; other interests preoccupied their minds. Dewey, however, kept alive an interest in the subject to the end of his life. His naturalistic logic is put forth as a hypothesis concerning how formal and empirical procedures can be functionally related within the total process of scientific inquiry. The postulate of naturalism, which underlies this hypothesis concerning logic, means that there is a continuity of organic functions with the higher symbolic functions. Dewey claims that logical forms have emerged from organic processes such as stimulus-response sequences, selection-rejection responses, and generalized ways of behaving. Logical procedures, however, are autonomous in the sense that they have functions which are different from the organic conditions which foreshadow them and out of which they arise. On this view, symbolic forms are not reducible to the organic processes out of which they emerge. If logical methods were explained as organic processes, the reductionist fallacy would be committed.

The naturalistic theory of logic, Dewey thinks, has several advantages. In the first place, since logical forms are natural, there is no need to project them into some transcendental realm, making them static and unchanging and giving them some metaphysical status of absolute certainty. It is not necessary to claim that logical forms, even the most abstract ones, are known only by intuition, for on his view, logical forms are functional in inquiry, and it is through their use that they acquire their meaning. Dewey's view of the emergence and functional use of logical forms releases the mind to construct new forms, to experiment with them, to test them in actual practice, and the task is not hindered by some emotional attachment to the absoluteness and finality of forms already discovered.

Dewey's treatment of logical procedures is in the context of the pattern of inquiry which starts with a problematic situation and moves to a settlement or solution of the problem. The various concepts and techniques receive their operational force and meaning in terms of the continuum of inquiry. Dewey admits that there are distinctions to be made between subject matters which are formal and material, abstract and existential. Scientific procedures use facts and ideas, observations and concepts, existential subject matters and abstractions. Dewey does not think that the formal methods should be divorced from the empirical methods; these two aspects within scientific method represent divisions of labor, and both are needed in solving a problem.

It is not possible here to survey the many special techniques and conceptualizations which make up Dewey's account of scientific method. This would involve summarizing all the elements treated in his *Logic: The Theory of Inquiry*. A few of the more commonly known procedures will be singled out in order to indicate Dewey's view of how these operate in his theory of inquiry.

Observational techniques make up a significant part of scientific inquiry, but observations are always made in regard to a specific problem at hand. Failure to relate observation statements to a problem results in a haphazard approach, making this observation here, another observation there, and so on, with no purpose in mind. Furthermore, observation is not simply looking and seeing and hearing. Observation involves an inference from what is seen to what is not seen, for without detecting connections among what is and has been observed, there can be no meaning to what one sees or hears. Besides being grouped around the problem at hand which determines their relevancy at the moment, observations are grouped in functional ways, such as those groupings which cluster around the prediction of the weather or those groupings which cluster around the functions of reproduction.

Observations cannot be made without the use of symbols, for symbols allow us to assimilate one event to another, to record observations made only a moment or even years ago, and to imagine observations of the same kind in future situations. Groupings of observations around specific problems, as these *kinds* of problems recur from time to time, show us that many of them can be treated generically. That is, groupings of observations are made in a particular situation and the same kinds of groupings of observations are made in another particular situation of the same kind.

The same situation never recurs again; each situation is unique in the sense that it occurs only once in space and time. Once experienced it passes into memory. It is not the same situation, but the same *kind* of situation which recurs.

A point must be made here about the clustering of observations around a problem or situation. Sometimes it has been thought by philosophers in the past that observation is connected with an operation of noting all the things in the universe which have certain similarities of colors, sizes, shapes, smells, and so forth. A moment's glance shows how far away from actual practice of common sense and science is such a method of assimilation and analogy. Let us say that we line up all the red objects in our experience. What would this tell us? What would be the meaning of this operation? The meanings of qualities, as we found before in the section on theory of meaning, are found in their functional relations in recurring problematic situations. A *red* pimple on the skin and a *red* traffic light are both *red*. But the quality of red functions differently as a diagnostic mark or sign in each situation, and it is the situation which fixes its meaning. On the other hand, by showing that observational groupings cluster around kinds of problems, it is possible to assimilate diverse kinds of quality meanings, such as a warm body with fever and a red pimple, when they are related to a case of measles. Without a problematic situation around which to assimilate diverse quality signs (and the observation of them), the process of assimilation of qualities on the basis of their similarities appears pointless.

Dewey shows how the various symbolic forms of logic can be interpreted in a functional way when incorporated into the total scientific method. In order to do this, he is compelled to rethink and to reformulate the conceptions and uses of most of the inherited, as well as of the contemporary, elements of logic. When he does this, he gives interpretations of the functional use of specific items in logic which are at variance with those of his contemporaries in the field. Their failure to see what he is trying to do often results in distorting his theory or making it completely absurd.[40] For instance, his interpretation of the functions of the various kinds of propositions in actual inquiry deals with propositions as neither true nor false. He asks: How are affirmative and negative propositions (All S is P and No S is P) used in physics or biology? What are the functions of particular propositions (Some S is P and Some S is not P) in chemistry or metallurgy? In a specific inquiry we are not concerned with the problem of a proposition of this kind being true or false. True or false applies only if a question is raised as to any proposition's veracity, but usually the truth of a proposition used in one inquiry has been determined in a previous inquiry. Take, for instance, the proposition "that is a red pimple," when red pimples are one of the diagnostic marks of measles and when it is known that if you have measles, then you should take certain precautions with the care of your body. If a question arises or has arisen as to the truth or falsity of whether the quality *is* a red pimple and of the final judgment of "that *is* a red pimple" or "it is not true that 'this is a red pimple,' " then truth or falsity is relevant. But note that in the case of the statement "that is a red pimple" functionally used in determining a case of measles, truth or falsity is not relevant; the proposition becomes evidential in the situation of determining if such and such is a case of measles.

When specific logical procedures are placed in the continuum of inquiry, then a different light is thrown upon their interpretations. For instance, Dewey treats the problem of induction by setting it inside the pattern of inquiry and explains its meaning in terms of its use in solving a concrete scientific problem, such as the determination of a bite of a certain mosquito as the cause of malaria.[41] If one does not follow this procedure, and if he tries to develop a concept of induction independently of how it is related to inquiry, then he is likely to set up superficial problems which contribute nothing or at least very little to the fruitfulness of induction in inquiry. Scientific method uses inductive procedures, as Dewey shows, but it uses them to solve a problem, and it carries out the process of induction only so far as is necessary to do this. There comes a time in a specific inductive process when it must show its relevance and fruitfulness to the solution of a problem. Furthermore, inductive procedures which are formulated in direct inquiry are not cut off from other procedures akin to them. Deductive processes and inductive processes work together, not in isolation, and both of these are never cut off from the development of a hypothesis and other data relevant to the problem at hand. It may be found that faulty inductive inference is the cause of a defective inquiry, but this can never be discovered until some kind of test is made which lies outside the inductive generalization which is selected as relevant. Inductive generalizations become more precise, dependable, fruitful, not through the number of instances by which we determine their formulations, but in their dependable use in the solutions of recurring kinds of problems.

In the treatment of Peirce's logic, it was noted that the hypothesis plays an important part in his view of the method of science. Dewey adopts the same position, generalizes upon it, and sometimes claims that it is this aspect of scientific thinking which distinguishes it from the older method, which was primarily that of definition and classification. Dewey popularized the terms "experimental method" and "experimentalism" as designative of the modern way of thinking. Furthermore, he, like Peirce, claims that the experimental method is not confined to the laboratory; it is a wider logical concept belonging to the manipulatory functions of the mind. Experiments can be conducted in the imagination, in the dramatic rehearsals of thought, and with slight modifications from one field to another, these experiments can be used in all problematic situations, including those of psychology and valuational behavior. It should be kept in mind that Dewey's fourth step in the pattern of inquiry is one in which the inquirer reasons out the consequences of any hypothesis. This is a kind of experimental thinking, and even the investigator in the laboratory does not limit his experiments to the test-tube variety. As he entertains some hypotheses, he can see in his imagination (in thought) what might result.

When Dewey adopts the term "experimental" to epitomize the main trend of modern scientific thinking, he does not intend that this method be taken as the only procedure used by modern science. In various places he lists other well-known procedures, such as observation, classification, definition, induction, deduction, and so on. If one were to list all the procedures he mentions and analyzes in his *Logic*, one would find one of the most exhaustive accounts of all the methods of science.

One other term which Dewey interprets in the total context of inquiry is one which has brought about extended discussion. Dewey views all the selected materials, existential and conceptual (material and formal), used in the solution of a problem as *data*.[42] These are taken in the most inclusive sense, and a sense which confuses his critics who think of data only as sense data or observation statements. When abstract conceptions, definitions, classifications, deductive procedures, and the like are designated as "data," this is a meaning of the term which is at variance with most of the meanings which have grown up in contemporary logical theory.

It is understandable that logicians and philosophers of science coming at the subject matters of their fields from different perspectives find Dewey's writings difficult to understand and, from their point of view, erroneous. Traditionally, propositions have been defined as statements which are true or false, but for Dewey they are said to be sometimes neither true nor false (as the truth of the statement "this is a red pimple" may not be in question when it is relevant to the inquiry concerning the truth of a diagnosis of measles). This is baffling and apparently contradictory to some logicians. Similarly, to say that color qualities may be data in some inquiries but not in others, while theories and logical deductions may be data in some cases, conflicts with traditional concepts of "data." If one attempts to see what he is trying to do, however, perhaps the issues can be cleared up to some extent. All of Dewey's writings on logical procedures, from the earliest to the latest, have been concerned with the unity of scientific method; over the years he tried to show the relatedness of formal methods to other methods of inquiry, for it is this dualism which he thinks is detrimental to the development of formal methods, of material procedures, and of science as a whole.

Many of the specific problems with which Peirce and Dewey were concerned in their theories of inquiry are now being analyzed and developed further by scholars in the field. This is what both of them desired. They thought of themselves as suggesting new directions in which the whole process of inquiry, of logic as they conceived it, could be developed.

12. Theory of Truth

In their conceptions of nature and experience, pragmatic naturalists hold that reality is changing and that knowledge which is built upon this reality necessarily changes with it. The absolutist view of nature as monistic, complete, and closed was destroyed by the evolutionary idea, and the pragmatic naturalists show that a new philosophy is needed to reflect a more accurate account of reality; thus, they conceive of a universe which is emerging, pluralistic, and open to new possibilities. The concept of truth which is all-inclusive, unchanging, and absolutely certain belongs to an older view of nature, a pre-Darwinian era, and now it becomes necessary to replace this view with a concept of truth which will fit the new world of nature and experience.

James points out these simple facts concerning the conditions of truth statements in a changing world. If reality changes, truth statements about reality must change too. But the old quest for certainty and the old monistic, absolutistic views were so deeply imbedded in the minds of his contemporaries that James set the philosophic world in turmoil with his ideas. How could truth change? Truth is truth, regardless of what anyone thinks about it. Our ideas of truth may change, to be sure, but there is *a truth* which is forever the same; thus, if James wants to talk about our ideas of truth changing, that is one thing; but to claim that truth itself changes, this appears philosophically irresponsible. The major difficulty, it seems, in understanding James's theory of truth is that it is set within the evolutionary view of nature in which change is basic. Two other conditions, however, are fundamental to understanding this view of truth; one is the pragmatic naturalists' philosophy of experience, and the other is the contention that scientific procedure is the ground upon which any idea or belief is established as true.

James holds that truth is a *property* of our ideas or beliefs.[43] This statement does not seem so radical when it is seen that people entertain many ideas and beliefs and some of these, of course, are false and some are true. If one were to say "the earth revolves around the sun," this statement would be said to be true, and the belief expressed by the statement would be said to be a true belief. In this manner we would be ascribing "true" to the belief, and thus the belief would have the property of being true. Ascribing "true" to the belief just mentioned does not take account of the grounds or evidence for the belief's being true. No scientifically-minded person today would accept this belief, or any other belief for that matter, purely on its face value and without concern for the methods and grounds upon which the belief achieved its status as being true.

James's philosophy of experience is also basic for an understanding of his theory of truth. It will be recalled from an earlier treatment that, for James, primal experience is a perceptual flow; there are feeling-states or pulsations of life moving through the human organism. This primal state is not definite in arrangement, is not formed or structured, and is not meaningful. Reality at this stage or level of human development is a flux which is neither true nor false; it is simply felt. Out of this perceptual flow, sensations and concepts emerge. Each person is given a block of marble, James says, and we "carve the statue ourselves." What he means by this is that we shuffle our perceptions of relations which are given to us in the perceptual flow; we arrange them and rearrange them. We read them in one serial order or another, class them in this way or that, treat one or another as fundamental until we construct logic, geometry, and mathematics, and so forth.

James's view of experience is at odds with previous notions of experience, and this gives some explanation, perhaps, why critics have been so violent in their reactions to his view of truth. On the perceptual side of experience, some who criticize James take for granted that the world comes to us as antecedent reality, ready-made, with sensory experience preformed. It is the business of philosophy, then, to formulate true ideas about what is *given*. This notion of the nature of experience James rejects. Sensationalistic empiricism, with atomic, discrete units already structured, is not his starting place. On the other hand, there are those who claim that it is the conceptual side of experience which contains the cognitive, the knowledge aspect, and that truth is a matter of clearness and distinctness of a concept or idea.

Concepts are related to each other according to the laws of thought; that is, they must be consistent with themselves; they must not contradict each other; they must be distinguishable from each other. For James the realm of truth implies much more than formal consistency.

James is a realist who holds that "all roads lead to Rome," and by this he means that all ideas or concepts must be led back to primary experience, to particularities which are immediately felt.[44] In this context, James's nominalism exhibits itself, a nominalism which holds that all concepts are verified for their truth function by testing them in the empirical world. When James says that the truth of an idea is determined by its practical character, he means that the idea leads to directly experienced percepts or feelings. "Practical" in this context has a philosophical meaning. Critics who single out the term "practical" for ridicule in James's theory of truth miss his main point, especially when these critics think that James had in mind the adopting of the meaning of "practical" used in American business life. He is partly to blame for this misinterpretation because he talks of the "practical cash-value" of an idea. What James intends is that ideas must lead us to particular realities, that ideas and concepts and principles must not get lost in abstractions which become divorced from life's problems, intellectual and social.

Another way of explaining James's point about the practicality of an idea is in terms of his meaning of verification. Truth is essentially bound up with the way in which one moment of our experience leads us toward other moments which will be worthwhile to have been led to. Let us say that a stranger asks me the way to someone's house. I tell him to follow a certain road and he will come to the house. As the stranger proceeds down the road and finally comes to the house, he can tell his host that I told him to follow certain directions (ideas) and these led him to the *particular* object he was seeking, the house. One part of the stranger's experience tries to get in touch with another part of his experience, and my ideas helped him get there. Since he was successful in finding the house, then the statements I made to him were verified as true.

It is some such meaning as explained in the preceding paragraph which James intends when he says that ideas must "work" or that they are "practical." Our experience at this moment can warn us to get ready for another piece of experience (as when a funnel-shaped cloud warns us of a tornado). Our present moment of experience can intend or "be significant of" a remoter object, this remoter object being envisioned or imagined during this present moment. This "leading on" aspect of ideas and concepts can take us toward objects, as just described, or it can lead into quarters where there are other concepts, that is, conceptual implications which broaden our theoretical horizons. Concepts leading into other concepts in theoretical constructions, however, must be brought back at some time and in some way to the particularized sensible world for their verification and check.[45] Verification of an idea is not achieved by tracing it back to its genesis, to the perceptual flow out of which it arose. Verification is always a forward movement, and this is why James holds that a concept leads to sensible effects which are other than the sensory counterparts which it describes and names. It is in this sense that ideas become true in the course of a search, in continuing inquiry which moves through time to a conclusion in a continuum of experience. It is obvious that ideas which do not lead to the particulars they aim for are false.

The process of verifiability runs into difficulty when the particularity which is sought is not accessible to observation with our present observational techniques. Take, for instance, the problem of verifying whether or not another person has a toothache. Obviously, we have not found at present any technical means by which another person can observe directly or feel directly the particularity of another man's ache. This problem of accessibility to particular objects for direct observation also enters into scientific endeavors. We cannot experience or feel or observe directly the occurrence of an electron. How do we verify statements about such inaccessible particulars, whether they be another man's toothache or the event of the electron? James says we postulate these particulars and follow out our ideas concerning them to their proximities, to the objects which we can observe which are nearest to them. In the case of the toothache, if we see the cavity in the tooth, touch the exposed nerve, and note the response, we say we are close enough to this particularity of experience to verify the man's having a toothache. In like manner we verify the existence of the electron. We observe the behavior of its immediate field, its surrounding conditions, and we postulate that the electron is there and functioning even though we do not have the technical means of observing it directly. Such problems as these do not destroy the importance of verification in the ascertainment of truth; they indicate merely the present state of the conditions of inquiry, and they point up the need for cautious procedures in making any statement concerning their truth.

We do not question every belief we have; we take many beliefs as potentially verifiable. We do not enter into a verification process unless some truth or belief is challenged. For ages people believed that the earth is flat, but this so-called truth was challenged, and it was found that it could not stand the test of verifiability. Conditions such as this in our intellectual history drove James into a consideration of the nature of belief and to an examination of how such beliefs once regarded as true change in their function and status. Most philosophers have been content to say that the old beliefs are no longer regarded as true, and new and better beliefs have replaced them. James is interested in how these changes in belief come about. An individual has a stock of beliefs which he carries around "under his hat," as James puts it. A new experience may unsettle one or more of these beliefs. (The entire stock of beliefs is not unsettled all at once.) When beliefs are unsettled, an emotional and intellectual turmoil arises in the consciousness. The strain may be precipitated by someone's contradicting these settled beliefs, or by an individual's finding his own beliefs contradict each other, or by his encountering facts which the old beliefs cease to satisfy. The individual tries to conserve his old beliefs (these are always dear to him), and so a new idea is often grafted on to the old. In this case the new truth is always a go-between, a smoother-over of transitions. New facts are "married" to old beliefs so as to have a minimum jolt and a maximum of continuity.[46] Loyalty to old truths is controlling; in fact, it is the first principle, for the obvious reason that these funded truths are the accumulated knowledge and wisdom of the race. Truths grow, however, and new facts are added to our experience in numerical fashion; thus we are obliged occasionally to make a rearrangment of a large portion of our stock of beliefs.

In attempting to distinguish his view of truth from the traditional ones, James adopts other terms which aroused philosophic criticism. He speaks of the truth processes as *"the expedient in the way of our thinking,"*[47] and he says that the leading-on aspect of an idea to its verification results in "satisfaction." James is a realist, and he claims that our ideas or beliefs, if they are true, must correspond to reality. The example of giving the stranger ideas of how he can find his way to the house at the end of the road illustrates the meaning of "expedient" and "satisfaction." The idea or belief which leads to reality in the most efficient and expedient way is its truth. One does not seek to get to reality (the house one is seeking) by a circuitous road or by oververbalizing the problem. Furthermore, when the idea or belief leads to the reality, there is an intellectual and emotional satisfaction concerning the outcome. The arrival at reality by following the belief or idea may take account of all the experience of the moment, but this singular experience may be narrow and confined, and this is why we must understand that, as James says, if an idea works "with all the experience in sight" it will not necessarily meet all future experience satisfactorily. This is why all beliefs regarded as true have a tentative nature to them.

Thus far the account of James's view of truth has been based upon his view of cognition. Difficulties emerge when we begin to consider his meaning of "over-beliefs" and the beliefs resulting from "forced options." There are theological and philosophical beliefs, speculative in nature, which cannot be verified on the view of cognition as previously explained. What does one do about beliefs in God and immortality? How does one decide between one religion and another and no religion at all? These beliefs cannot be verified by a process which leads directly to some particularity in experience. For instance, there is no particular object called "God" which the belief leads to and which we can directly experience. James appears to throw such problems over into the psychology of belief and to ask if there is some other way we can estimate or appraise these kinds of beliefs. At this point he seems to broaden the pragmatic method of ascertaining truths in the scientific sense. He claims that his method is one of "settling metaphysical disputes that otherwise might be indeterminable," and he says that one might ask: "What difference would it practically make to anyone if this notion rather than that notion were true?"[48] In other words, since these speculative beliefs cannot be verified by testing their agreement with reality, by observing that they lead to empirical particularities, then one must find their meaning and truth in their effects upon other kinds of human behavior. James thinks that metaphysics is like magic; it tries to solve problems with words. But if one were to ask: "What effects does believing in monism or pluralism have upon man's behavior?" then one might have a way of determining if these speculative beliefs amount to anything. Does believing or not believing in God or immortality make a difference in one's behavior? If no discernible difference can be found in the effects of believing or not believing, then the issue is dead. Here James seems to shift the meaning of the word "practical" from the sense in which he uses it in regard to scientific beliefs to a sense which implies psychological responses. He tends to think of practical not in terms of the satisfaction which comes when a belief leads to a felt particularity which the belief directly aims at, but in terms of satisfactions which are felt in other parts of experience. It appears that James has mixed psychological and emotional meanings with logical and scientific meanings and has left the matter confused. Be that as it may, this dimension of James's view of truth cannot be dismissed in a casual manner. Objects and beliefs arising out of the stream of consciousness, such as dreams and fictions, do have effects upon human behavior, and somehow an accurate view of their function and status must be developed in a total philosophy of experience. The ideas and beliefs found in poetry and art undoubtedly influence human conduct, and these somehow must be incorporated into a comprehensive view of truth.

At times James seems to make truth a species of the good. He says: *"The true is the name of whatever proves itself to be good in the way of belief, and good, too, for definite, assignable reasons."*[19] Using the example of foods, he goes on to say that certain foods are agreeable to our taste, but not only this, for they are good for our teeth, our stomach, and our tissues. In like manner, certain ideas are agreeable as supporting other ideas we are fond of, and they are helpful in life's practical struggles. They are agreeable and supporting, as food is pleasant and nourishing, because of discoverable objective characteristics which they possess. These truths are better for us to believe, and we cannot keep apart what is better for us and what is true for us. Truths are useful in the sense that what makes for human happiness is true, and those beliefs which do not make for human happiness are false.

For Peirce and Dewey, the existence of such emotional responses may be interesting to a psychologist but irrelevant to the determination of truth in a logical and scientific manner. The fact that people are psychologically affected by a controversy is no proof that the controversy is logically defensible. The individual or social acceptance of a belief on the basis of emotional satisfaction may be accidental, that is, not grounded upon a method of inquiry which is objective, public, and self-critical. Peirce and Dewey generally agree with James's account of the ascertainment of scientific truth; but James's account of truth becomes blurred and open to a host of difficulties when the emotional and psychological overtones of a belief are considered.

It should be recalled that Peirce and Dewey set their discussion of the knowing process inside the limits of doubt, a doubt which starts with a problematic situation on one side and with a settled belief on the other. The removal of doubt eventuates in belief or knowledge. The term "belief," however, has many meanings. In some uses of the word, says Dewey, it refers to "the settled condition of objective subject-matter," and if it is used in this sense, there is no objection.[50] But the word "belief" also refers to "a mental or psychical state," and this designates something personal and subjective. This confusion in meanings of the word suggests to Dewey that some other word ought to be adopted which carefully designates the objective nature of the situation and which rules out the personal and subjective factor.

Sometimes the word "knowledge" is used in an objective way to mean the settlement of a problematic situation. But this term also suffers from ambiguity. Sometimes the word means "a fixed external end," thus it carries metaphysical connotations.[51] Furthermore, this latter meaning of knowledge views knowledge as something distinct and separate from the evidence and the method by which knowledge is ascertained. In his later writings, Dewey prefers the term "warranted assertibility" as a substitute for the term "truth."[52] He interprets truth as the final judgment which eventually solves a problem or resolves an indeterminate situation.

The notion of truth as the outcome of successful inquiry, or the judgment which solves a problem, as held by Dewey, is essentially the same as the view held by Peirce. Dewey says that Peirce has given the best account of truth he knows, and he quotes with approval this passage from Peirce: "The opinion which is fated to be ultimately agreed to by all who investigate, is what we mean by the truth, and the object represented in this opinion is the real."[53] A more complicated version of this notion of truth is stated by Peirce: "Truth is that concordance of an abstract statement with the ideal limit toward which endless investigation would tend to bring scientific belief, which concordance the abstract statement may possess by virtue of the confession of its inaccuracy and one-sidedness, and this confession is an essential ingredient of truth."[54] Truth, then, is that upon which all who investigate by means of the scientific method agree.

For Peirce, Mead, and Dewey, inquiry starts from a problematic situation, moves through the rigorous methods of science, and eventually comes to a judgmental conclusion. All the data (data interpreted in the broad sense) used for the solution of a problem—the observations, physical manipulations, experimentations of thought and experimentations in the laboratory, symbolizations, propositions of all kinds, inductive and deductive procedures, and all the other aspects of inquiry—move toward the goal of final judgment, a judgment which is carried by symbols. Final judgment is the outcome of inquiry and satisfies the requirement of solving the problem. If the final judgment solves the problem at hand, it is warranted as true; if it does not solve the problem, then it is false. It is in this sense that final judgment in the solution of a problem is warranted or unwarranted.

As final judgment is carried by symbols, there is a sense in which pragmatic naturalists have a semantic theory of truth. This must be understood, however, in the context in which pragmatic naturalists conceive of the way in which the procedures of inquiry are tied to final solutions and the manner in which they conceive of a theory of meaning and symbols. For example, if anyone doubted the statement, "Snow is white," then a procedure of inquiry would be initiated to determine whether or not such a statement is warranted. That is, the statement, "Snow is white," is held as a conclusion or judgment which has eventuated from a problematic situation in which it was uncertain whether or not snow is white under all conditions or recurring kinds of situations. Once the statement has been warranted by the procedures of observation (taking account of all the problems of perceptual errors), experimentation under various conditions, concepts of what "snow" is in terms of its chemistry, and many other operations, then it can be said that "Snow is white, if and only if under the conditions determined by scientific inquiry, it is warranted that 'snow is white.'" It is a conclusion, however, from the funded experience of the past, from observing snow under many conditions and at many times and places. The history of the occurrence of perceptual error in the growth of knowledge cautions us about taking any perception or any statement about perceptions at face value. All statements concerning perception and all perceptions themselves must be investigated by the most refined of scientific instruments and procedures to gain that kind of reliability which one seeks in an experimental theory of knowledge.

Traditional theories of truth have been designated as

the correspondence theory and the coherence theory. The terms "correspondence" and "coherence" are adopted by the pragmatic naturalists, but they interpret both in functional ways within their view of inquiry. Mead says that "truth expresses a relationship between the judgment and reality."[55] He says: "The judgment comes with healing in its wings. It might be called a reparations theory, for, as we all know, a reparations commission requires first of all a formula, a healing formula. Most reparations commissions are no sooner organized than they adjourn, to be called together when a committee, appointed to discover such a formula, can report. Such a formula is a judgment. Its relationship is not so much that of correspondence as of agreement. The judgmental reconstruction fits into organized reality."[56] Thus, the pragmatic naturalists claim that a judgment growing out of the process of inquiry must "agree" with reality.

All inquiry from the beginning of a problematic situation which sets the stage of inquiry to the final solution which resolves the problem has coherence. There must be no formal contradictions occurring within the inquiry; this much of the traditional coherence theory of truth is correct. The coherence of an inquiry, however, means much more than the absence of contradictions in thought processes. Mead contrasts the pragmatic naturalist view and the traditional view of coherence this way: "If coherence means such a dovetailing of the hypothetical reconstruction with given reality, we might call the relationship that of coherence. But coherence theories of truth have in view rather the coherence of the structure of the judgment, assuming that as a thought structure it must be consonant with a thought constructed universe, if only it be correctly thought. That is, coherence refers to the formation of the hypothesis rather than to its agreement with the given conditions of further conduct."[57] Coherence within an inquiry means that all the data, conceptual and material, hang together and are related to the final judgment. So-called "independent" propositions which cannot be deductively inferred from each other cohere around a central problem, thus giving the process of inquiry a contextual unity.

Dewey once wrote that truths are rare and precious attainments. There are many meanings, many beliefs, many suppositions, many statements, and some of these are verified in the solutions of problems. Those judgments which appear to solve problems in the present may be upset by further investigations tomorrow. There is nothing absolutely final about any judgment; it is always tentative. Verification of judgments must be taken in the long run of human experience, and evidently this is what Peirce means when he says that truth involves "endless investigation" approaching that "ideal limit" which is the goal of scientific inquiry. The attainment of truth is accomplished by a strenuous discipline which is careful, cautious, and persistent. All inquirers who use the discipline of science undoubtedly know how rigorous is the method and how rare is the product.

Suggested Order of Readings

1. Peirce, *Collected Papers of Charles Sanders Peirce*, vol. 5, ed. Charles Hartshorne and Paul Weiss (Cambridge: Harvard University Press, 1931–35). "The Fixation of Belief," pars. 358–87.
2. Dewey, *Logic: The Theory of Inquiry* (New York: Henry Holt and Company, 1938). Chap. 6, "The Pattern of Inquiry."
3. Dewey, *Logic: The Theory of Inquiry*. Chap. 3, "The Existential Matrix of Inquiry: Cultural."
4. Mead, *Mind, Self and Society*, edited with an Introduction by Charles W. Morris (Chicago: University of Chicago Press, 1934), p. 42–82.
5. Peirce, *Collected Papers*, vol. 5. "How to Make Our Ideas Clear," pars. 388–410.
6. James, *The Writings of William James: A Comprehensive Edition*, edited with an Introduction by John J. McDermott (New York: Modern Library, 1968). "What Pragmatism Means," pp. 376–90.
7. Dewey, *Logic: The Theory of Inquiry*. Chap. 22, "Scientific Laws—Causation and Sequences."
8. Dewey, *Logic: The Theory of Inquiry*. Chap. 1, "The Problem of Logical Subject Matter."
9. James, *The Meaning of Truth* (1909; reprint ed., Cambridge: Harvard University Press, 1975).
10. Mead, *George Herbert Mead: Selected Writings*, ed. Andrew J. Reck. (Indianapolis: Bobbs-Merrill Company, 1964). "A Pragmatic Conception of Truth," pp. 320–44.

PART 3

VALUE

13. General Theory of Value

Each of the founders of pragmatic naturalism made contributions to what are generally called the value fields, to ethics (moral philosophy), social philosophy, aesthetics, and religion. One of Dewey's most significant contributions to the movement has been that of tracing out the implications of basic ideas in theory of experience and theory of knowledge into a general theory of value. On this subject his *Theory of Valuation* is an important work. Dewey also wrote major works in all the specific fields of value. James wrote a classic in the field of religion, *The Varieties of Religious Experience*. For the most part, however, the views of Peirce, James, and Mead in the specific fields of value are scattered throughout their writings and must be gleaned from their treatment of particular problems.

In the history of philosophical thought the specific value fields developed first, and apparently without the guidance of a general theory. The notion of a general theory of value has developed within the last century.[1] This intellectual condition poses some questions: Do the specific fields of value have a general theory which underlies them but which has never been made explicit? Is there an assumed general theory which affords the basis for demarcation of the boundaries of the specific fields and which is the foundation from which their respective methodologies develop? At present we do not know the answers to these questions. Some thinkers, including Dewey, believe that currently there is a need for a general theory of value. Dewey writes: "Till this field is reasonably settled, discussion is a

good deal like firing bird-shot in the dark at something believed to exist somewhere, the 'where' being of the vaguest
sort."[2] Construction of a general theory of value, however,
poses difficult and challenging problems. In the first place, a
general theory which makes coherent all the subject matters
and methods of the specific fields of value requires a comprehensive grasp of each of the fields. In the second place,
there is required some hypothesis concerning the interrelations of the various fields. For instance, what are the relations of good, social justice, beauty, piety (religion) to each
other? These problems are major ones, and other complex
difficulties will be shown in what follows.

At the present stage of theoretical construction about
all that can be done is to present some hypothesis about the
general field of value and hope that subsequent experience
and thought can evolve an adequate solution.[3] In line with
the pragmatic way of thinking, Dewey poses the matter as a
problem, and then he seeks to locate and define the difficulty. From ancient and medieval times was inherited a
view of value which lodges all particular goods in what were
thought to be the unchanging forms of nature. The inherited
view also claims that beyond nature there is a supernatural
and transcendental realm which contains values which are
permanent and eternal. Since the scientific revolution, however, there has been uncertainty about the goals which should
direct human life. In the first place, scientists have shown
that nature is changing; new species have arisen from old
species; some species have disappeared and others seem
doomed to extinction. The changing orders of nature put a
strain upon beliefs concerning some final or ultimate end
toward which all creation was thought to be moving, and
these beliefs, in turn, brought questionings concerning the
final and ultimate goal or goals. In the second place, scientific beliefs are tentative, not absolute; they are the most
dependable beliefs we have, but they are always accompanied by an element of scepticism. As nature itself is

changing and evolving, the beliefs about nature must change too. With the old beliefs concerning some permanent and fixed end or purpose of human life challenged, a new problem arises. What goals should or ought to direct human life? What kinds of goals or purposes should be pursued? How are beliefs about what should direct conduct constructed? And when beliefs about what should or ought to direct our conduct are put forth, what is their relation to scientific beliefs? Dewey thinks that this latter condition presents the central problem of our age. He writes: "The problem of restoring integration and co-operation between man's beliefs about the world in which he lives and his beliefs about the values and purposes that should direct his conduct is the deepest problem of modern life."[4]

According to Dewey's analysis, belief in some kind of absolute or transcendental value stems from the quest for certainty. The natural world in which we live undergoes constant change; some things are relatively stable, while other things are relatively unstable. The longing for something to believe in, for something secure, for "something to hold on to," in a precarious world has had a tremendous hold upon the psychological and emotional in human beings. Where securities cannot be elicited from the relatively stable parts of nature, they have been invented. Humans have selected those parts of nature which are valued in ordinary experience, have abstracted from these, and have constructed a realm where they are held to be unchanging and absolute. Ideals and goals regarded as unchanging give a feeling of absoluteness and certainty about values. When the tentative nature of scientific beliefs invaded the picture of nature and of human life, then the feeling of absoluteness was destroyed and modern life appears to swim in a sea of uncertainty.

Human responses to the emerging scientific picture of the universe have been varied. Some people still cling tenaciously to their claims that values are absolute and unchanging in spite of the tentative nature of scientific beliefs about the world. A sharp distinction is sometimes made between science and value; value is then elevated into a realm which goes beyond science. It is claimed that the subject matters and methods of value (usually the methods of intuition and abstract reason) are distinctively different from science and that some of the methods of science, experimentation, for instance, cannot apply. Others have responded by claiming that, after all, values are what each individual thinks or feels is valuable; thus value feelings and thoughts are purely subjective. A theory which has enjoyed wide currency in contemporary times is the "emotive" theory, which in its most extreme statement appears to hold that value expressions are ejaculatory; that is, they are like interjections in grammar. Words such as "good" or "bad" do not state anything or say anything, not even about a person's feelings. Such expressions simply evince or manifest the latter.[5]

The pragmatic naturalists reject the foregoing philosophical analyses of the present situation in the confusion in values. The situation, while perplexing, can be arrested by starting on a different line of attack in thinking and studying about values. The proper starting place, they say, is a behavioral one. They hold that we need to observe human behavior in order to see what each individual *selects* and *rejects* from the array of objects within the scope of a particular person's environment. It is noted that certain objects are prized and cherished and loved; other objects are rejected. What is prized, what is cared for, what is loved may be taken as objects of value. Prizing one's home, caring for the health of the body, loving one's family, taking pains about one's work, cherishing some art object, enjoying a piece of music or poetry, working for some social cause, devoting time and effort to international peace, are some instances of a person's observable valuational behavior.

The objects loved and cared for are dependent upon particular situations in which these objects function as values. For instance, fire is valued when it functions in situations where warmth is needed for the health and comfort of our bodies or where it is useful in cooking our meals. When fire destroys our homes or our forests, however, then it is not a valued object in those situations. Instances such as these can be multiplied. Critical analysis is needed in each situation in order to determine if some object is or is not a value. Again, some objects are valued at one time of an organism's development and discarded at another. A baby finds its nursing bottle a source of nourishment, therefore a value; adults, however, find other means and sources of nourishment and put away childish things. Much of the business of life is knowing when to give up an object of value which no longer meets our needs. Because value objects are loved and cherished, because they are accomplished with strong emotional attachments, value adjustments are the hardest to make. Keeping abreast of life's changes and keeping experience integrated and serene at every stage from childhood through old age is an ideal sought by all who take the value problem seriously. Since life does not remain abolutely stable, since it shifts and is constantly on the move, value behavior takes two dominant forms: 1) We try to preserve some object of value already in existence, to guard it against the constant threats of extinction. 2) We attempt to bring into existence some object which will meet the demands of the situation, in which case the sought after object takes on the quality of becoming a value.

The objects we prize and care for are under continuous threat of being destroyed, and this condition exists for two reasons: 1) Our biological organisms are changing and developing throughout our lives, thus our responses to a certain value object may waver and finally cease. Changes within ourselves may cause a value object held at one time in life to be rejected at another time. These organic changes, such as the one mentioned above in the movement from infancy to adulthood, may affect what we love and care for. 2) The environment which sustains each individual's life may change. Economic depressions may upset our carefully planned economic values; a flood may destroy our homes; a loved one may die. These environmental changes, along with our organic changes, always put some valued object in peril.

When some object held as a value is threatened or lost, human beings may respond in various ways. The response may take the form of resorting to some kind of impulsive behavior, to activities which are neurotic, to explosions of verbal expressions (such as swearing), to escape-behaviors such as taking to alcohol or drugs. In extreme cases of the breakdown of value structures, the maladjustment may lead to suicide. In every new value situation previously formed habits project themselves with a force which often complicates matters. Values and practices of a rural culture project themselves into an urban setting, the old values and habits of family life of pioneer times project themselves into a complex industrial situation, and the old values and habits frustrate and confuse because new values and habits are needed with life's changes. Again, some responses to a value situation take the form of adopting an authority who prescribes a solution, an authority who is too often without expertness and qualification in dealing with value problems.

When a value situation occurs, pragmatic naturalists hold that it should be treated like all other situations demanding inquiry. Thus, they hold that the general method of scientific thinking should be applied to value situations. Note that it is the general method of scientific thinking that is adopted; some specific methods of scientific procedure may not be applicable to this or that value situation. This is the case, however, with every application of scientific method in general; in every situation, whether in astronomy or psychology or value studies, one must select from among the various specific procedures those which are useful. The pattern of inquiry, it will be recalled, begins with a doubtful situation, a situation in which conflicts, obscurities, and confusions are present. The objects we love and cherish may conflict with each other, both in their conditions of attainment and in their relations with each other when attained. One may desire an art object; obtaining possession of it, however, may disrupt one's financial security. Desire for an education may conflict with the care for one's family. When a value situation occurs, one begins by locating and defining the problem, by entertaining ideas and hypotheses for its solution. One does not rush into action without deliberation; one first reasons out the broad consequences of choosing one value over another. These broad consequences involve other parts of character and life, including the family, the community, and humanity at large. After carrying out this kind of deliberation, the best hypothesis is chosen and acted upon. Time and experience will show if the decision is intelligent.

It was noted previously that the pragmatic naturalists think that value studies should begin with observations of the behavior of individuals, with what each person selects and rejects from the environment. Observations should be made of what human beings love, cherish, care for, or as is sometimes stated, of what they desire. When the term "desire" is introduced into the discussion, it is adopted with a special meaning.[6] Desire is not simply a mental occurrence, it is the projection of a goal involving effort to achieve. If a person saves money, denies the self of some pleasures, works long hours so that a trip can be taken to a foreign country, then we say that all these observed activities denote a desire to travel. Desiring must not be confused with wishing, however, for wishing is not accomplished with activities which we call "effort." Thus, a person who wishes merely dreams of traveling abroad and does nothing to bring about the actualization of this goal. While desires are always specific activities, they may be grouped around certain larger goals, and these larger goals are called "interests." Interest activities usually require a long time-span for accomplishment. For instance, interests in international peace, in social reform, in education, are lifelong activities.

Observing and recording what people select and reject, what they prize and care for, gives us a sociology of value behavior. This procedure tells us what people actually *do* love and prize. The statements about what people do enjoy or have enjoyed are factual statements like any other statements of fact in science. Dewey thinks that the traditional empirical theory of value rests upon a calculation of what people do enjoy or have enjoyed in the past.[7] If this were all there is to the value problem, the task of formulating value theory would not be difficult. We could gather facts about what are prized and cared for, organize the facts into some kind of pattern or patterns, and claim that what most people love and enjoy *ought* to be loved and enjoyed. This procedure, while preliminary to the development of a general theory of value, sidesteps the genuine problem, for what people have loved or desired is not always lovable or desirable. Traditional empirical value theorists have tended to make what is desired by humans equal to what is desirable, and for the pragmatic naturalists this is generally an error. It may be true that what is desired is intellectually and critically desirable, but this can be known only after inquiry into the value situation.

"Some things sweet in the having are bitter in aftertaste,"[8] writes Dewey; thus some object prized or desired may lead to consequences which are destructive of other values, and in some cases may even lead to death. The crucial problem of valuational behavior centers around the relation of the desired to the desirable. While desires have some critical reflection attached to them, more often they need a more comprehensive treatment in terms of the broader and more precise methods of intelligence to determine if what is desired is desirable. The concept of the desirability of an object is constructed by looking into the conditions and the consequences which its being desired makes. In constructing the desirability of a desired object, one may draw upon the whole of human knowledge. Scientific beliefs about the object are indispensable in constructing the desirability and undesirability of an object. Take, for example, the scientific determination of the effects of an insecticide such as DDT. This insecticide is useful in controlling certain insects, and thus it takes on value. But the chemical components of this insecticide do not break down, or at least at the time of this writing no way has been found to break them down. One of the consequences of the use of this insecticide is that it builds up in the bodies of fish, animals, and humans and becomes harmful to the existence of all. The consequences of the use of this insecticide are determined by inquiry in the scientific laboratory; thus the conclusion is a scientific fact. But human response to this scientifically determined fact, the selection or rejection of it, goes beyond a bare description of a fact; it takes on a functional importance in valuational situations. It is now judged to be undesirable as an object of value in some situations.

A desired object may change its status and function as a value when a broad vision of the consequences is ascertained. If its being desired meets no objections, that is, if common sense and scientific imagination can detect no disastrous consequences, and if this value will not put other critically analyzed values in peril, then we can say that the desired object is desirable. It may be argued, of course, that when an object has stood the test of critical analysis and is cherished more deeply because of this test, that it is still a desired object. This is true, but it is now a desired object which enters a new plateau of experience; it is desired because it is desirable. Experience and inquiry show us that there is a significant difference between a desired object subjected to inquiry and accepted as desirable and a desired object which fails the test of critical scrutiny and is rejected.

It appears that more and more scientific determination of the consequences flowing from certain objects is making inroads upon the value selections of our lives.[9] There are objects which are desired, of course, which science shows to have disastrous consequences. Bringing our valued objects in line with what scientific determination and intelligent imagination determine as valuable is a matter of education.

The foregoing outline of a general theory of value is put forth as a hypothesis. It is a framework within which to carry on inquiry into specific problems of value and into the problems of constructing a more precise and fruitful general theory of value. One of the primary problems facing current investigation is the development of a language of value.[10] While the pragmatic naturalists have contributed some linguistic terms for the treatment of value, these terms have not become universally accepted. There is the further problem of the scientific development in psychology and sociology, for these fields are the bases from which the study of valuational behavior must be further developed and systematized. Dewey and others have tried to make more precise some psychological terms pertinent to value theory, terms such as prizing, desire, willing, interest, and so forth. But there is a whole range of psychological terms and their denotations which needs more precise analysis, terms such as motive, intention, habit, impulse, emotion, and many others. Until the field of value is more precisely defined, it is difficult for sociologists to proceed in describing, organizing, and ranking various kinds of valuational behaviors. One of the most difficult problems encountered in constructing a general theory of value concerns the development of a methodology. Any methodology which is adopted must take account of the relation of descriptive propositions to prescriptive propositions, of the relation of the "is" to the "ought." The logic of evaluation and its relation to procedures in the several natural sciences is a challenging undertaking.

In the meanwhile without guidance of a well-developed general theory of value, we must remain content with what has been thought and critically analyzed in the specific fields of value. The moral life is one which we have sought to achieve and to value. Aesthetic experiences undergone in everyday life have been refined into objectified expressions (painting, sculpture, music, poetry, and the like). Many have held that democracy is a value, a value for which some have given the full measure of their devotion. The religious life is a life in which all the values of an individual cohere, and when ideals and goals are critically analyzed and organized into a unity of feeling and thought, then this goal becomes the ultimate commitment.

14. Moral Philosophy

William James came upon the philosophic scene during a period when the arguments over determinism and freedom seemed to have reached an impasse, and some philosophers claimed that nothing more could be said upon the subject. James revived the issue, however, because it is a vital one for him. If man has no freedom, then moral decisions and actions involve no real possibilities and human conduct can be judged neither good nor bad.

James wrote a famous essay, "The Dilemma of Determinism," and the views he puts forth stimulated discussion of the problem of determinism and freedom which extends to the present. The ideas about determinism contemporary with James had reached a stage of thought where, as he says, one was either a "hard" or "soft" determinist. Hard determinism, a view which James called "old fashioned," adopted words like "fatality, bondage of the will, necessitation, and the like."[11] During James's time, soft determinism was the more popular view; it repudiated words like "fatality, necessity, and even predeterminism," and held that soft determinism is the real name for freedom. Freedom in this context means "necessity understood and bondage to the highest is identical with true freedom."

James is not satisfied with these philosophical statements about this aspect of human experience. We do not live in a block universe in which every bit and piece of experience fits into a unitary scheme. We live in a pluralistic universe where there are continuities (causal ones), but our experience also contains disjunctions, real gaps, in which one part of experience cannot be causally related to every other and to some monistically conceived whole. Human freedom, he claims, is set within a context in which there are real instances of indeterminism or real instances of chance. At these junctures in experience we can initiate new lines of activity; we can act as causal agents. Take, for instance, the person who commits treachery and murder. If one holds to a rigid determinism, can the person make judgments of regret which are meaningful? Can others pass moral judgment upon him if he cannot be blamed or praised for originating certain actions? James thinks that in a monistic deterministic view of experience judgments of regret are out of place. He puts the dilemma this way: "Murder and treachery cannot be good without regret being bad; regret cannot be good without treachery and murder being bad."[12]

For James the clue to the moral dimension of life is found in the fact that humans are free to act, and the acting becomes objectified conduct. Human beings are the sole causes and originators of some actions at least, and for these they must assume responsibility. At certain junctures in experience where discontinuities and gaps occur, where these gaps cannot be causally related to any past and where the future is open, then real possibilities appear, and a person has the potentiality of becoming a causal agent; that is, he can initiate new or at least different continuities. As a causal agent his actions become objectified conduct and are subject to judgments of morality. The act he performs in these kinds of situations may be either good or bad, and he can be praised or blamed for what he does. The act performed, however, carries no metaphysical guarantee of success or failure; the act involves a risk which is the condition of freedom of the moral life.

William James says that "there can be no final truth in ethics anymore than in physics, until the last man has had his experience and said his say."[13] James believes that the individual has impulses, desires, intuitions which are spontaneous. This spontaneity is the source of new ideals and principles which cut the ground from under any claims of final and absolute views. The starting place of James's account of the moral life is found in his belief that an individual even in his solitude has preferences. Human desires and demands upon life generate ideals and goals to be brought into existence. When individuals' solitary desires are joined in social life, numerous ideals and preferences emerge. In a limited social life it may be possible for people to be indifferent to each other's ideals and preferences; in this case there would be little moral unity. In fact, however, social situations in which individuals act produce claims made upon each other, and these claims are the source of obligations. Experience teaches that some claims are more authoritative and more demanding than others. The ideals of philosophers are one part of the social life and they take their place alongside the ideals and claims of other groups; thus the philosophers' ideals become part of the common lot of preferences. Whatever claim is put forth and however a claim is justified, whether by a philosopher or by someone holding that the Deity demands it, the truth is that some human response must be made to it. Even a rejection of the claim is one kind of human response to any ideal. It is in feelings, desires, and responses of humans to various ideals and claims that terms such as "good," "bad," and "obligation" have their source.

Some of the reciprocal claims and obligations which spring from feelings, desires, and responses are more far-reaching than others. Philosophers have tried to find an essential commonality in the many moral systems. Some hold that obligation is a mean between two extremes; others have said that the common element is to make others happy; others have held that our willing should follow our reason, and so on. According to James, about all that can be concluded from a survey of the different ethical systems is that none of them has given general satisfaction. Thus, he concludes that the essence of good is simply to satisfy demand. But demands are many, and they cannot be brought under a single law anymore than the phenomena of physics can be brought under a single law.

In a world constituted as is the one in which we live, it is impossible to satisfy all human demands. Some ideals must be "butchered," and this is the tragedy of the moral situation and of each moral decision. To be objective we ought not deny any ideal a hearing. This means that we should try to satisfy as many demands as we can in choosing to act toward the best whole, or to put it another way, we should attempt to awaken the least sum of dissatisfactions. Thus, those ideals are written highest which prevail at the least cost, that is, in whose realization the least number of other ideals are destroyed. James thinks that the course of history has been an attempt to find a more inclusive moral order, a way of life in which more and more desires and demands can be satisfied. A moral prophet proposes a new ideal which will bring about a larger ideal whole; the moral conservative tries to preserve the goods already gained. The moral philosopher must include the prophet and the conservative in his account.

According to James some ideals are easygoing in the

demands they make upon us; others are more tyrannical. Some ideals can be put aside casually, but other ideals return to haunt us. This tyranny that certain ideals hold over us means that they are felt as imperatives. Peace of mind can come only when we keep the imperative goods at the top of our scale of values. The ideals which demand the most of us create a strenuous mood, causing us to be indifferent to a present ill. The more imperative ideal needs wilder passions to arouse it. Big fears, great loves, and intense indignations are required to bring this ideal about. The most penetrating appeals are to the higher fidelities—justice, truth, and freedom.

James links impulse to reason and imagination, and nowhere is his position made more relevant to concrete problems than in his essay, "The Moral Equivalent of War." He holds that the "military feelings," the feelings of the strong and hardy life have been inherited from the past.[14] These feelings which generate military ideals are so ingrained in human experience that "showing war's irrationality and horror" makes no effect upon us. In fact, we seem to glory in the horrors of war and to take a peculiar fascination in it. The strong and hardy life appeals to the military patriots and the romantic historians. These feelings have a positive value and must be kept alive, else "history would become insipid indeed." James rejects the fatalistic view that war is inevitable and claims that war making is subject to "prudential checks and reasonable criticisms" just as are other parts of experience. The extreme ambitions of war must be replaced with other ambitions of the hardy life. The impulses which make for war have a military content, and these impulses, though not negated, must be turned to other activities where the character which these impulses breed can be given a different content. Priests and medical men have some of the same impulses which make for the strong military character. What needs to be done is "to inflame the civic temper as past history has inflamed the military temper." Along the same line of argument James claims that much of morality is touched with religious faith, and he claims that even if there were no God, man would invent one "simply as a pretext for living hard, and getting out of the game of existence its keenest possibilities of zest."[15]

Peirce, Mead, and Dewey agree with James in rejecting moral dogmatisms of all kinds. Mead in his account of moral behavior, for instance, rejects that view of evolution in which behavior is determined wholly by environment, a view which is a kind of dogmatism.[16] Mead rejects the other extreme which holds that morality is built upon a transcendental ideal of the perfection of the self. Again, he thinks that the Utilitarians are wrong in making the attainment of the greatest sum of pleasures the *summum bonum*. These theories, whether teleological and spiritual or mechanistic and materialistic, claim that the moral goal is given in advance. Mead objects to the view which maintains that there is a determining moral environment which goes back into the past and antedates moral consciousness itself. The consequences of a determined moral environment are tyrannical in that the end is imposed from without and moral necessity is made independent of activity itself. On this view, human beings would find an already existent ideal and adapt to it, and this means that they would try to act toward a distant goal which is not their own. Mead thinks that many publicists and social reformers wish to train people to be led unwittingly to socially worthy action, but action which is not meaningful to the individual.

For Mead, intelligence is purposive and moral activity is one kind of intelligent or purposive behavior.[17] The moral end is not given by a determining environment, but the motive for moral action is the recognition of the end which arises in experience and in each individual's consciousness. The interpretation of our moral experience must be found within experience itself. If we appeal to a moral order which transcends the moral situation, we rob ourselves of a certain intellectual interest. Transcendental orders of morality stimulate an intellectual interest which is confined to matters of agreement or disagreement with them; furthermore, the moral reaction to such orders turns out in the final analysis to be only emotional. In a real, practical moral situation, however, the response is different. We may respond to well-organized cues by well-formed habits (accommodation); or we may adapt and reconstruct habits by a new interpretation of the situation (adaptation). It is in the latter type of response that moral issues develop. If we presuppose a fixed order of morality, then we are robbed of the experience of evaluating our conduct to determine what is and what is not worthwhile.

Mead defines moral values in the context of a problem which has arisen in experience. A young man wishes to go to college, but he finds that he has people financially dependent upon him so that he is compelled to make a living. In the ordinary way of analyzing his problem, one value is thrown over against another. In other words, the young man must select one value and reject the other. Mead's significant insight, an insight which he shares with James, is that the young man should try to reconstruct his life in such a way that he can encompass both values. By reasoning out the implications of realizing or giving up the values concerned, the meaning and importance of these values are made more vivid. Mead thinks that this is essentially what we do in scientific situations when we are faced with certain facts. A fact is given relevance by noting what happens when it is ignored or left out of a problematic situation. He thinks that reconstructing experience in an intelligent manner requires doing justice to all values involved in each problematic moral situation. The treatment of values, then, follows the same pattern of inquiry as the treatment of facts. An adequate hypothesis must apply to all facts; an adequate hypothesis in valuational and moral behavior must apply to all the values involved.

Mead's analogy between a scientific situation of a re-search problem and the inquiry situation of a moral problem does not ignore a very important difference between the two inquiries. In a research problem we may suspend work until a satisfactory hypothesis can be found; in a moral problem we must act. Often this means that we cannot take into account all of the values in each moral situation, but we must not dismiss them completely. In fact, we should merely postpone them; the surrendered values become our ideals. These unrealized ideals demand realization; they abide in our moral consciousness until the day when we do them the justice they claim.

The application of intelligence to the problems of morals is an approach which Mead and Dewey share. Within the context of scientific method and its operations, Peirce sees a new dimension. Peirce thinks that there is a "built in" condition of morality in the nature of scientific activity. "A scientific man must be single-minded and sincere with himself," says Peirce, or "love of truth will melt away, at once." The very conditions of the scientific attitude mean that a person must be honest and fair-minded.

The problematic situation which generates moral inquiry is a theme in Dewey's philosophy as it is in Mead. Dewey is concerned, first of all, with an analysis of how a moral situation can be distinguished from other kinds of situations. He finds the demarcating principle in the concepts of moral choice and moral decision as described by Aristotle.[18] The moral situation grows out of conflicting goals of personal life. There are many acts, he says, which have no moral quality. At the same time, he recognizes that any situation may become moral. Take a case of opening or closing a window. Ordinarily such an act is trivial and involves no great consequences. On the other hand, if opening a window endangers someone's health, the action takes on a moral quality. Each of our lives is intertwined with other individuals and with our social institutions. Individuals do not exist in a vacuum. A moral situation emerges when: 1) the character of an individual's life is involved in a choice among alternatives, and 2) the institutions of an individual's social and community relations are deeply and broadly involved. Dewey defines character as consisting of all of a person's habits, where habits are taken to mean his generalized ways of behaving.[19] When we speak of a strong character, we mean that a person's habits interpenetrate and buttress each other; one's habits are integrated and without conflict. On the other hand, a weak character is one in which habits conflict. The weakness of one's character is one's vacillation; one lies in one situation, tells the truth in another; one keeps some promises and breaks others. Part of the moral enterprise is that of building strong moral character, and a moral situation arises when one's character is at stake. Humans are social beings, however, and if an act has broad consequences, if it affects the family, the educational, economic, and political institutions, then it takes on moral quality.

It is not easy to know when an act is morally significant and when it is not.[20] Determining what kind of problem is present is all important, for to set up a problem as moral, when in fact it is not, leads to confusion in inquiry. Furthermore, there is the tendency of some people to moralize about every little act, even when it is as inconsequential as taking a drink of water. To drag morals into every situation is silly. On the other hand, to overlook the implications of a truly moral situation may lead to personal and social disaster.

Dewey thinks that many moral theorists have given biased reports of moral experience. They have emphasized one part of moral experience to the exclusion of others. In order to make his analysis vivid, Dewey organizes theories of the past under three main divisions: 1) those which make ends or goods uppermost; 2) those which emphasize rights, duties, obligations; and 3) those which make approbation the standard of virtue. After showing the relation of reflective morality to the ends of conduct and maintaining that desire cannot be separated from thought, he proceeds to make a critical analysis of the major moral theories from the Greeks to the present.

Some moral philosophers have placed emphasis upon the attainment of pleasure as the goal of life. They look to the future consequences of an act to determine if it is good. This procedure forms part, but not all, of the Utilitarian doctrine. Dewey finds fault with this group on many scores, but mainly he objects to making pleasure a criterion of the good. He thinks that we do not calculate what pleasures and pains we might encounter in the future when making a genuine moral decision. Pleasure may accompany a good, but it is not the criterion of a good. In our world, he says, pleasures are not to be shunned, for we endure enough pain in the normal course of living. Pleasures are accidental and have a short temporal span. But moral happiness is a condition which endures; it is a quality of life which is sought for and constructed through each moral decision that is made; it is a consequent condition of the moral self.

There is some truth, however, in considering the future consequences of an act. It is an error, however, to think of the future as something disconnected from the present. The future is simply a part of the present act; it is an imaginative projection which *is* present here and now; the thought now present concerning future consequences enhances or mars the present. The Utilitarians are correct in emphasizing the importance of looking to the future consequences of an act, but they are wrong in holding that we can calculate the pleasures and pains we will have at some distant date.[21] Experience shows too many times that our projections concerning what pleasures and pains we will experience at a later time are not accurate. Making projections a part of the present deliberation, however, is an important contribution to moral theory.

Some theories of the moral good stress the present enjoyment to the exclusion of any vision or concern for future consequences. The immediate present absorbs all the attention, and the admonition to "eat, drink and be merry for tomorrow you may die" is the guiding rule. The present moment of life is important, and if one does not attend to matters of the present but lets his projections about the future completely occupy his mind, then he is likely to end up in dreams, illusions, and fantasies. For pragmatic naturalism, a balance between the two theories, that of attention to the future and that of attention to the present, yields a more intelligent view of the treatment of the good. Other pleasure theories recommend avoiding entanglement of the individual in external circumstances; this view belies the nature of social life and the consequences which flow from individual acts. A balance between social and individual concerns is more rational. There are others who make success the end of the moral life, but this is usually success interpreted in the narrow sense of monetary gain. There is a partial truth in the view that success or achievement is important to the moral life, but it is success or achievement in terms of moral quality. Some moralists reject completely the view of pleasure as good, and they advocate a denial of pleasure as the goal of life. This view is called asceticism. There is some truth in this approach to the moral life, but not in the sense in which it is usually taken. The moral ideal requires denial of some pleasures of the moment, the exercise of restraint in the interest of the achievement of new goals. Asceticism carried to the extreme, however, cuts the nerve of moral action generally and makes one indifferent to many values which are integral parts of the moral self.[22] The moral self is a synthesis of many goals and interests, of many actions and habits, of many choices and decisions. The unification of all the goals and interests can be gathered around the ideals of happiness of the individual and the general welfare of humanity. This is a goal which unites the individual and the social, the present and the future, the sacrifice of present pleasures to the fulfillment of happiness. As inquiry and scientific investigation continues, the specific empirical elements in the concept of happiness and general welfare may change. Almost every philosopher with a theory of the good will hold that health is a part of the general notion of happiness of the individual and of the general welfare. But health is an abstract term, and its specific aspects may change as science determines more and more what constitutes health.

Some moral theorists have made the concept of duty or obligation the primary concern of the moral life. Immanuel Kant, for instance, put forth a view which made the "categorical imperative" the most important law of morality. His famous statement reads: *Act only on that maxim whereby thou canst at the same time will that it should become a universal law.*[23] Kant selected certain duties to illustrate his view. Keeping a promise, for instance, is a moral duty because "to make a lying promise" is a contradiction of the meaning of promise. Suicide is a contradiction of life itself. Denial of self-realization is a contradiction of the purpose of a rational being. Kant claimed that any consideration of the consequences of an act degrades the moral motive; the only good is a good will, he said, a will determined by reason and a will indifferent to the demands of impulse, inclination, and desire. One should perform his duty regardless of the feelings present in the moral decision.

Dewey's theory of the origin and function of moral obligations and duties runs counter to that of Kant's. Dewey holds to a view of the origin of obligations similar to that of James. Obligations and duties are made in relation to others and in relation to ourselves by the very nature of our social life.[24] Children have a claim upon parents for nurture and protection; thus it is a parental duty to care for them. Friends have claims upon each other due to the very nature of friendship. Citizens in a community have reciprocal claims upon each other. In the course of social life many obligations and duties emerge; they emerge first in habits of social interaction and then as general rules of social living. These rules are general (generic) and they are defined and classified as of certain kinds. The difficulty with Kant's law of morality is that it does not account for generic ways of behaving, for the various obligations and duties which have arisen in social interaction. Kant seems to make each moral situation unique and to make each decision and act unique. This approach results in making every case of a moral decision and act a law unto itself, thus not a law at all, for to be a law requires connections with similar *kinds* of cases.[25]

For the pragmatic naturalists rules and laws regarding obligations and duties are important, for they are summaries of past experience and guides for present moral decisions. The use of rules is a shortcut in the ascertainment of what is "right" to do in a situation which falls under a general category. These rules are not absolute; they are constantly under scrutiny by the method of intelligence; they are evaluated and either discarded or retained as significant. New occasions emerge in experience which require new duties, and one of the great moral lags in modern life is that new duties have not emerged to cope with the changes in social life. The duties and obligations of slave to master and master to slave have become defunct in Europe and America. The obligations and duties of wife to husband and husband to wife are changing from the old Puritan patterns. An industrial urban society generates conditions of social relationships different from those of rural life. The obligations of a father to educate his child has now been transferred to the community, the state, and the nation.

Dewey finds that Kant's idea of universalizing an act does have great merit, but not in the sense in which Kant intended it.[26] Dewey thinks that universalizing an act makes us aware of the broad consequences to which the act leads. Telling the truth, keeping promises, being honest are all conditions of a decent personal and social life; in fact, these duties are so important in human life that it appears that a good life, or perhaps any life, would be impossible without them. Keeping a promise, for instance, has emerged in social interactions among individuals as a kind of social faith, a social faith which is a condition and integral part of community life. The moral virtues are vital to social life because of the ways in which they function. Moral principles are vital to any moral theory, but moral principles are not regarded as absolutes or transcendental rules to be plastered down on any and every situation. Moral principles are treated as *hypotheses*, or working ideas, which are selected as being relevant to certain kinds of moral situations.[27] For instance, a moral principle like that of forgiveness of an offender applies to certain kinds of situations; but when forgiveness encourages a criminal to continue his antisocial habits, then forgiveness does not fit this situation as a relevant moral hypothesis.

Moral rules or laws have a significant function in aiding one to have ready-made formulae for use in particular situations; thus they have a generality which goes beyond particular cases. But these rules may work for hardship in certain cases and they will need to be reevaluated. Moral rules are important because they afford an impartiality in their application, thus they reach for objectivity and justice in the treatment of each individual. In the theory of pragmatic naturalism, the right and the good do not stand in opposition to each other; behaviors which are right and good cooperate and blend their functions into a harmony for the total moral life.

There are still other moral theorists who, like Hume, make approbation and disapprobation the central part of moral philosophy. Dewey shows that those who make approval and disapproval the basis for a standard of moral experience are looking backward to acts already performed. The method starts with the approval or disapproval of a particular person or group, and proceeds to construct an ideal spectator who views the act as would an impartial and far-seeing objective judge. This method is apparently based upon the way in which standards of excellence are built up in society. Experience accumulates around certain kinds of problems, whether these problems be those of excellence of work such as building a house or excellence of living which is the moral life. Thus standards are evolved, and historians of the moral life have described and catalogued these emerging standards. The standard of justice is an example. The ideal of justice has grown with the accumulation of experience, and its justification as a moral standard is found in its usefulness. The theory of Hume, as well as others of his kind, has great significance, for moral standards do seem to emerge in the manner which they describe. What is needed, thinks Dewey, is that moral standards be related to a moral end, an end which is primarily concerned with the happiness of the individual and the general welfare of society.

The moral theories of James, Mead, Peirce, and Dewey have many elements in common. They reject moral dogmatism, authoritarianism, and they attempt to construct a theory of reflective morality. Their account does not tell us what is specifically right and wrong in each concrete situation, but it does provide a method by which an individual can analyze each moral situation he encounters. It is a method which allows the individual to entertain several hypotheses and to think out the implications of each. Thus on this view the mind of man is liberated from moral dogmatism and is free to discover the unique good of each situation.

15. Social Philosophy

Social philosophy is a value study because various forms and functions of societal life are prized or rejected, defended or attacked. The history of human life consists of numerous wars defending or attacking social and political ways of life. We fight to "make the world safe for democracy," to "destroy capitalism," to "contain communism," to promote or destroy fascism. Social and political organizations grew out of primary associations; these forms are "not outside human desire and judgment," thus they become matters of deepest value.[28] From this broad base pragmatic naturalists interpret this field of value, for any group which organizes itself around desires and interests, which shares goals and ideals, which puts forth programs and policies may be said to have a social philosophy. Social philosophy as viewed by the pragmatic naturalists is problem-oriented; social problems occur in a wide context of culture, some more far-reaching in their consequences than others. While there is general agreement among the pragmatic naturalists on the approach to social problems, each man selected what he held to be important at various times in his life.

For William James the most important issue in social philosophy is the encouragement of individualism.[29] His general evolutionary views, carried over into psychological and social realms, take account of what he called "social mutations." These social mutations are centered in the deviation of individuals from the norms of social behavior. Without these innovations there can be no progress. James takes a strong stand against the kinds of intolerance which smother individual variations in conduct. He claims that often we are blind to the feelings of people different from ourselves; yet it is just these contrasting feelings, aspirations, and strivings of others which make them unique. Individual uniqueness is a person's democratic right, and this uniqueness demands respect.

James never developed a systematic social philosophy, but at times he did speak out strongly on specific issues. He detested the drift toward social organizations which herded and branded individuals. In one of his most memorable passages, he writes: "The first thing the intellect does with an object is to class it along with something else. But any object that is infinitely important to us and awakens our devotion feels to us also as if it must be *sui generis* and unique. Probably a crab would be filled with a sense of personal outrage if it could hear us class it without ado or apology as a crustacean, and thus dispose of it. 'I am no such thing,' it would say; 'I am MYSELF, MYSELF alone.' "[30] On the whole James pins his faith in individuals. Individuals have developed some common habits in American life, habits which James thought are fruitful for hope in the future. These are mainly the good temper held for the opposite party in politics and the resentment toward those who break the public peace.

Mead's social philosophy develops from a broad intellectual base. Recent developments in anthropology, history, economics, political science, and sociology offer new perspectives, for these sciences have made it possible to "take the role of others." By looking backward we can observe the direction of the movement of the social process; but this looking backward is really a construction in the present, and this constructed past aids in setting up goals for the future. These goals should not be utopian, however, as some Christians and utopian socialists have urged. For Mead, we "fashion hypotheses and test them and intentionally reconstruct the institutions within which we live."[31] This scientifically oriented approach means that Mead rejects fixed interpretations of history whether those of Hegel or Lasalle or Marx. Herbert Spencer's theory of evolution is rejected because Spencer made adaptation a static end or goal of evolution. Mead maintains that social values change as do the tastes of people from age to age. New hypotheses need to be put forth as new social problems arise, and Mead's social philosophy in general is a kind of social experimentation.

John Dewey has often been called "the philosopher of American democracy."[32] His tireless efforts to democratize the schools, to liberalize our social institutions, to champion the cause of free inquiry, and to elevate the quality of cultural life, lead some commentators on his thought to view these matters of primary importance in his career and to designate him primarily as a social philosopher.[33]

Dewey is perhaps the foremost advocate of democracy in the twentieth century, but he is also a severe critic of what often assumes the name of "democracy" in theory and practice.[34] Democracy in America, he claims, has occurred as a result of accidental conditions. By this he means that there has been no conscious and deliberate planning for activities guided by some democratic idea or ideal. Democracy has grown up haphazardly; it has developed from the pressures of many persistent social habits. When Dewey says that democracy has been more or less accidental, he does not mean that there have not been *causes* for the forms which have evolved. Foremost among the causes which produced what we call democracy today was fear of government.[35] The impulse of fear set the individual over against any political public when organized into a state. A short step in theory and practice makes this fear of the state and the kind of individualism it fostered into a view that the individual is independent of any and all associations. Since individuals are social, however, the "old" individualism is a distortion of that social existence. Individuals do organize into groups around common interests and goals. The philosophy of the "old" individualism based on fear of the state and on the assumption that individuals are independent was transferred to the belief that the emergent social organizations were also independent of each other and of the state. In fact, a laissez faire philosophy was transferred from the atomistic individualism of the old European world to the new American world of powerfully organized economic and social groups. These new power groups nurtured the old suspicion of any control by the political public. It was assumed that the state is hostile to the individual even when he expresses himself through the new social organizations. Furthermore, the emergence of the view that there are natural laws in economics which guarantee social harmony without the intervention of a political public gave theoretical and practical support to laissez faire philosophy.

The democracy which as emerged is the result of impulsive activities and habits which are not always intelligently formed. But uncritical impulsive activities and habits, fears, and suspicions, hardly serve as positive conditions for the growth of creative democracy. From these impulses, however, came the demand for the individual's right to vote, and the laissez faire theory released the impulses of initiative, inventiveness, foresight, and planning on the part of some members of society.[36] The individual's sovereignty gave him the right to make many decisions having social consequences. The means of counting these individual decisions brought forth the idea of majority rule. Thus, majority rule is a method of calculation of the coincidence of atomistic reactions. Majority rule takes many forms, as any student of elementary political science knows; it may become the majority of one, or two-thirds or some other agreed upon dividing line between majority and minority. Under some conditions where individual purposes and desires are extremely diverse, a system may be devised whereby a coalition of minority parties will add up to a majority count. When majority rule means only a calculation of the conjunctions of the uncritically formed impulses and desires of aggregations of individuals and when this kind of rule is imposed upon the lives of others who are in disagreement, then this form of so-called democracy often becomes tyrannical over minorities.

The point of departure for Dewey's analysis of social philosophy is with associated behavior, a behavior which involves consequences of an individual's acts upon other people. The effects of human acts, some of which are perceived, lead to an effort to control these actions "so as to secure some consequences and avoid others." Dewey takes this clue and remarks that "the consequences are of two kinds, those which affect the persons directly engaged in a transaction, and those which affect others beyond those immediately concerned." He goes on to say: "In this distinction we find the germ of the distinction between the private and the public. When indirect consequences are recognized and there is effort to regulate them, something having the traits of a state comes into existence. When the consequences of an action are confined, or are thought to be confined, mainly to the persons directly engaged in it, the transaction is a private one."[37] The line between the private and the public affairs of life cannot be drawn without close scrutiny as to which activities affect the general welfare and which do not. Some activities once held as private have been perceived to have broad public consequences, and a reversal of their legal status and function takes place; other activities held to be of public concern have been shifted to the private realm since the general welfare is not at stake. Current discussions concerning sexual behavior and the use of drugs are cases at point, for these kinds of activities must be evaluated in terms of effects or noneffects upon others.

The "political public" or state arises when the indirect consequences of individual or group activities become the concern for the general welfare of all groups. Governing rules or laws are instituted to control the acts which produce broad consequences to human life. Thus, there is a sense in which every political public within a society "represents" the needs and concerns of that society. What has emerged in most European and American nations holding to some variation of the philosophy of the old individualism is the institution of elected officials determined by each individual's right to vote.

Certain familiar words have arisen in the folklore of democracy, words like equality, liberty, and fraternity, and each of these terms has its causal roots in some historical condition of the past. After these terms are located and understood in their historically causal settings, Dewey reworks their meanings and incorporates them into his own democratic theory. Sometimes Dewey speaks of democracy as "a way of life," and by this he means that democracy is a name for certain impulses, habits, and methods of solving problems of individuals and for certain procedures and policy-making decisions of institutions. In his view of the democratic way of life, terms like equality, liberty, and fraternity take on special meanings.

Equality does not mean equality of natural endowments.[38] It means equality before the law, that is, equal treatment of all in the administration of law. An individual is equally an individual among others; one is afforded the right to express one's own judgments; one has an equal right to all the facts which bear upon one's making a decision. Each has an equal right to the development of one's capacities and to the satisfaction of one's needs. Every person has a right to the conditions of achievement in terms of his needs and capacities. A child, for instance, has a right to expect its parents and its society to provide it with the conditions for growth. The needs and capacities of individuals vary, and equality means that each person is equal to every other in terms of the claims of one's individual needs. This view of equality is important to Dewey, for it guarantees that the less gifted are protected from oppression.

There is an old cliché which states that freedom or liberty is "the right to do as one pleases as long as it does not interfere with the rights of anyone else." The statement is so vague that it allows almost any meaning one wishes to be read into it. For Dewey, freedom or liberty is the power to do things or the power to form purposes, but it is a power to do things which fits into a system of liberties at any given time. Liberty means that no person can do anything that is denied to others with the same qualifications; an individual's freedom must fit into what others can and cannot do. Dewey holds that the first ten amendments to the United States Constitution are concerned with basic freedoms of action and experience, for they set the conditions which lead to the most important freedom of all—*freedom of mind*.[39] Freedom of mind is the basic freedom, for it means equal opportunity for individual development, and Dewey does not think, as some do, that this freedom is incompatible with equality. Freedom means equality when each person's claim to the conditions of qualitative development is guaranteed by society.

An individual is not born free. Each is born dependent upon others; each is at the mercy of others for survival and continued existence and growth. A baby's random activities and impulsive behavior are channeled into social habits from the days of its birth. Freedom to formulate goals and purposes, to reflect and to deliberate, to choose among alternatives and to decide, are transcendent of dependence upon others and of the causal conditions which operate in most forms of his behavior. Thus freedom and equality are achievements. Freedom and equality are not given to man by the benevolent hand of nature, nor are they inherent in man's physiological and psychological structures. The old natural rights theories sometimes assumed that freedom and equality are antecedent to man's achievement and all that is needed is protection of them against the encroachment of political authority. This is a common philosophical fallacy; that is, the assumption that an antecedent reality given in experience needs only clarification for its realization; this appraoch substitutes the antecedent reality for the conditions of the achievement of an ideal or goal. On Dewey's view, freedom and equality are not given, but are *values* to be prized, and their attainment requires moral effort.

Fraternity or cooperation has an origin similar to that of equality.[40] The original condition of humanity is association, and a minimal amount of cooperation is required by the very nature of associated behavior. The child, for instance, must be protected, loved, and cared for by the group. Cooperation on the higher levels of association, however, must be learned. It becomes something which must be valued and prized, and, like friendship, which is the highest form of cooperation, it has a moral basis.

With the foregoing interpretations which Dewey gives to equality, freedom, and fraternity, it can be seen that he relates the impulses, habits, desires, and method of the mind to the culture as a whole. When these functions suffuse a culture, it is then that it can be said that democracy is a way of life. This way of life, however, needs more philosophical justification than has just been given. Equality, freedom, and cooperation can exist as habits of a people, but they may have arisen accidentally, that is, they may have causes and not reasons for their occurrence. They may not be cherished and prized as values, and they may not have a rational or theoretical justification. This is why Dewey is uneasy about the habits and impulses which have grown up with so-called democracy. He thinks it is possible to redirect, to recondition, and to drain off such impulses and habits to support totalitarian institutions and states. This is why guiding ideas and ideals are needed to make democracy secure.

Right to vote, majority rule, elected officials, representative government are not truly safeguards of a democracy. All of these so-called democratic procedures can and have been used by any kind of totalitarian government. It is possible for a government to allow its people the right to vote, to have majority rule, to have elected officials, and to claim that their officials "represent" the people, yet have a single list of candidates. Even the presentation of more than one list of candidates does not guarantee a democratic way of life. This is why democracy must rest upon something more basic, so basic that, although the particular political methods may change, the guiding ideas and ideals remain more or less stable. For Dewey, there are three kinds of basic democratic ideals: 1) Any government is designed to serve and service the community; 2) the community is to share in the choosing of those who govern it; 3) the community is to share in determining the governing policies.[41] Using these ideals as a guide, the specific methods of democracy, such as majority rule and elected offficials, can be judged as to whether or not these methods are really serving and servicing the community.

The ideals of democratic life should be buttressed by other methods which are more vital to democracy than those mentioned above.[42] First among these methods is *consultation*. Consultation of all concerned with any decision which affects their lives should be a way of life in the home, the school, the economic institution, and the political organization. Democracy means *discussion*, a method of communication whereby desire and interest, hurt and pain, pleasure and welfare of each individual get a chance to be heard. Along with consultation and discussion goes *participation* in group activity. The method of *persuasion* as opposed to coercion, brute force, and irrational appeals is another democratic procedure. There must be *voluntary choice* which involves access to the facts necessary to make the choice, and thus insures the freedom of mind of each individual. Finally, there is *evaluation*, which is a means of taking account of the consequences of the decision made;

this means that every individual has a right to express his judgment concerning how the decision affected his own life and the lives of others.

Some critics have said that Dewey's view of democratic ideals and democratic methods is unrealistic.[43] The self-styled authoritarian claims that Dewey's method allows the stupid, the mediocre, the undeveloped, and the immature to make decisions when, in fact, they are incapable. These criticisms miss the point of Dewey's democratic way of making decisions. In the first place, Dewey's view is based on the fact that every individual has something which is valuable to contribute to the group and that no one individual has a monopoly on knowledge, or experience. By allowing consultation, discussion, participation, persuasion, voluntary choice, and evaluation to operate, all opinions will have a hearing, and the final pooled intelligence will be a contribution of all members of society, mature and immature, more or less intelligent, informed and ignorant. Furthermore, the decision reached and put into practice will be that of the people concerned and will not be one imposed from without. The fear of democracy by the authoritarian creates the conditions of dictatorship, for the authoritarian claims that only he has the intelligence and experience to rule; the lack of democracy, however, creates the conditions for revolution, often violent in form.

Dewey's democratic theory is built upon his general theory of value and upon his moral theory described in preceding sections. He holds that human desires are consolidated into interests, and in social life these interests are organized into "publics." Since desires and interests are social in character, groups organize themselves around these in a pluralistic society; that is, a pluralistic society allows persons to communicate and to organize themselves into interest groups without any or with very little interference on the part of political authority. As Dewey sees contemporary societal life, there are too many interest groups and too many publics. These groups, for the most part, have selfish goals; they want to extend their own power over others. These selfish interest groups often come into conflict with each other. Dewey rejects that view of democracy which maintains that the ideal is one in which conflicting interest groups are so balanced that no one group becomes powerful enough to dominate all the others. On this view it is the function of political authority to curb any dominant group. Against this view of the role of political authority, Dewey proposes that there be developed, through education primarily, a consciousness of a "larger public," a "great community," in which every person's interest is related to the general welfare of the whole and in which the general welfare is fashioned so as to secure the happiness of each individual. Thus, no individual or interest group should formulate goals and pursue them without relating them to the goals and interests of the larger community. For Dewey, community means democracy.

The ideal we should pursue, says Dewey, is one in which each group's interests are subjected to critical scrutiny in order to evaluate them as desirable or undesirable. The interests of various individuals and groups are integrated with the whole society, and the whole society appreciates and protects the uniqueness of each individual. These conditions are not present in contemporary society composed of publics which work at cross-purposes, which seek to limit the freedom of other publics, and which often seek annihilation of all competitors. The result is a chaotic, unplanned, competing, angry society.

Within the framework of Dewey's theory of democracy, there remains a problem of paramount importance; it is the relation of the expert to the nonexpert in a democratic way of life. It is generally recognized that some ways of life are better than others, that some objects of value are more desirable than others, that some actions and consequences have a quality of excellence more than others. The more mature in experience are the experts, like the physician, the teacher, the lawyer. Thus, there arises the problem of the relation of the expert to the nonexpert, of the mature to the immature. The problem concerns how the mature person shares with the immature, for he may share dictatorially or democratically. The manner in which mature ideas about the management of life are brought to the immature is the main problem of education, a problem which is as wide as the whole transmission of culture. This topic is treated subsequently in more detail under the philosophy of the educational process.

For Dewey the ultimate test of any social philosophy is the *quality of life* it produces.[44] Criteria for judging social philosophies may be put in a series of questions. How many consummatory value experiences (enjoyments) does any social philosophy foster in particular individuals, and how wide is their accessibility to these enjoyments? What are the effects of social policies and programs on the lives of individuals who are involved in them? Are the individual's memories made more adaptive or are they cut off from the present experience? Is imagination made more fertile or is it diverted into daydreaming? Is the individual's perception heightened or dulled? Is ability to think and to solve problems stimulated to creativity, or is thinking channeled into intellectual busywork? These questions concerning the vitality and accessibility of an individual's value experiences, concerning the quality of one's perceptual, memory, imaginative, and intellectual life can be asked of any policy or institutional practice. When these questions are faced realistically, the weakness of antidemocratic and authoritarian philosophies will come to light; the value of democratic procedures will become apparent.[45]

Dewey objects to the emphasis in some social philosophies on the opposition of the individual and the social. On his view there can be no dualism of this traditional kind; the individual is social by nature, and one's own happiness is involved in the welfare of others. The intimate connection of the individual and the social means that one ought to have a part in the planning of programs affecting one's own life and interests. This is what Dewey means by a "planning society," a society in which purposes and goals are proposed and explored in thought and judged acceptable or unacceptable by all who are involved in their consequences. Since the problems of individuals and groups are always changing, and since valuings and evaluations are always on the move, there can be no absolute blueprint for society. A planning society, which Dewey advocates, is different from a planned society; the latter is imposed by a hierarchy of authority, often indifferent to the desires and interests of individuals.[46] An intelligent society, like an intelligent individual, is one in which inner forces such as desires and interests are carefully evaluated and the external conditions (the environment) are cautiously managed to bring about the common good of all.

16. Philosophy of Art

Peirce says that he worked "with intensity for many hours a day every day for long years" to train himself to the study of feelings.[47] On one level of experience Peirce holds that feelings are primary, and he designates these as belonging, in his terminology, to the category of Firstness. When the aesthetic is limited to these primary feelings, however, confusion may occur unless it is clear that the term "aesthetic" may refer to constructed and refined meanings which are a synthesis of primary feelings, interactions, and continuities of experiences lived through and consummated. Toward the end of his life Peirce said that he had not worked out an adequate theory of the aesthetic, although it was a topic to which he gave a large amount of study.

The idea of linking the constructed and refined objects of art with the primary experiences out of which they arise is a common theme of all pragmatic naturalists. William James observes that the emotional, which serves as the original material of the aesthetic, is found in the stream of experience.[48] Dewey says in *Art as Experience* that there has been a wall built between art objects and the experiences out of which these works have arisen. He thinks that one of the contemporary tasks is "to restore continuity between the refined and intensified forms of experience that are works of art and the everyday events, doings, and sufferings that are universally recognized to constitute experience."[49]

Human feelings and emotions are those aspects of experience which the artist seeks to transform, intensify, and express. At first, feelings are mere feelings, gross and undifferentiated. These perceptual feelings then become differentiated and refined through interactions (transactions) and continuities of experience. Some of these perceptual feelings emerge into sensations, some into concepts, some into desires, and some into emotions. Sensory and conceptual feelings are basic to knowledge; desires are basic to morals; and emotions are basic to art.

Emotions are nurtured by the kinds of experiences each undergoes in one's early transactions with one's world. Adults around a child teach it that certain kinds of activities and feelings are called "fear," or "anger," or "love," or the like, because of the consequences to which they lead. Fear is an activity and feeling related to other parts of experience, an instance of which would be the fear of a rattlesnake. Love is related to certain objects or persons, an example of which is the love of family. The specific objects feared or loved may vary from culture to culture, but emotions are generic aspects of all human experience.

When we look into our own experiences, we find that much of our everyday existence is permeated with feelings of fear, love, hate, anxiety, elation, and many other emotions. No exhaustive list of human emotions can be compiled, for there is always the possibility that new feeling-states will emerge from the stream of experience. This does not mean that emotional meanings are purely subjective states of feeling, for experiences which take on emotional meanings arise from responses to objects which have certain qualities; thus an emotionalized object is the result of an interaction of organism and environment. For instance, the fear of a rattlesnake is not a bare feeling locked in some individual's private experience and consciousness. Qualities of the rattlesnake, such as its poisonous fangs, bear direct relation to other parts of man's experience. The emotional response to the rattlesnake is as much a part of objective experience and its meaning as is the zoologist's classification of it as a reptile.

In living from day to day, individuals undergo different kinds of emotional experiences. Each life is punctuated with feelings of frustration and fulfillment, with problems lived through and solved or unsolved. If an individual endures, some of the problems must be solved, for if life were one long continuous series of frustrations, one would become completely neurotic and would eventually come to death. On the other hand, if human life were a monotonous plateau of rest and fulfillment containing no shocks or problematic situations, then no thought, no sensation, no desire, and no emotion would arise. Dewey says: "Emotion is the conscious sign of a break, actual or impending."[50] Emotions such as fear, hope, joy, and sorrow are qualities of a divided response; thus emotions emerge out of the clashes and conflicts of life. James had pointed out that emotions are responses of the organism itself to its own attitudes under certain conditions. For instance, we run away from an object, and the running creates the emotion of fear. Mead thinks that Dewey improved on James's theory by showing that unless there is some inhibition of the activity of running, there would not emerge the emotion of fear.[51]

James shows that life is an affair of "flights and perchings." We live through an experience, an ongoing affair, "a flight"; we come to the end of that experience, and there is a time when we say it is over, finished, consummated. Our "perchings" are momentary, however, for new problems arise, and new flights must be made. A day in the life of an individual is a series of experiences strung along one after the other. One arises in the morning and puts on clothes, and this experience is completed. One eats a meal, and this experience has a beginning, a continuity, and an end. The other activities undergone and performed throughout the days and years make up an individual's life.

Some of the experiences which compose the ongoing of life have meanings which are deeper and broader than others. These kinds of experiences emerge above the routine; they reach down to the depths of our lives; they are filled with emotional meanings and we remember them thereafter. Even the simplest of experiences have moments when we exclaim: "That *was* a meal to remember!" or "That *was* a ball game!" These emotional experiences have a pervasive quality which is absorbing; they draw all the divergent and conflicting elements in the situation into a synthetic whole. As the consummation of the experience nears, the memories of the beginning and of its movement flood in upon us. We feel the fullness of that moment, and all the parts of the experience, the feelings, the interactions, and the continuity merge into an emotionalized whole. A life would be dull indeed without the aesthetic aspect of experience emerging now and then in its stream. Once the emotionally dramatic has been experienced, this germ of aesthetic form finds many expressions. The experience may be relived in song, in story, in poetry, in painting, or in any of the other means of expression. Storytelling appears to be one of the first forms of art. The storyteller dramatizes in narrative the happenings of work, play, and social life. The moments when emotional meanings are uppermost in experience are the raw materials of refined art. As Mead says, aesthetic appreciation is making the enjoyed meanings which have been experienced a part of living. And Mead goes on to say that "our affective experience, that of emotion, of interest, of pleasure and pain, of satisfaction and dissatisfaction, may be roughly divided between that of doing and enjoying and their opposites, and it is that which attaches to finalities that characterizes aesthetic experience."[52]

Not every experience, of course, has aesthetic quality. When the aesthetic quality is absent, then life is dull and uninteresting. Habits which are not aesthetically grounded are routine and mechanical. Activities flowing from mechanical habits are monotonous, things to get done, and when finished, to escape. Habits which are artistically grounded are of a different sort, for activities flowing from these kinds of habits are interesting and enjoyable to perform. There is a world of difference between habitual activity which is mechanically dull and habitual activity which is artistic. The artistic activity, no matter how difficult and challenging, contains no resentment when performed; every action, gesture, symbol, and object is loved for its own sake.

Some experiences come to an end where the feeling of tragedy is uppermost. Not every experience is exciting, exuberant, joyful; some experiences are frustrating, disappointing, melancholy. When one is compelled to submit to a course of experience which cannot be changed, as in the case of death of a loved one or in the case of great loss in all that has been planned and worked for, then there emerges a tragic sense of life. Depressions, war, and death are encountered. In these experiences the aesthetic may be present, but it is aesthetic experience with a different kind of content.

The raw materials of art are the emotional experiences lived through to some kind of consummation, whether tragic or fulfilling. Many of these experiences are unplanned and accidental. They become, however, the materials out of which refined and intensified aesthetic experiences emerge. Emotions are highly complex parts of experience. They are not easily given expression, as any poet or painter knows. Emotional expression must not be confused with the biological explosions of energy or the random activity of a human being. If a child stomps its feet in a fit of rage, he is not necessarily expressing himself. Usually the child's activities can be understood in terms of some causal conditions preceding the stomping of the feet. Such energetic outbursts are physiological and do not belong to the arena of aesthetic expression. On the other hand, the poet who tries to weave together in words the meanings of anger or love or rage has a major problem on his hands in trying to express these complex emotions. Dewey writes: "Expression is a clarification of turbid emotion; our appetites know themselves when they are reflected in the mirror of art, and as they know themselves they are transfigured. Emotion that is distinctively esthetic then occurs."[53] The refinement of the emotional means that the ordinary feeling is made over, transformed into something more meaningful.

Refinement of emotional experience is not a duplication of the original either in the attempt to reenact it or in the attempt to symbolize it in any of the media of the arts. New elements are woven into the original experience, thus the original experience is transformed and made deeper and richer in meaning. Sometimes we may think that a picture which is an exact copy of the original is art, but artists dislike duplications and reproductions of experience of the bald and unimaginative type. An artistic and creative photographer does more than represent the facts and meanings of life which lie on its surface. The creative photographer looks for that certain expression of the face, that certain stance of the body, that certain mannerism of a human being which reveal the deeper and more substantial meanings of the subject's life and character. The great artist puts meanings into the "expressive object" which must be pried out, for the meanings found there are of such intensity and range that the spectator and interpreter can always anticipate finding new ones. The depth and range of meanings of the aesthetic experience constructed in refined works of art make it possible for us to "live with them." We can return to great works of art again and again and always find suggestions for new meanings.

Every person is moved emotionally by some line of poetry, some strain of music, or some painting which intensifies life. The aesthetic experience expresses itself in many forms and in many media. What one artist seizes upon to make into an expressive object, another may ignore. One artist is intrigued with lines and planes and sees primarily the abstract qualities of an object. Another may seize upon the sensory impressions of colors, of sunlight and shadows, of moonlight playing upon ripples of water. For the pragmatic naturalist there is no preconceived theory of what subject matters are appropriate for artistic expression, and there is no preconceived technique of how any material should be expressed. The forms of experience are many and varied, and as long as form and content can be worked into a unity which makes an aesthetic experience, then that experience should be allowed to express itself in all of its depth and range of meaning. The media of artistic expression are many. The poet, novelist, and dramatist work with the media of linguistic symbols; the painter thinks with colors, lines, surfaces, and shapes; the musician works with sounds and rhythms.

Pragmatic naturalists are averse to the use of the term "beauty" when beauty is taken to be an analytic concept. The analytical view of beauty rejects a work of art if the latter does not fit into a preconceived definitional mold. When the aesthetic qualities of ordinary experiences evoke a certain kind of emotional response, it is common to speak of these as beautiful. We also speak of works of art as beautiful when their aesthetic qualities evoke a similar response. Such experiences are many and varied; their meanings are rich and difficult to classify. Thus for the pragmatic naturalists beauty is a synthetic concept under which are gathered different kinds of art as well as those works which are individually unique.

Mead and Dewey made protests against the manner in which modern society has cut the refined products of art from the life and culture out of which these arise. Greek art, for instance, is an expression of the times in which it was produced. Mead went so far as to claim that certain values of Greek art were values for them which subsequent generations can never recover.[54] Even with the greatest of imagination we cannot recapture the feelings, the experiences, the outlook of the Greeks who enjoyed meanings which their art had for them. The symbols they used held social meanings for them. (Symbols here are interpreted broadly to include nonlinguistic symbols, such as those found in painting, sculpture, dance, music and the like.) Each age creates its own artistic expressions. Great art endures because it has some meanings which cut across the centuries, which appeal to the universal in experience, which all can find worthy of enjoyment, contemplation, and appreciation. Since we cannot transport art objects of another age into our own times, we must enter into the life of the culture which produced them and see them as parts of other people's aspirations and defeats.

The idea that art objects are products of the times in which they arise can be misunderstood, for this theory can be interpreted to mean that the artist's creation is only a vehicle of social meanings. It is true that an individual artist does not live in a social vacuum; the self is all that has been experienced. Some parts of experience the individual has loved and cared for; other parts have been rejected. Rejection of parts of the culture and its time is the beginning of the criticism of life. The individual's selections are of objects loved with great intensity. In this sense the artist is the severe critic of experience and its most devoted lover. The artist is not simply a reporter of the facts of experience or a recorder of what human beings have felt most deeply. The artist's world is a world which emerges above the commonplace, although the commonplace may be the point of departure. The artist sees meanings in the commonplace which others lost in its movement do not see. Transformations of the ordinary are made into unique creations; the artist's experience is thus transcendent and autonomous in a vital sense. The artist stands on a mountain peak and with a new perspective finds new meanings and new forms of experience; creativity emerges in this kind of experience.

The mountain peak of creativity from which the artist's perspective is gained links with the rest of life. Mountain peaks do not float on a sea of nothingness; they are parts of the earth from which they have thrust themselves. The transformed meanings embedded in art require some ordinary meanings to be transformed, otherwise art is divorced from life, is isolated and irrelevant. The greatest fallacy of the social conception of art, however, is that it dissolves the artist into his culture and reduces his autonomy and creativity to its antecedent conditions. The experiential and cultural connection is found in every work of art, but the work is more than its antecedents, more than its constituent parts. A creative work of art is a new form; it carries new meanings; it evokes a new experience.

Dewey once said that one of the clues to the understanding of a culture is found in the appreciation that culture has for its artists.[55] When a culture has some measure of social unity, when the feelings and aspirations of its people are integrated, when they love and appreciate the expressions of this unity given by their artists, then art is central to their lives. Dewey claims that today, however, social unity is lacking in our culture; our feelings and aspirations are in

conflict; and the artist is pushed to the outer rim of importance. Where social unity is not present, then art is one
means of escape. Furthermore, many artists capitulate to the
business interests and make their art commercial, while
other artists revolt against the business culture and become
artistic bohemians. This condition turns the aesthetic impulse in directions of escape; experiences become esoteric or
expressions of the neurotic.

If one is not a creative artist, then one may become an
interpreter and critic of art objects for oneself and others.
Some individuals are makers of art and art critics as well.
Mead thinks that it is the task of the interpreter to discover
the emotion of the artist, to discover the value or values in
the work of art. Some questions may be asked which will
illuminate the function of the interpreter and the critic. Has
the artist achieved his value? What means has the artist
used? How does the form selected express his value? Does
the work of art arouse the same emotions in others as it
arouses in the artist? Does the work of art communicate?
The interpreter and critic, Dewey holds, is not a passive ob-
server nor a mere spectator. Emotional meanings of the artist must be re-created. In doing this the interpreter and the
critic undergo a kind of aesthetic experience; they enter into
the feelings and understanding of the meanings of the art
creation. This is why Mead writes: "The great critic is able
to present the work of art to his audience so that the audi
ence is able to feel that value as he himself feels it; then he
turns to the work of art and shows why and how it has suc-
ceeded in bringing out that value."[56]

There is another aspect of the pragmatic naturalist's
philosophy of art which should be mentioned, if only as a
warning to some who may distort the aesthetic experience.
There is a tendency on the part of some people to inject
morals into every aspect of aesthetic experience. The vogue
of teaching moral and spiritual values in the public schools
has taken the turn sometimes of setting up moral criteria to

which all art objects must conform. This interpretation is rejected in the pragmatic naturalist's philosophy of art. If the experience which the artist is expressing happens to have a moral quality to it, then it is proper that this moral quality find expression in the art object. Where the aesthetic experience and its expressive object have no moral quality inherent in them, dragging in a moral meaning distorts and falsifies the experience.

When Mead and Dewey interpret art as having the possibility of being as wide as the experience of humanity, they open the road for making the aesthetic uppermost in ways that liberate the emotional life. They make the aesthetic quality of life as lived in the ordinary and in the refined experiences found in special media a carefully and lovingly constructed achievement. Appreciation of the aesthetic follows from heightened and enhanced experience.

17. Religion and the Religious

The pragmatic naturalists inherited an intellectual world in which traditional supernaturalism was one of the oldest and most widely held interpretations of human experience. Some thinkers like Thomas Paine had advocated a kind of minimal supernaturalism which went by the name of "Deism." By mid-nineteenth century Ralph Waldo Emerson and others had founded a school called "Transcendentalism," a version of an outlook which emphasizes the mind and its intimate relations with a God-Mind or Spirit. The view of ultimate reality as Mind or Spirit is called "philosophical idealism," and James had, as his colleague at Harvard, Josiah Royce who was one of America's leading idealists of the time. Opposing supernaturalism, transcendentalism, and idealism was the philosophy of materialism, a view which claims to be scientific in its outlook. Philosophical materialism denies that there is any supernatural or any metaphysical entity such as spirit or mind. Materialists hold that matter in motion is basic reality, and they generally believe inquiry should be limited to observable events and to cause-and-effect relationships which are scientifically determined. All beliefs, they say, which go beyond what can be verified by observation are speculative, and one should take a sceptical or agnostic view toward them. When Darwin's theory of evolution is added to the basic concepts of materialism, then the traditional beliefs about God, nature, and man are severely challenged.

The foregoing views of experience created a serious conflict in William James. He thinks that physical objects and organisms are real parts of experience, but he rejects the materialist's reduction of all emergent forms of experience and nature, including religious responses, to the physical or material. James also thinks that ideas and ideals are parts of experience, but he rejects the idealists' notion of an Absolute Mind or Spirit. The beliefs of this latter group allow the finite parts of experience to be dissolved into an organic and absolute whole. James admits that the hypothesis of the Absolute Form might be true, but he claims that as yet we do not have empirical evidence that it is true. Furthermore, he thinks that the philosophy in which the source, meaning, and outcome of everything in nature and experience depends upon the Absolute discourages human endeavors. Darwin had shown that life is in a precarious situation in its evolutionary development, that all human living is a venture and a risk, and that we cannot be sure where all will come out. To believe that there is an Absolute which is securely bound to all the finite items of living is to nurse a delusion. One might wish that this Absolute Being exists, says James, but the evidence at present is insufficient.[57]

For James the philosophic choice among super-naturalism, idealism, materialism, or some other philosophy is a forced option. Thus he argues that if one had to choose between an infinite, absolute God on the one hand, and a finite God on the other, then it seems that a finite God suits best the facts of experience as we know them.[58] The practical implications of the latter view are that God need not be held responsible for all the cosmic evils and maladjustments of nature and that human moral choices and actions are determinate and significant. A finite God needs human beings in making and directing an evolving world, and human beings need God in the process of living.

There has always been some speculation as to whether or not James really believes in the existence of a being called "God," or whether he believes in the existence of the "idea" of God. That the idea of a supernatural Being and the idea of a Being such as the idealists define are found in symbolic meanings, most philosophers would admit, although there are some who claim that these ideas are meaningless. Furthermore, most thinkers say that the idea of God has had great influence upon human behavior throughout man's history. Sometimes James writes as if he is interested only in the symbol meaning or idea of God, and in these passages he seems to view the notion of God within the framework of his pragmatic method when applied to psychological matters. At other times, it is clear that he believes that there is an aspect of experience which he calls "divine" or "the religious." Most students of James's philosophy hold that James really believes in the existence of a Divine Being, but a Divine Being of finite dimensions.

Peirce says that he came to the study of philosophy by a road other than the religious. He was struck by the majesty of God through his study of scientific objects. The idea of God, as he interprets it, involves a kind of kindredship of the heart of the universe with the hearts of human beings, a view which has affinities with philosophic idealism. Peirce's philosophy is usually classified as a kind of realism, rather than idealism, but it is not a type of realism which cuts human life off from the universe; there is a kind of inner harmony between the universe and human beings. He says that "every single truth of science is due to the affinity of the human soul to the soul of the universe, imperfect as that affinity no doubt is."[59] For Peirce there is a continuity between the human mind and the "Most High"; humans are made in God's image.

Peirce holds that the hypothesis of God has pragmatic value; that is, the idea of God can be an ideal for human life. By musing upon the idea of God with scientific singleness of heart, one will be stirred to the depths of one's nature by the beauty of the idea and its practicality. He thinks that this musement on the idea of God has affected his own life and the lives of others. The idea of God, he holds, is so obvious that he does not see how any reasonable person can doubt it. Some people may not recognize God because the idea is so familiar to them; an awareness of His reality may be taken for granted, for it is known that many people do not recognize things which are nearest and which should be most obvious to them.

Peirce admits that he has not worked out all of his ideas on the subject of the Deity. There are scattered insights here and there in his writings, but these are more suggestive than conclusive. He thinks, for instance, that human beings cannot know what the mind of God is like, and every attempt to grasp the nature of God's knowledge evades us. Humans are cocksure and conceited, trying to escape a confession of total ignorance when they try to prescribe what God will do, and Peirce goes so far as to say that, in fact, every attempt on the part of humans to predict what God will do is simply a lack of sanity. He holds that God's knowledge is something utterly different from our own, that it is more like willing than knowing. God's omnipotence is not at all what the traditional theologians have described, for God's omnipotence means that He is freed from all experience, all desire, all intention. Peirce goes so far as to say that "God is disembodied spirit which probably has no consciousness."[60]

Peirce's idea of God contains some difficult philosophical problems. He is suspicious of definite theologies, yet he thinks it obvious that every person sees the nearness and beauty of God. He says he finds some force in the arguments for the existence of God, yet he denies that one can argue by means of induction, hypothesis, and deduction for the existence of God. At times he says that God is unknowable, yet he accepts doctrines which seem to be very precise in the characteristics attributed to God. He seems to hold that God does not interact with the world, that God's relation to the world is a mystery, yet he holds that God loves all human beings. He says that God is not immanent in the world, yet God is creative without being immanent. These puzzling and seemingly contradictory beliefs about God perhaps can be reconciled, but as they stand they seem inconsistent with each other and with the rest of Peirce's philosophical system. However, for those interested in developing a view of God through rational speculation, the musings of Peirce have suggestive value.

Mead offers a psychological and sociological interpretation of how philosophies of traditional supernaturalism became a part of human thought-life.[61] The self, he says, is more than a purely sentient organism, more than a living machine, and the self is not at home in the universe in the same sense that organisms are at home. According to Mead, the explanation of the development of supernaturalism is found in the fact that the self has always had a desire for a better society. The ability to construct goals, to project them, and to symbolize them leads man to express this desire for a better world in many ways. In traditional religion sometimes this desire for the better takes the form of a retreat into the past to some Golden Age; sometimes this desire takes the form of a withdrawal to some hoped-for world to come, as the Kingdom of God in this world or the next. This demand for an ideal existence is closely related to the projection of the self into another world which gives rise to the idea of immortality.

Mead thinks that there have been three significant points of view concerning the relation of man to the universe as a whole. First, there is the attitude of the agnostic who claims that there is no way of inquiring about the relationship. Second, there is the attitude that "religious experiences" have import and are a means of bringing out the meaning of life. Third, and this is Mead's own view, human value experiences "can be conceivably analyzed and brought back to the relation which we have to society as a whole."[62] He thinks that the self is continually trying to extend its control. In the early days of the human race, the attempt to extend this control was by means of magic. At present science has developed to help society achieve its goals. Magic and science do not always disagree on ends; they are different means to the same goals. In the past when humans were frustrated in reaching their goals, they looked for some power outside the world to help them. This is an error, says Mead, and it offers no help in solving problems. He thinks that with science as a tool, we can now construct new goals and achieve them as never before. To Mead it makes no difference whether one calls this latter kind of adjustment religion or not; on his view, the construction and achievement of goals is the most significant development in man's history.

Mead is willing to grant that, at times, Christianity includes in its theology the idea that all persons belong to a universal society in which the interests of each would be the interests of all, a notion which is found in all universal religions. At times Christian doctrine has held that this universal society is possible if humans were only reasonable. On the other hand, the Christian doctrine of human life as depraved and its concept of the world as an expression of Divine Will tend in the opposite direction. The development of science has now made obsolete many of the older formulations of ends and means. Mead thinks that we are on firmer ground if we work toward social goals under the guidance of science. In one of his most significant writings on this problem, he says: "We are coming nearer than ever before to understanding what is involved in providing the community with the goods it needs for its life. In a word, science is enabling us to restate our ends by freeing us from slavery to the means and to traditional formulations of our ends."[63]

In his *Varieties of Religious Experience*, James makes religious impulses rather than religious institutions the subject matter of his study. He claims that his work is a study in human psychology using the data of personal religious documents. In order to circumscribe his topic, James advances a definition of religion which he thinks wide enough to include all that various students might deem the religious. "Religion," he writes, "shall mean for us *the feelings, acts, and experiences of individual men in their solitude, so far as they apprehend themselves to stand in relation to whatever they may consider the divine.*"[64] James maintains that an individual's total reaction to life can be called "religious," and his definition is wide enough to include those religions which have no gods. For James, religious feelings and impulses are no different in kind from other feelings and impulses; that is, religious fear is a kind of fear and religious love is of the same kind as other loves. Thus, there is no separate, discrete religious emotion.

Another element which enters into James's view of religious experience is that the unseen, the ideal, is real in human experience. Many religions have capitalized upon this element of the ideal in human experience and have projected a world beyond anything we call nature; this ideal may take the form of an unseen, otherworld, or an unseen heaven, or an unseen Absolute which draws all human actions toward itself once individuals let it take possession of them. For James it is a fact that the unseen, the ideal, is a part of the real, whether or not it meets the description given it by supernaturalists and idealists.

Many of the ideas put forth by Dewey in his work, *A Common Faith*, share affinities with James's views found in *Varieties of Religious Experience*. For Dewey there is no separate emotion called "religious." Humans have total reactions to life, and these total reactions compose one's meaning of the religious. There is a reality of the unseen, of goals and ideals. Dewey objects, as does James, to defining the religious in terms of supernaturalism alone. Dewey starts his analysis of religion and the religious by showing that supernaturalists and atheists agree upon a definition of God which is supernatural, the one accepting the existence of such a God and the other rejecting the belief in such an entity. Dewey thinks that we should divorce the truly religious elements in experience from their connections with traditional symbols, beliefs, ceremonies, and institutions. He thinks that the term "religious" should refer to a *quality* of experience, for religious quality is often obscured by the numerous beliefs, creeds, rituals, and institutional practices which surround it.[65] Furthermore, he holds that "a religion" usually contains beliefs about the world and superworld, but these beliefs have now been shown to have no scientific standing. Anthropology, philology, and history have cut the ground from under many of the special claims concerning nature and many of the world religions. Comparative studies show that there is no common denominator of religious beliefs, not even in the idea of gods or a God.

In order to sharpen the distinction between the religious and a religion, Dewey says that one may view "religious" as an adjective and "religion" as a substantive noun. The adjective "religious" refers to a quality of experience, and not to any specifiable entity, nor to any institutional organization, nor to any system of beliefs. The religious is an attitude taken toward the whole of life. The wholeness of life has a moral dimension, but it involves more than morals; it contains intellectual and emotional dimensions. The religious aspect of experience involves the existential and the ideal. The ideal, however, is not a romantic fancy or some Absolute or some abstract concept cut from naturalistic roots. The relations of the actual to the ideal, of needs to goals, of means to ends are vital ones. How to bring ideals into actualities, how to make needs and desires correspond to goals which are desirable, how to relate purposes and ends to means—these activities involve the direction of the whole self and of the universe which that self envisions. How to inquire, to plan, to control, and to bring all aspects of life into a synthetic unity are the most challenging problems of human existence. When these moments of unity are achieved, the individual is religious. On the other hand, an individual may live a fragmented life without relating one part of experience to other parts, without relating the total self to the total world in which one lives and moves; in this case, the unity of experience which possesses a religious quality does not emerge.

Dewey thinks of nature and experience as a series of processes, of functional relations. When this view of human life and nature is understood, the following words of Dewey point up a new interpretation of the religious: "The idea that 'God' represents a unification of ideal values that is essentially imaginative in origin when the imagination supervenes in conduct is attended with verbal difficulties owing to our frequent use of the word 'imagination' to denote fantasy and doubtful reality. But the reality of ideal ends as ideals is vouched for by their undeniable power in action. An ideal is not an illusion because imagination is the organ through which it is apprehended. For *all* possibilities reach us through imagination. In a definite sense the only meaning that can be assigned the term 'imagination' is that things unrealized in fact come home to us and have power to stir us. The unification effected through imagination is not fanciful, for it is the reflex of the unification of practical and emotional attitudes. The unity signifies not a single Being, but the unity of loyalty and effort evoked by the fact that many ends are one in the power of their ideal, or imaginative, quality to stir and hold us."[66]

In another significant passage Dewey writes: "These considerations may be applied to the idea of God, or, to avoid misleading conceptions, to the idea of the divine. This idea is, as I have said, one of ideal possibilities unified through imaginative realization and projection. But this idea of God, or of the divine, is also connected with all the natural forces and conditions—including man and human association—that promote the growth of the ideal and that further its realization. We are in the presence neither of ideals completely embodied in existence nor yet of ideals that are mere rootless ideals, fantasies, utopias. For there are forces in nature and society that generate and support the ideals. They are further unified by the action that gives them coherence and solidity. It is this *active* relation between ideal and actual to which I would give the name 'God.' I would not insist that the name *must* be given. There are those who hold that the associations of the term with the supernatural are so numerous and close that any use of the word 'God' is sure to give rise to misconception and be taken as a concession to traditional ideas."[67]

The foregoing passages from Dewey have evoked considerable controversy. Some of his followers think that Dewey should not have used the term "God" at all, for the term has too many associations with traditional supernaturalism. Some interpret Dewey as a humanist, but this view Dewey denies.[68] Dewey says that he is a naturalist, the main difference between humanism and naturalism being that the former interprets ideals as purely human projections of the imagination, while the latter holds that "there are forces in nature and society that generate and support the ideals." In Dewey's own context of thought, however, it seems that he is trying to rescue the term "God" from its traditional associations. He is trying to open the way for a new and creative insight concerning the nature of the truly religious.

Dewey shows that there is not a discrete, separate kind of experience called "religious," as there are discrete kinds of experience called economic, political, aesthetic, and so forth. By freeing the religious from the view that it is a separate compartment of experience, Dewey tries to make the religious a quality of many different kinds of experiences. On his view, religious quality can emerge in family life, in economic life, in political life, and in social life generally. The religious quality emerges in the various aspects of experience when that intellectual, moral, and aesthetic unity is found which binds one to oneself, to other human beings, and to the world.

Suggested Order of Readings

1. Dewey, *Value: A Cooperative Inquiry*, ed. Ray Lepley, (New York: Columbia University Press, 1949). "The Field of Value," pp. 64–77.
2. Dewey, *Theory of Valuation*, International Encyclopedia of Unified Science, vol. 2, no. 4 (Chicago: University of Chicago Press, 1939).
3. James, *The Writings of William James: A Comprehensive Edition* (New York: Modern Library, 1968). "The Moral Philosopher and the Moral Life," pp. 610–29.
4. James, *The Writings of William James: A Comprehensive Edition.* "The Moral Equivalent of War," pp. 660–71.
5. Mead, *George Herbert Mead: Selected Writings*, ed. Andrew J. Reck (Indianapolis: Bobbs-Merrill Company, 1964). "The Philosophical Basis of Ethics," pp. 82–93.
6. Mead, *George Herbert Mead: Selected Writings*, ed. Andrew J. Reck, "Scientific Method and the Moral Sciences," pp. 229–47.
7. Dewey, *Theory of the Moral Life*, ed. Arnold Isenberg. (New York: Holt, Rinehart and Winston, 1960).
8. Dewey, *The Public and Its Problems* (New York: Henry Holt and Company, 1927). Chap. 5, "Search for the Great Community."
9. Mead, *The Philosophy of the Act*, edited with an Introduction by Charles W. Morris (Chicago: University of Chicago Press, 1938). Chap. 23, "The Aesthetic and the Consummatory."
10. Dewey, *Art as Experience* (New York: Minton, Balch & Company, 1934). Chap. 4, "The Act of Expression"; Chap. 5, "The Expressive Object."
11. James, *The Writings of William James: A Comprehensive Edition.* "Pragmatism and Religion," pp. 461–72.
12. James, *The Varieties of Religious Experience* (New York: Modern Library, 1936).
13. Peirce, *Collected Papers of Charles Sanders Peirce*, vol. 6, ed. Charles Hartshorne and Paul Weiss (Cambridge: Harvard University Press, 1931–35), pars. 395–587.
14. Mead, *The Philosophy of the Act.* Chap. 25, "Science and Religion."
15. Dewey, *A Common Faith* (New Haven: Yale University Press, 1934).

PART 4

EDUCATION

18. Societies and Their Schools

Educational theories and practices have been of vital interest to the pragmatic naturalists. Peirce made some observations about education, but these are made primarily from the point of view of an inquirer and not as one directly involved in the teaching experience. Peirce's experience as a teacher was limited, and after he left the classroom at Johns Hopkins, his primary contact with formal education was in the form of occasional lectures. James, Mead, and Dewey were professional teachers, directly involved in the daily tasks of preparing lectures, leading discussions, and directing research. They view education and philosophy as intimately related to the total development of human life. Dewey writes: "Education is the laboratory in which philosophical distinctions become concrete and are tested."[1] Philosophy remains purely dialectical and verbal unless related to action, and the kind of action which is most significant is that involved in education taken in the widest sense. Furthermore, reconstruction in philosophy, when related to education, results in the reconstruction of individual and social life.

In 1894 Dewey left the University of Michigan to assume a new position at the University of Chicago as head of the Department of Philosophy, Psychology, and Pedagogy. One of the enticements to Chicago, besides a reunion with his former colleague, James H. Tufts, was the opportunity to establish a laboratory school in education. The school opened in 1896, and Dewey remained associated with it until 1904 when he left Chicago to go to Columbia University in New York City. Mead joined the faculty at Chicago in 1894 and became actively involved in the laboratory school.

The decade of Dewey's residence in Chicago when the laboratory school was established was one of the most creative in the history of American education. During this time Dewey gave many addresses and wrote many articles and books about the theory and practice of education. The philosophy which guided the laboratory school gradually evolved, and the principal ideas are contained in Dewey's works: *My Pedagogic Creed* (1897),[2] *The School and Society* (1900),[3] and the recently published class notes, *Lectures in the Philosophy of Education: 1899*.[4] After leaving the laboratory school Dewey continued to write on education, and two of his most influential works are *Democracy and Education* (1916) and *Experience and Education* (1938).[5] In 1892 James was asked to address the teachers of Cambridge, Massachusetts, on the relation of psychology to education. These lectures were later published under the title *Talks to Teachers on Psychology* (1899).[6] Mead's articles on education are few in number, but his writings have had a lasting influence on the development of the pragmatic naturalists' philosophy of education.[7]

Pragmatic naturalists believe that education is a vital function in any society. Dewey describes a society as "a number of people held together because they are working along common lines, in a common spirit, and with reference to common aims."[8] The institution of education has emerged because societies have sought to transmit certain beliefs, practices, and values to their younger members. Education is necessary if any society is to perpetuate itself, and thus there is an intimate relation between any society and its schools.

A brief glance at some of the relations of societies and their schools reveals that the nature and function of formal schooling depends upon the values and purposes held uppermost by each society. At times education serves the ruling class to keep the disinherited and the ignorant in subjection; at other times education performs the function of liberating the capacities of human beings. Sometimes learning is an activity which concerns a special social class; this was the case especially in those ages before printing was invented. In those times the high priests of learning were responsible for the acquisition and preservation of knowledge, while the masses had no access to this dimension of human experience. With the invention of printing an intellectual revolution occurred. Books, magazines, journals, and newspapers made ideas accessible to a larger populace, and the clamor arose for the widening of education to more people. In recent years the widespread use of the media of radio and television has brought about a communications revolution and a still wider dissemination of knowledge.

Societies and their schools operate in a world of social change. Change, of course, is a generic trait of experience and nature. Some societies may resist social change, others may welcome it, but no society can escape it. Sometimes social change is rapid; sometimes it occurs at a slower pace. When the pragmatic naturalists were formulating their ideas on education in the later years of the nineteenth and early years of the twentieth centuries, social change was accelerated, perhaps more so than at any time in human history. In America the rural farm was being replaced by the urban-industrial life. Industry and division of labor were eliminating household occupations. Manufacturing centers, rapid means of transportation and communication, wide distribution of products were taking place. This rapid social change was affecting almost every phase of human life, and its impact was growing upon the schools. There arose a demand that the schools take over industrial training of workers, and, as will be shown subsequently, the pragmatic naturalists opposed narrow views of vocational training in the schools; they had definite ideas about the role of education in an industrial society.

The pragmatic naturalists lived in the midst of these sweeping social changes, and they tried to come to terms with the emerging conditions by offering some theories concerning the direction change should take through education. When they came upon the scene, most of the ideas about schools and their functions in society had been handed down with certain modifications from medieval times. Reading, Writing, and Arithmetic, or the three "R's," had been used to fulfill the need of giving certain members of the populace just enough learning to enable them to take orders and to carry out certain menial tasks. The goal of a wider, more liberal and humanistic education combined with the mastery of emerging scientific methods and subject matters was yet to be developed.

In adjusting to social change some societies demand that their schools reflect the status quo; Dewey points out, however, that societies are changing, that social change is natural, and about all the term "status quo" means is resistance to any innovations in what is currently practiced. The justification for preserving and making inflexible some habit or practice of the present is sometimes based upon the notion that human nature does not change, that it is constant in its basic constitution, and that there are fixed characteristics in all which educators must build upon for the formulation of what is essential educational subject matter and method. According to the pragmatic naturalists, the notion of a fixed human nature is unrealistic, for scientific studies of humans show that children have plasticity; human beings develop varieties of impulses, habits, and customs. Advocates of status quo practices are defending already developed social habits and customs, and often these practices lack relevance to the new conditions and problems which are encountered.

Thus, one aspect of the relation of societies and their

schools is the social and political pressure from groups which desire to retain what is traditional, the already developed. These pressure groups are fearful of social change, and they attempt to impose upon the schools programs which they think will secure the inherited and often outmoded values they are afraid of losing. Accordingly, some groups demand required reading of the Protestant Bible, compulsory teaching of the Constitution of the United States (usually with biased interpretations), the signing of special loyalty oaths by teachers, and the revision of textbooks which will conform to their own prejudices. Such requirements are external and verbal, but status quo advocates think the schools can safeguard society by imposing such practices upon the young and their teachers.

Sometimes the advocates of the status quo require that their schools be institutions of indoctrination and that their teachers impose upon the pupils a certain kind of mental discipline. The common notion of mental discipline includes rigid conformities of actions, beliefs, and values. The use of rote memorization, repetition of social and political creeds without discussion, the adoption of authoritarian methods of teaching are some of the traits of formal schooling which has as its aim indoctrination and mental discipline. Instances of this kind of education are found in our own times in the educational theories and practices of fascism, in certain types of communism, as well as in some institutions of Europe and the United States. These social philosophies have invaded the schools in order to capture the minds of the young and to impose upon them predetermined and narrow sets of beliefs, practices, and values. Pragmatic naturalists have been critical of education as indoctrination, and they maintain that this kind of teaching destroys desire to learn; it cripples the mind so that it is unable to think for itself.

Groups with narrow and selfish interests often make demands upon the schools, and one of the most persistent pressures has come from the new industrial and commercial classes which insist that the schools train their future employees. Vocational training became a controversial issue during the formative years of the educational theories of the pragmatic naturalists. Dewey opposed the kind of vocational training which is concerned only with the acquisition of industrial and commercial skills. Vocational training which is concerned with routine skills does not give the pupil insight into the processes which underlie the industrial revolution and its meaning for human life. Vocational training is often similar to the apprenticeship training which developed during the Scholastic period, and this method fails to be effective and meaningful in modern times. Furthermore, even if the schools were to adopt a program of industrial training, technological forces are changing so rapidly that the skills and the materials the students learn will soon become obsolete. Dewey thinks that most skills and materials of vocations can best be learned "on the job."[9]

Industrial education, according to Dewey, has a much deeper and broader meaning than the narrow connotation of the learning of practical skills for the purposes of making money and meeting the needs of industry. Industrial education should give insight into the scientific, technological, and humanistic dimensions of the industrial order. Attention should be given to the scientific concepts, principles, and methods involved in the industrial transformations of nature; thus, industrial education is a theoretical or intellectual affair. The study of the industrial order, however, should not be confined to its narrow technological achievements. Most important is the consideration of the moral and aesthetic consequences involved in the industrial way of life. The impact of the industrial revolution upon human life, the new social relationships which developed, and the moral problems emerging from this way of life should be the concern of industrial education. The place of the artist in this society, the attitude toward his works, and the value placed upon them should be concerns of industrial education.

Dewey's ideas about industrial education were not adopted by the schools. Technical and commercial schools were established for the purposes of preparing students for future jobs in industry. Elementary and secondary schools with traditional curricula adopted programs which included manual training and commercial subjects. Understanding and control of the industrial order for humane and moral purposes, a program which Dewey consistently pleaded for and worked for, were ignored. The new social relationships of human beings to each other, of capitalist and worker, of producer and consumer, of urbanite and farmer, were not studied in the schools, were not subjected to moral evaluations, but were left, for the most part, to be accommodated by the processes of power struggle and conflict. The emphasis upon human transformation of nature through technology and industrial goals, through desire for new products, made increased production the supreme value of the industrial order. The emphasis upon increased production, however, has brought with it some undesirable consequences. Failure to understand the ways in which nature has been exploited, the ways in which the by-products of industrial transformations have polluted the planet, the ways in which some species have been made extinct, and the ways in which our own existence is now threatened—all point up the importance of Dewey's view of industrial education. Had the schools followed his lead on the meaning and purpose of industrial education, the ecological plight of modern life might have been avoided.

During the formative years of the pragmatic naturalists' views of education one of the most vital issues was that of the education and preparation of teachers. Previously it had been generally held that anyone who had gone to school was prepared to teach. Critical examination of the teaching-learning experience, however, revealed that this experience is a science and an art. During Dewey's years at Chicago a controversy arose over the philosophy of education of teachers. Dewey championed the "laboratory idea" of teacher preparation and rejected what he called the "apprenticeship idea."[10]

The apprenticeship idea of education of teachers, a view which Dewey strongly opposed, starts with imitating the techniques of the "master" teacher. Apprenticeship training means that lesson plans are predigested and handed down to subordinates whose duty it is to put them into practice. Certain prescribed methods of teaching are followed without question. Apprenticeship training means that the mechanics of the classroom are predetermined by some group outside of the classroom situation. Educational apprenticeship requires ability to carry out orders, to follow prescribed rules, and to act with a minimum of reflective thinking. The subject matters or "lesson plans" are worked out in advance, and the teacher is expected to cover all the material at designated times in the day, the week, and the school year. This kind of educational practice damages the minds of both the apprentice and the pupils; it dulls the impulses of innovation, invention, and creativity.

On the other hand, the laboratory idea of education, the view which Dewey advocates, involves the development of inquiring minds on the part of the beginning teacher and of the students. The laboratory idea means that attempts are made to develop habits of critical thought, the habits of personal inquiry. The beginning teacher observes each student's ongoing life, the impulses which move that life, and the interests which hold attention. The beginning teacher observes the interactions of students with each other and his or her interactions with them. How mind meets mind is perceived; critical analysis and evaluation are made of what is seen; that is, to the observations are brought theories of perception, stimulus-response, motivation, habit formation, and discovery. Thus, the teacher brings to the educational situation a critical mind, an openness to new ideas, and an experimental approach to the teaching-learning process.

The laboratory idea as over against the apprenticeship idea was an issue on which Dewey felt deeply, and it appears that the conflict between his view and that of others was one of the reasons for his leaving Chicago and giving up his work with the laboratory school.[11]

Dewey once wrote that the schools are chaotic in their programs, particularly in the United States, because the society in which they operate is chaotic. Goals and purposes of various social groups are in conflict with each other, and the schools simply reflect this condition of society.

Dewey made a plea that the schools become experimental institutions for individual and social reconstruction. This process of reconstruction, of deliberately effecting social change, became the primary theme in his writings on education. The school should become a community of inquirers, of people who live and learn together, of situations in which innovation, initiative, and creativity are encouraged in each child. The children and teachers, however, have wider interactions than those of the little world within their schools. They are related to a larger society. Educational administrators, teachers, and students sensitive to the genuine needs of society can become creative agents for the enrichment of culture. There seem to be no other alternatives: either the schools yield to the conservative forces, to the status quo advocates, and to pressure groups with selfish interests, or they become independent and creative in promoting new possibilities and directions for human life. Dewey and his followers thought that the schools should become the agents for directing social change. Social change is going on anyway, but it needs intelligent direction and ought not be left to the haphazard planning of competing and conflicting social forces.

William James points out that a child's interactions in

the early days and years of its life are most important in shaping the child's future. School experience, of course, is only one of the interactive processes which the child undergoes; he interacts with a social and natural world beyond the school. This primary concept of childhood experience led to the slogan usually put in the following way: "Education is going on all the time." In other words, education is as broad as the transmission of culture, and that transmission takes place through the child's parents, playmates, adult friends, and those in social groups of the larger society. This is an important educational insight, but the idea has often been abused by those who do not understand its full meaning. The bare fact that culture is transmitted in the interactions of a child with its society does not always mean that the transmission is qualitatively good and fruitful. On the one hand, the transmission may be haphazard, lacking in selectiveness, purposiveness, and intelligence; it may or may not be judiciously done. Many aspects of the culture can be transmitted, such as superstititions, false beliefs, errors, outmoded habits, prejudices, and harmful impulses. On the other hand, a judicious transmission of culture selects and promotes scientific truths, evaluated goods, and creative aesthetic experience.

Since education is as broad as the transmission of culture, then education is everyone's responsibility, whether or not one is connected with formal schooling. The parents of a child transmit meanings of impulses before the child enters school; they instill habits; they encourage or indoctrinate goals and ideals of living. Most of the child's interactions are subject to some kinds of interpretations, groovings, controls, or guidance; at the same time, some of the child's interactions are random, pointless, or harmful. When all the members of the institutions which make up a society realize that education is as broad as the transmission of culture, then they bear some responsibility for what is transmitted to the child. The important point, however, is not that transmission of culture takes place; that is a bare fact of social life. The quality of the transmission should be the chief concern.

Another slogan which developed out of the philosophy of pragmatic naturalism and its relation to education is that the teacher "shares" experience with the students. On the lowest level of interpretation, "sharing" simply means "interaction" of teacher and pupil. Any and every interaction of one human with another can be interpreted as a kind of sharing, whether or not there is any judicious concern for what is shared and how it is shared. When the pragmatic naturalists use the term "shared experience," they mean something more than mere interactions of one person with another. Shared experience means that the adult, the mature in experience, shares his understanding of the *connections and relations* in nature which have been scientifically determined; the mature in experience shares *a method of inquiry* which yields statements which are warranted or scientific truths and a *method of evaluation* which makes values secure. The mature in experience, whether or not a professional teacher, has the responsibility to share those truths and goods which have been intelligently grounded. Thus, anyone who attempts to share what has been learned about experience must understand the connections found in experience and the method by which those connections are ascertained; otherwise, the transmission of ideas, values, and practices may lead to chaos and disaster. Uncritical transmission of culture can be the blind leading the blind. This is why everyone who attempts to teach needs to develop goals and ideals of education and to have some understanding of intelligent methods employed in the educative process.

19. Ideals and Goals of Education

Human beings are goal-seeking in many of their activities; the ability to construct ends-in-view and to move toward the accomplishment of some of these goals is a distinguishing mark of the species. The pursuit and achievement of goals gives meaning and purpose to living. Behavior that is not goal-directed is impulsive, or it is a matter of routine habit. Specific goals grow out of specific problematic situations, and they are unique in that they occur in particular times and places. Kinds of situations recur, however; thus there emerge ends or goals which are generic to past and present experience. General goals have a cumulative force persisting from the past; they occupy attention in the present, and they become imaginative ideals demanding actualization. Since the emergence of purposes, goals, and ideals is integral to the pragmatic naturalists' metaphysics of experience, and since education taken broadly is a transmission of that experience to succeeding generations, then it follows that ideals and goals are central to their philosophy of education.

Goals are narrow or broad in scope depending upon the problems with which they deal. The end-in-view which a person carries in the mind when moving on a continuous route from home to office may be viewed as a practical and somewhat limited goal. The end-in-view or goal a person has in mapping out a career is much broader, involves contributory activities and goals, and stretches across many areas of experience. There are still other goals which belong to human life as a species. These comprehensive goals cut across broad areas of experience, and they are the guiding ideals of human life; they are abstract and general in the sense that they are not tied down to any immediate time and space, but they are not abstract in the sense that they are unrelated to all concrete experience. If the term "ultimate" be allowed interpretation in this sense, then pragmatic naturalists hold that there are ultimate goals or ideals with which philosophy and education are concerned, and there are proximate goals which are more immediate in their demands and more concrete and empirical in their contents.

For the pragmatic naturalists one of the most important ideals of education is the *intellectual ideal*. They hold that one of the foremost functions of education is to teach a child how to think, how to inquire, and how to formulate judgments. Dewey says that with the development of "methods of controlling investigation and controlling reflection, the intellectual ideal can and must in the long run change more and more from one of information to one of ability to use the methods of inquiry and verification."[12] As experiences of human beings accumulate, there is a multiplication of studies. The teacher finds himself overwhelmed by the vast accumulation of information, and there is an increased need for some principle of unity and simplification if the amalgamated mass of subject studies is not to fall into disorganization or crumble under its own weight. There is an important place for subject matters in the curriculum, as will be shown later. The primary emphasis, however, is upon science as an attitude of mind and as a method of inquiry. For Dewey it is not enough that a child know the accumulated achievements of past inquiries; the important thing is that the child learn to inquire for himself.

Dewey thinks that the steadying and centralizing factor in education is the attitude of mind and habit of thought which we call "scientific." Encouragement of an inquiring mind in each child may seem a tremendous task to a teacher engaged in day-to-day activities of keeping a group of youngsters occupied and busy; but Dewey believes that there is an important connection between the early impulses of children and the refined disciplines of scientific investigators. The child has curiosity, imagination, and a love for experimentation which are akin to the same attitudes of the mature scientist.

The early impulses of children are random, however, and may develop into habits of perception which are lacking in sustained attention; this may lead to hasty, heedless, impatient glancing over the surfaces of things. These early impulses may turn into haphazard guessing, into what may be called a grasshopper-type mind, flitting from one stimulus to another. Thus habits of credulity may alternate with habits of incredulity. Beliefs may be based upon whim, emotion, or some other accidental circumstance. Dewey is aware of the dangers of the impulses of children developing into nonscientific attitudes, into attitudes which foster enslavement because unhindered and unreflective activity is at the mercy of appetite and chance stimuli.

When pragmatic naturalists use the term "mental discipline," the term has a special meaning. The original impulses of the child are transformed into inwardly controlled activities. The goal of education is the development of a mind which can think independently of any external tutor. A free mind is one which can think for itself, and, for Dewey, freedom of the mind is the first freedom.

When the intellectual ideal is described as individual ability to think, "thinking" has a meaning different from that put forth by others. Learning to think is not a matter of memorizing the definitions of a large number of concepts, nor is it a matter of thinking the great thoughts in the patterns of the great thinkers of the past. Learning to think starts with a problem which is vital to the child; with the aid of the teacher the child learns the methods by which problems are solved. The child learns to look at data deliberately, that is, in terms of the causes and consequences of the problem. The child learns to judge whether there is enough evidence and evidence of the proper kind in order to make a judgment. The child learns where to look for evidence and how to judge if the facts and concepts gathered are relevant to solution of the problem at hand. This kind of thinking requires attention, persistence, and carefulness on the part of the inquirer. For the pragmatic naturalist this kind of thinking is the intellectual ideal of education.

Another concern of education is the *moral ideal*. This ideal, like the intellectual ideal, is one of creating the conditions and of guiding the child so that the child can make independent moral judgments. The moral ideal is the development of a certain quality of life, of a certain kind of moral self, a self in which impulses, habits, and activities have an operational unity. Moral behavior or conduct is concerned with the consequences of the activities of an individual upon the formation of personal character and upon the lives and characters of others. The aim of moral education is the control of conduct, and conduct is behavior with a moral meaning.

Dewey says that "everyone knows, the direct and immediate attention of teachers and pupils must be, for the greater part of the time, upon intellectual matters. It is out of the question to keep direct moral considerations constantly uppermost. But it is not out of the question to aim at making the methods of learning, of acquiring intellectual power, and of assimilating subject matter, such that they will render behavior more enlightened, more consistent, more vigorous than it otherwise would be."[13]

Deliberation in morals follows the intellectual pattern of inquiry as conceived by the pragmatic naturalists. Children must learn to recognize a moral problem when it appears. They learn to compare cases, to assemble facts about the ills from which human beings suffer, and to generalize upon the goals which these ills point to by putting them into classes. Like all other kinds of deliberation, deliberation in morals means that judgment and choice must precede action.[14] Thinking out the implications of proposed moral hypotheses requires moral imagination, and moral imagination is something which is not automatically achieved; it must be cultivated in the child by the teacher. Moral behavior stems from human ability to set up goals, from the ability to manipulate various stages of the act before the final overt action is consummated. Moral imagination is required so that, beginning early in life, a child is sensitized to the consequences of its actions upon others and upon the development of its own life.

The moral ideal in education, like morals in every other aspect of human experience, concerns "nothing less than the whole character, and the whole character is identical with the man in all his concrete make-up and manifestations."[15] As pointed out in the section on Moral Philosophy, the organization of the interests of life is uppermost. Intellectual concerns and moral concerns are separable only in abstraction. Dewey makes the further point: "The most important problem of moral education in the school concerns the relationship of knowledge and conduct. For unless the learning which accrues in the regular course of study affects character, it is futile to conceive the moral end as the unifying and culminating end of education."[16] This means that "all the aims and values which are desirable in education are themselves moral."[17] Pragmatic naturalists do not make a sharp demarcation between the individual and the social; thus "apart from participation in social life, the school has no moral end or aim."[18]

The social nature of the moral life leads directly to another ideal of education, that is, the *social ideal* of the democratic community. Moral behavior may be conceived narrowly or broadly, and there has been a tendency in the past to emphasize the development of individual character apart from a person's interaction with others. "There is also an ideal provided from the processes of education, formal and informal," says Dewey. "Education should create an interest in all persons in furthering the general good, so that they will find their own happiness realized in what they can do to improve the conditions of others."[19]

The school is a miniature social group, on the one hand, and has continuity with the community on the other. In the miniature social group, the child enters into interactions with others. In solitude it might be possible for the child to build up by reading alone some store of information. But genuine education takes place in situations in which the meanings of symbols are understood in communications involved in work and play. It will be recalled that in Dewey's description of democracy a group or public should consider its goals in relation to the general welfare. To fail to do this, in extreme cases, is to foster the group interests of gangsters and thieves, for these interest groups set up goals which do not mesh with the rest of society. To use the school to put forth the goals of one special group at the expense of the rest of society falls into the same category and makes the same mistake. Furthermore, it fosters slaves rather than free individuals, for individuals are not free when grooved into some narrow or parochial interest.

The school in a democracy attempts to help children see the kind of society and life which Dewey put forth in his outline of democratic ideals. This means that there are two fundamental considerations which will protect the school and the child from being isolated: 1) the many and varied interests of the community and of humanity as a whole are constantly shared and critically analyzed; 2) the interplay with other forms of association outside the school are sufficiently full and free for the child to learn what life is all about. Approaching the problem of teaching democracy in this manner, of having the student see the various interests of all groups in society, will enable evaluation of which ones are working toward the democratic ideal and which are not. The full and free interplay with other forms of association allows the student to respond to a diversity of stimuli and to see the effects of individual and group actions upon the environment and upon other human beings.

Throughout his writings on education Dewey objected to the great humanistic achievements of man being cut off from his industrial activities. He thinks that our industrial life, as well as the entirety of our cultural life, should be humanized with science, morals, and art. Industrial life has developed because of the great advance of science and technology. But industrial life is mechanical, drab, and self-defeating when cut from its intellectual foundations, from moral considerations, and from artistic refinements. Industrial and technological life needs the enlightenment of moral evaluations made by its participants to humanize it and make it responsible to humanity at large. And these participants in the industrial enterprise need the aesthetic sensitivity which infuses their lives with meaning, refinement, and enjoyment.

Thus, another concern of education is the *aesthetic ideal*. The pragmatic naturalists do not make a dichotomy of life experience and the refined products of art. The aesthetic is an aspect of experience which "absorbs into itself memories of the past and anticipations of the future," and when an experience has these qualities, it becomes an aesthetic ideal.[20] Writing on art in education, Dewey says: "A study of education in its earlier forms, not only in savage communities, but in a civilization as advanced as the Athenian, reveals the great role played by the arts. Anthropological investigations have confirmed the obvious educational influence by showing the great part played by the arts in the life of the community and in determining progress."[21] The aesthetic is primarily concerned with the emotional aspect of experience, and it is the emotional which produces "unity of attitude and of outlook and imagination."

The arts are fundamental to the development of civilization; they are not luxuries or ornaments to be tacked on to an otherwise drab experience. When the arts are assigned a trivial role in formal schooling, there is a great loss to the educational experience. Aesthetic experience begins in a school when a group activity is of "joyous character," when "some event or fact of common value is the natural soil of artistic creation in the school as well as out." The aesthetic element takes on significance in education because "it trains a natural sensitiveness and susceptibility of the individual."[22] The emotional enters into the responsiveness of the child to ideas and acts. Aesthetic quality can become an integral element in moral and intellectual experience.

Dewey thinks that we have reversed the process by which children come to love and appreciate art. The starting place should be with the child's impulses, for there are found in a child's life impulses and desires to tell and to represent. Aesthetic appreciation of great works of art does not come first; the art impulse appears in early life, and appreciation comes later as an achievement.[23] The art impulse emerges when man "attempts to enhance and perpetuate his images that are charged with emotional value by some kind of objectification through action. The outcome inevitably is marked by certain factors of balance, rhythm, and constructive order, and by the function of representation, i.e., of recording in some adequate way the values to which emotions cling."[24] The feelings which children can develop for great art masterpieces must first be cultivated in their own experiences; then children can understand how the great artists have objectified emotion.

There is a tendency on the part of some teachers to inject morals or grammar or history into every aesthetic experience and into the study of art and the appreciation of it. Sometimes the effort to teach moral and spiritual values in the schools has taken the form of setting up moral criteria to which all art expressions must conform. Dewey objects to this use of art: "Literature is not to be used as a means for any other end than this gathering together, in a vital and readily appreciated way, of scattered and inchoate elements of experience. It is not, for example, to be made a means of moral instruction or consciously impressing a specific moral lesson. It is ethically important simply because it presents in a form easily grasped and likely to be enduring values which are themselves felt to be intrinsically important. Any attempt at definite formulation and impressing of these values and the kind of conduct they require is certainly detrimental to the literature as art, and is very likely to be harmful to the moral influence which the values might exercise, if left undisturbed in their proper medium of feeling and imagination. The same principle holds, of course, of methods that utilize literature simply as a means of teaching grammar, information about the history of literary men, antiquities, or any of the diverse topics which have been hung upon literature as upon a peg."[25]

Critics of the pragmatic naturalists' philosophy of education have pointed out that in this philosophy there are no absolute goals to which the educator can look for guidance.[26] This objection has come mainly from theologically oriented critics who have not accepted a naturalistic philosophy in which goals are always on the move, or, if these critics have accepted a process philosophy, they have attempted to impose some final and completed goal upon the process. Some critics have failed to grasp, or have rejected, the starting place of the natural movement of experience for the development of a philosophy of education. The natural movement of experience begins with the impulsive energies of the child, with activities currently going on, with capacities and potentialities empirically grounded, with acquired habits, and with perplexities, ends-in-view, and interests current in the child's life. The process philosophy of pragmatic naturalism claims that goals are generated out of direct experience and out of the funded experience of the

human race. These goals are more or less stable, but are not fixed and permanent.

The way in which goals are conceived and modified in a process philosophy can be illustrated by taking a brief glance at the history of the goal of health. Health becomes a problem when some perplexity or frustration in the ongoing of life is encountered. The survival of life and the avoidance of death as human problems stretch back to the dawn of human consciousness. The efforts to find some connections in experience to make life secure have taken many forms, forms which start with the magical and the superstitious, with the development of the practices of the witch doctors. At times practices like bloodletting were regarded as cures for certain diseases. Then came the development of the germ theory, and this brought a host of scientific ways of treating diseases. The use of vaccines, of antibiotics, assists the achievement of health. Throughout all this history, and there is much more that could be mentioned, the concept of health itself was modified. What is regarded as a healthy state of the human organism today differs in many ways from what was regarded as a healthy person centuries ago. The fact is, of course, that the concept of health is a rather abstract concept; it is a synthesis of many investigations and appraisals. The goal of health has more or less stable aspects to its development, but it cannot be fixed and permanent in its content; any attempt to absolutize the concept of health at some stage in its history is a sure way of inviting human disaster.

Intellectual, moral, social, and aesthetic ideals are analogous to the abstract concept of health. They are refinements of experience which have been criticized and evaluated, thus, modified and recreated over the centuries.

Some statements made by Dewey on educational goals have become the slogans of his followers and the source of criticism by others. Dewey once wrote that "the educational

process has no end beyond itself; it is its own end."²⁷ Again, he says: "Since growth is a characteristic of life, education is all one with growing; it has no end beyond itself."²⁸ The interpretations of these statements reach a point of absurdity when taken out of context. Dewey's contention has been made to mean that growth is purely quantitative, meaning increase in size or the accumulation of more and more experiences on the analogy of the accumulation of money. Sometimes the statements have been taken to mean that growth could be increase in evil, falsehood, and ugliness.

The concept of growth for the pragmatic naturalists has a special and refined meaning; it means transformation, emergence, development. The concept rests upon the pragmatic naturalists' view of experience as having continuities within it, continuities which reveal a connection between the less complex and the more complex functions of behavior. Emergent functions in the continuity of experience cannot be reduced to some prior physical or physiological condition. The physical and the physiological are integral to a self-developing life, but life for human beings is more than the physical and the physiological, important as these processes are for the general concept of growth in the overall view of life. On the human level, growth involves the emergence of symbolic behavior, of communication, and of the expansion of meanings. Language functions expand human life; they allow us to develop in thought a method of inquiry, to plan, and to have foresight of the consequences of our actions. But the development of the physical, the biological, and the symbolic functions are only conditions for the development of meanings. Meanings are perceived in the interconnections of experience and nature. Meanings make up what is called "mind," and mind is a set of meanings.

The development of a child's life may be viewed, then, as a growth of meanings, a growth of the perception of the interconnections found in experience and nature. At any

stage of a child's growth, the meanings it has acquired are integral to its understanding of life and the value placed upon objects. Dewey persistently reiterates the importance of living in the present, but living in the present involves meanings which stretch the present into a reconstruction of the past and an imaginative projection of the future. He says: "To live in the present is compatible with condensations of far-reaching meanings in the present. Such enrichment of the present for its own sake is the just heritage of childhood and the best insurer of future growth."[29] So important is this growth of meaning in individual and social life that Dewey makes it the most important heritage we can pass on to posterity.[30] The growth of meanings encompasses all of human cognitive experience; meanings are the fundamentals both of science and of human values.

When goals are discussed in the context of the pragmatic naturalists' educational philosophy, the question is often asked: Growth toward what? The answer to this question has been given in the preceding paragraphs; it is growth toward the intellectual, moral, social, and aesthetic ideals of life. The growth of meanings in these dimensions of experience and the blending of them into one continuous individual life gives human life quality and excellence, the only reason for human existence. A summary of the ideals and goals of education may be put in terms of the ideals and goals of all life; Dewey writes, "Nothing but the best, the richest and fullest experience possible, is good enough for man. The attainment of such an experience is not to be conceived as the specific problem of 'reformers' but as the common purpose of men."[31]

20. The Educative Process

Theories of learning which Peirce and James initiated, and which Mead and Dewey expanded, led to one of the most comprehensive and influential philosophies of the educative process in recent history. Human educational processes cannot be effective without some theoretical understanding of the organic and environmental materials with which the teacher works. The education of children builds upon what we know of the natural sciences, the social sciences, and the humanities. The education of children must take account of how children function and how they develop. To set up goals and adopt methods of education without taking these factors into account is to commit educational suicide.

Knowledge of the studies of the various fields of human activities, however, will not automatically produce a workable philosophy of education which eventually results in fruitful practices. William James notes in his famous *Talks to Teachers on Psychology:* "I say moreover that you make a great, a very great mistake, if you think that psychology, being the science of the mind's laws, is something from which you can deduce definite programmes and schemes and methods of instruction for immediate schoolroom use. Psychology is a science, and teaching is an art; and sciences never generate arts directly out of themselves. An intermediary inventive mind must make the application, by using its originality."[32] James went on to make this observation: "The best teacher may be the poorest contributor of child-study material, and the best contributor may be the poorest teacher."[33]

Dewey makes the same distinction between general psychology as a scientific study and educational psychology which is concerned with the science and art of teaching. He says that "no educational procedure nor pedagogical maxim can be derived directly from pure psychological data."[34] General psychology treats of the details of the so-called mental life, whereas educational psychology is concerned with a selection of those materials and the use of them toward growth and development of the individual.

The point which James and Dewey are making in the foregoing quotations is that the teacher selects materials from the various sciences concerning human behavior which will enable the teaching experience to be effective; the purpose in the teaching-learning situation is not to study children as the psychologist does in analytic and abstract ways, but to guide them in concrete and ethical ways. This does not mean that the teacher can ignore the knowledge which the various sciences have produced about human life; the teacher must use the inquiries of the scientists, but the purpose of the teacher is different from that of the strictly scientific investigator in most respects. James shows how important is the teacher's art when he says that it involves "a happy tact and ingenuity to tell us what definite things to say and do when the pupil is before us."[35] There is an "ingenuity in meeting and pursuing the pupil," a "tact for the concrete situation," and these are "the alpha and the omega of the teacher's art."

The psychology of learning which has dominated many schools in America has been based upon a view of human consciousness which Mead and others call the "associational type of psychology." On this view, the materials of the curriculum are presented as "percepts capable of being assimilated by the nature of their content to other contents of consciousness."[36] Advocates of the associational theory hold that the structure of an idea is all important and that the lines of association of an idea with other ideas will guarantee their abiding in consciousness. Consciousness, on this view, is looked upon as a storehouse of ideas, materials, and methods waiting there to be tapped when called upon. This philosophy of the development of the human mind, which may be called the "traditional," has been prevalent in America for the last one hundred years, and it is the source of one side of the conflict over methods of teaching, the goals of education, and the selection of curriculum materials.

The pragmatic naturalists developed new views of human consciousness. James maintains that consciousness is not an entity; consciousness is a function of the experiencing organism. Furthermore, the world does not come to the child ready-made or structured; it comes as a "blooming, buzzing confusion." In the beginning of a child's life, percepts and ideas are not structured, and they become meaningful only through his responses within his environment, natural and social. As the child moves through its life, through the continuity of its organic responses, excitations are encountered, some of which become stimuli bringing forth responses. These responses are seriated and gradually make up the structured functions of the organism. A child learns to use gestures and symbols, to communicate; experience takes on meanings in terms of connections and relations which are recognized through personal responses and through the guidance of adults. When symbols enter into a child's experience, it learns to take the role of others, and taking the role of others is a precondition for the developing self.

The traditional view of a child's consciousness and of the development of the conscious life makes the assumption that there is no content to consciousness; it maintains that the business of education is to present structured ideas to the mind, to "stuff them in," so to speak. Ideas, many of them abstract, are then presented to the consciousness to be absorbed, and are then ready to be repeated on demand; on this view the child's impulses have little or no part to play in the development of the intellectual life. As a place where these ideas are presented and where the child receives them, this classroom is nonactive, nonemotional, and nonsocial. Pragmatic naturalists disagree with this traditional view of the development of human consciousness, and they hold that the practices built upon the traditional view distort and damage the development of the child's total life. Mead writes that "it is impossible to fully interpret or control the process of instruction without recognizing the child as a self and viewing his conscious processes from the point of view of their relation in his consciousness to his self, among other selves."[37]

The child is a developing self, a self which interacts with other selves and with nature. These interactions are the lateral dimensions of its development, while the continuity of its life is the longitudinal.[38] A child develops by participating in what Mead calls the three general types of human activity—work, art, and play.[39] Work is an endeavor "in which a definite end is set up, and the means are chosen solely with reference to that end." The artist is concerned with "the feeling of appropriateness and consistency in the means which he uses for the expression of his idea." Play, however, is different from work and art. Play is spontaneous activity; in play there is no consciousness of an end-in-view. According to Mead, play should occupy a significant role in a child's life, for play aids the child's activities to become coordinated. These coordinations of the organs of the body cannot be forced; they must be developed through the spontaneity of the child's life. "It is the formation of these coordinations that represents on the side of the nervous system the process of education."[40] A baby's movement of its limbs, its rhythmic kicking, is not done for any purpose; it is a kind of free play. These movements become the preconditions for walking, and walking involves other organs of the body besides the limbs and feet; in fact, walking involves the whole organism. This spontaneous energy of the child affords the conditions of the child "taking possession of and making itself at home in new-won coordinations, that are later to be the highest value to man."

The pragmatic naturalists' way of approaching the child as a developing self, a self with actions, impulses, habits, goals, and purposes gradually evolving, is set against the view which is called the "intellectualistic" which adopts the perceptual and ideational assumptions of the associationalist psychology. The role that play should take in education in effecting coordinations in the nervous system of the child is ignored by the associationalist psychologists and educators. As a result, the advocates of the traditional view of consciousness accuse the pragmatic naturalists of being "anti-intellectualistic." This issue, however, is one concerning how the self develops, and it is not a matter of ignoring or not ignoring the intellectual aspects of the educative process. How does the child learn? How does the child learn to think for itself? How does the child learn to have some measure of control within its environment? Previously it was pointed out that Dewey made a connection between the early impulses found in children and the refined activities of the scientific investigator. The child has an impulse to handle things, to move about, to hunt and uncover, to mix things together, and to take them apart, to talk and listen. These impulses of the child have a connection and continuity with the many refined activities of the sophisticated scientist in the laboratory. The latter has organized impulses into dispositions of inquiry.

If inquiry involves handling things, moving about, uncovering, mixing things up and dividing them, talking and listening, then the traditional classroom with its neat rows of desks (often made to fit adult bodies) and the rigid discipline of sitting still, of talking only when reciting, of minimal interactions with other students and the teacher are not conducive to the child's growth in intellectual functions. The student's laboratory is a world to be investigated, parts of it are to be experimented with, and the world is not confined to the space within the walls of a classroom. The new classroom is one in which the walls have been pushed apart and the student moves out into the fresh air of a living, changing, developing world, a world of rocks and plants and animals, of human beings with their social activities and organizations in which the child lives and moves and "finds out" for itself. The process of finding out is a delight to the child because it is the self feeling its way into new and exciting experiences.

As the child moves in its natural and social environment, some stimuli are agreeable, while others are disagreeable. There may be causes for this condition, some perhaps due to the physical constitution of the child, some learned, and some conditioned. It is a basic fact of organic life, however, that we tend to repeat experiences which are agreeable and to disregard those which are disagreeable. When the pragmatic naturalists take note of this elementary fact of human life and capitalize upon it in their views of the educative process, the critics from the traditional school often reply that this starting place is definitely wrong, for the latter believe that the learning process should be laborious and painful, and if anyone who learns finds it a delightful experience, then it must be due to coddling and pampering the child. The experimental test of these two theories must be brought back to the child's own life development; the pragmatic naturalists show that the child's life is intellectually more adept, socially better adjusted in controlling its experiences, aesthetically more creative, and morally more fulfilling, when learning is a delight.

Often the distinction is made between the immaturity of children and the maturity of adults, and these two concepts are set in opposition to each other.[41] Immaturity in the traditional sense is taken to mean that the child is deficient in adult ways. The pragmatic naturalists think of immaturity in a different way; immaturity means capacity or potentiality. In the older view of immaturity the child is thought to be a kind of modeling clay to be shaped into the image of an adult. The child's interactions with its world at its level of experience are ignored. The child's future is mapped out in advance. This procedure leaves the child no choice; it lives at the mercy of the adults who groove its capacities from the beginning, and it is censured and punished when it does not conform. This procedure thwarts the child's attainment of its own individuality, and in the long run society suffers because of the sealing in of the child's creative powers.

The pragmatic naturalists claim that the child has plasticity, a plasticity which, at first, refers to the child's random activities, to its energetic impulsion.[42] These impulses take on meaning from the adult world, it is true, but the important point is how the impulsive activities of a child are given meanings and how these meanings function in a creative life. Impulsive activities are the springboards to new experience; they are the activities and movements which can be guided either by the child itself (and this is the ideal way) or by others toward a galaxy of goals, purposes, and ideals. The uncritical handling of a child's impulses and the dogmatic censorship of many of its actions can produce a smoldering resentment and can result in a violent revolt against the adults with whom it has direct interactions and against the members of the larger society with whom it has indirect interactions.

Impulsive activities become clustered around a habit. Habits are ways of behaving; they are generalized in that they cover a variety of activities which cut across situations occurring in different times and places, but which become organized into pervasive kinds. The habit of driving an au-

tomobile illustrates this point. Alertness in selective perception, caution as to the conditions of the road and of
traffic, fear of accidents are some of those impulses which
cluster around the habit of driving. Manipulating the steer-
ing wheel, working the accelerator pedal and the brake,
watching for signals and signs, listening for horns and sirens,
and many others, are activities involved in the occasion in
the exercise of the habit of driving an automobile. Habits are
the way the organs of the body establish control within the
environment. Habits are like tools in that they enable one to
use natural conditions as a means to an end. Habits have a
way of projecting themselves into new situations; they are
persistent and pervasive. Well-formed habits offer economy
and effectiveness in the control they secure. They are means
of accommodation when the environment cannot be
changed. Habits are creative when they are means of adaptation, when parts of an individual's life can be made over.

It is important for the adult teacher to develop a theory
of human nature and to capitalize upon the processes which
are already moving in a child's life. Usually there have been
three ways by which the child is approached.[43] The oldest
and most common method of approach to the child is that of
control. Control means that certain life processes moving in
a child's life are ignored and there is an authoritarian attempt to groove the behavior of the child in ways acceptable
to the adult. Naturally, there is some resistance in the impulsive activity of the child when this is done, and, in adult
terms this resistance is often called "stubborn," "hard-
headed," "recalcitrant," and "strong-willed." Discipline is
needed, according to the authoritarian view, a discipline
which crushes the ongoing impulses, which curbs them, denies them an outlet for expression, and which seeks to control them by forcing them into adult patterns. This approach
to a child's life makes it feel like a prisoner, cowed and un-
loved.

A second means of approaching the child is by means of

what may be called *direction*. Here the main emphasis is upon directing the child to a predetermined goal, an end which does not take account of the capacities of the child or the means by which it can move from where it is to some higher plateau of understanding and control. Too often direction means the ability to carry out orders of an adult, even though the adult sees the situation as one in which the child is assuming responsibility for its own future. This approach to the child imposes upon its impulses an authoritarian plan of development, and it stresses the discipline of school as the preparation for future life. The approach ignores the capacities, impulses, and desires of the child; it is told that it must develop other attitudes than those which are expressed. Furthermore, this approach often takes the course of pointing out the end or goal the child is to achieve without aiding it with the means by which the goal is to be accomplished.

A third approach to a child's development is that of *guidance*. The pragmatic naturalists find this approach the best means of bringing the child to a fruitful educational experience. Guidance is a kind of cooperation of teacher and child. The teacher recognizes that the child has its own personality structure and functions; that is, it has impulses, habits, meanings, and some methods of accommodation and some methods of adaptation already moving in its life experience. On this view, the teacher works with the capacities of the child, not against them. Capacities are taken in a broad sense; for instance, physical dexterity must not be grooved into or toward any particular occupation. Reflex actions, ability to manipulate objects, sense of rhythm, adeptness with symbols, and so on, have hundreds of different outlets in a culture where occupations and professions are not inherited. The teacher makes his or her own activities and those of the child work together. Joint activity in the uses of the immediate environment involves sharing the meanings of physical and cultural elements in the situation in which learning takes place. It should be remembered that physical things, for instance, have no meanings within themselves; they are given meanings by the way they interact with one another and by the way they function in a culture. The teacher shares these meanings with the child. Since the human organism very early sets up goals or ends-in-view, the setting up of goals within the child's immediate situation is important. The goal must belong to the child or one worked out in cooperation with the teacher, not a goal imposed from without. Once some goal, which the child cares for, is adopted, the child can move toward the goal by a kind of internal impulsion. Although some specific goal chosen by the child, the drive and effort expended, do not impress the adult as important and effective, there are no shortcuts to intelligent self-direction. Internal direction is not something which can be commanded or produced effectively by scolding or by bribing.

Understanding a child's impulses and habits is most important for a philosophy of guidance. The manner in which habits are changed or modified and impulses reconstructed is significant. Dewey writes: "We cannot change habit directly: that notion is magic. But we can change it indirectly by modifying conditions, by an intelligent selecting and weighing of the objects which engage attention and which influence the fulfillment of desires."[44] The intelligent teacher selects an object which engages attention. This procedure is not easy, for what engages attention in one child will not engage attention in another. Even when the attention is created, there is the further problem of the attention span of individual children, a span which changes from age to age of the child and which varies from individual to individual. The particular object chosen to engage attention cannot be prescribed in education texts; this must be left to the ingenuity of the teacher. The object must be an element in the present situation which the child can seize upon to start a sequence of activity toward an end-in-view which is related to it. The orderly sequence from object of attention to end-in-view carries with it its own disciplines of impulses, habits, perceptual selection, and control.

Guidance excludes freedom of activity where this means "uncontrolled activity." The permissive attitude so often identified with "progressive" education is the opposite of extreme authoritarianism, and neither of these philosophies is supported by the pragmatic naturalists. The goal sought by Dewey and others is the child's own internal development and control of its life and environment. This condition cannot be developed by allowing the child to follow any and every impulse which emerges in its consciousness; this procedure makes the child's life chaotic. And internal control cannot be achieved by authoritarian means; this procedure makes the child's life dull and conformist.

The emphasis upon the teacher taking account of the ongoing life of the child resulted in a view which came to be called "life-centered" education. From what has been said, it might be thought that the child-centered approach in the educational process excludes the consideration of subject matters. This contention would be a mistake, for subject matters are important in the educational process. The ongoing activities of the child are emphasized by Dewey because in traditional education the child's impulses, habits, goals, capacities, and personality functions have been ignored. In *The Child and the Curriculum* Dewey shows that both elements, the child's life and the subject matters of knowledge, are vitally important.[45] He thinks that there is no gap "in kind" between the experiences of children and the subject matters studied. The basic elements in the child's experience are the same as those in the logically organized subject matters of textbooks. The child's ongoing activities and the logically organized subject matters are both essential, and the teacher is an expert guide in bringing these together in an educational experience. This must be done in such a way that the experience of learning is vital and a personal one for the child. The activities engaged in, the symbols used, the goals achieved must be integral to the child's life. If the symbols used in communication are foreign to the child, it may be made to repeat them, of course, but they will remain outside of its meaningful experience. Furthermore, if outside motivation, such as pushing, drilling, prodding, or sugarcoating, is used, then the child will not have a lively interest in learning as an experience worthwhile in itself. When such methods fail, too often the adult blames the child for not being concerned and interested. The fault is not with the child but with the adult who will not take the time to understand the child and to engage its impulsive activities in the direction of the logically oriented subject matters.

Emphasis upon the concern and care for the development of the individual child in the educative process may lead to the inference that this kind of individualism is antisocial or, at least, is unconcerned with the social dimensions of an individual's life. It is true that individuality is an important value for pragmatic naturalists. Individuality, however, is a social concept. An individual is not isolated from nature or from other human beings; one lives and moves and accomplishes one's life fulfillment in a society. Dewey thinks that the terms "individual" and "social" should be hyphenated so that "individual-social" indicates that each term is an abstraction from an ongoing process. Furthermore, he thinks that the word "individualism" is ambiguous. The kind of individualism he rejects is that "laudation of selfish energy in industrial accomplishment with insistence upon uniformity and conformity in mind."[46] "Individuality," he thinks, is a better term, for it suggests "uniqueness of quality, or at least distinctness."

Dewey has been an outspoken critic of the attempt to classify individuals into a kind of social stratification through mental testing or intelligence tests. This procedure, he claims, ignores specific individualities, and it imposes a caste system of fixed intellectual classes. It is a method of classification, not discrimination, and results in a classification which represents "mediocrities instead of individualities." He says that the division of children into superior, middle, and inferior classes ignores their most cherished qualities as individuals. "An individual is not conceived as an individual with his own distinctive perplexities, methods, and rates of operation."[47] The method fails to deal with individualized minds and characters and submerges individuals in "averaged aggregates." If mental tests are employed, they should be used to aid in the determination of the individual's needs.

Individuality is not a gift, either from nature or society; it is an achievement. This idea is a common theme running through all of the writings of Peirce, James, Mead, and Dewey. The conditions of achievement of individuality involve the energetic impulsions of the individual guided by his own choosing of social, of intellectual, aesthetic, and moral ideals; on the other hand, the achievement of individuality rests upon a condition in which society values the contributions of its individual members. When both of these conditions are met, then society and the individual are no longer viewed as separate entities but as aspects of one process of a creative life and culture.

Suggested Order of Readings

1. Dewey, *Democracy and Education* (New York: Macmillan Company, 1916). Chap. 1, "Education as a Necessity of Life"; Chap. 2, "Education as a Social Function."
2. James, *Talks to Teachers on Psychology: And to Students on Some of Life's Ideals* (New York: W. W. Norton & Company, Norton Library, 1958). Chaps. 1–4.
3. Mead, *George Herbert Mead: Selected Writings*, ed. Andrew J. Reck (Indianapolis: Bobbs-Merrill Company, 1964). "The Psychology of Social Consciousness Implied in Instruction," pp. 114–22.
4. Mead, "The Relation of Play to Education," *University of Chicago Record* 1, no. 8 (22 May 1896): 141–45.
5. Dewey, *Experience and Education* (New York: Macmillan Company, 1938). Chap. 1, "Traditional vs. Progressive Education."
6. Dewey, "Individuality, Equality and Superiority," *The New Republic*, 13 December 1922. Reprinted in *Characters and Events*, vol. 2 (New York: Henry Holt and Company, 1929), pp. 486–92.

Notes

INTRODUCTION

1. Dewey, *Logic: The Theory of Inquiry* (New York: Henry Holt and Company, 1938), pp. iii–iv.
2. John S. Brubacher, *Modern Philosophies of Education*, 3d ed. (New York: McGraw-Hill Book Company, 1962), p. 312.
3. Dewey, "The Development of American Pragmatism," in *Philosophy and Civilization* (New York: Minton, Balch & Company, 1931), p. 13.
4. Dewey, *Experience and Nature*, 2d ed. (London: George Allen & Unwin, 1929), p. 151.
5. I am indebted to Charles Morris for the term "The Pragmatic Movement"; see his *The Pragmatic Movement in American Philosophy* (New York: George Braziller, 1970).
6. See, for instance, the following selected works about Peirce: Justus Buchler, *Charles Peirce's Empiricism* (New York: Harcourt, Brace and Co., 1939); James K. Feibleman, *An Introduction to Peirce's Philosophy* (New York: Harper and Bros., 1945); W. B. Gallie, *Peirce and Pragmatism* (Harmondsworth: Penguin Books, 1952); Thomas A. Goudge, *The Thought of C. S. Peirce* (Toronto: University of Toronto Press, 1950); Thomas S. Knight, *Peirce* (New York: Washington Square Press, 1965); Edward C. Moore and Richard S. Robin, eds., *Studies in the Philosophy of Charles Sanders Peirce*, 2d ser. (Amherst: University of Massachusetts Press, 1964); Murray Murphey, *The Development of Peirce's Philosophy* (Cambridge: Harvard University Press, 1961); Manley Thompson, *The Pragmatic Philosophy of C. S. Peirce* (Chicago: University of Chicago Press, 1953); Philip Wiener and Frederich H. Young, eds., *Studies in the Philosophy of Charles Sanders Peirce* (Cambridge: Harvard University Press, 1952).

Selected works about James: Gay Wilson Allen, *William James: A Biography* (New York: Viking Press, 1967); Bernard

F. Brennan, *William James* (New York: Twayne Publishers, 1968); Walter Robert Corti, ed., *The Philosophy of William James* (Hamburg: Felix Meiner Verlag, 1976); E. C. Moore, *William James* (New York: Washington Square Press, 1965); Lloyd Morris, *William James: The Message of the Modern Mind* (New York: Charles Scribner's Sons, 1950); Ralph Barton Perry, *The Thought and Character of William James*, 2 vols. (Boston: Little Brown and Company, 1935); John K. Roth, *Freedom and the Moral Life: The Ethics of William James* (Philadelphia: Westminster Press, 1969); John Wild, *The Radical Empiricism of William James* (Garden City, N.Y.: Doubleday & Company, 1968); Bruce Wilshire, *William James and Phenomenology: A Study of the "Principles of Psychology"* (Bloomington: University of Indiana Press, 1968).

Selected works about Mead: Walter Robert Corti, ed., *The Philosophy of George Herbert Mead* (Winterthur: Archiv für genetische Philosophie, 1973); Grace Chin Lee, *George Herbert Mead: Philosopher of the Social-Individual* (New York: Kings Crown Press, 1945); David L. Miller, *George Herbert Mead: Self, Language, and the World* (Austin: University of Texas Press, 1973); Maurice Natanson, *The Social Dynamics of George H. Mead* (The Hague: Martinus Nijhoff, 1973); J. W. Petras, ed., *George Herbert Mead: Essays in His Social Philosophy* (New York: Teachers College Press, 1968); Paul E. Pfuetze, *Self, Society, and Existence: Human Nature and Dialogue in the Thought of George Herbert Mead and Martin Buber* (New York: Harper Torchbooks, 1961).

Selected works about Dewey: George Dykhuizen, *The Life and Thought of John Dewey* (Carbondale and Edwardsville: Southern Illinois University Press, 1973); Richard J. Bernstein, *John Dewey* (New York: Washington Square Press, 1966); Jo Ann Boydston, ed., *Guide to the Works of John Dewey* (Carbondale and Edwardsville: Southern Illinois University Press, 1970); George R. Geiger, *John Dewey in Perspective* (New York: McGraw-Hill Book Company, 1964); James Gouinlock, *John Dewey's Theory of Value* (New York: Humanities Press, 1972); Sidney Hook, *John Dewey: An Intellectual Portrait* (New York: John Day Company, 1939); Robert J. Roth, *John Dewey and Self-Realization* (Englewood Cliffs, N.J.: Prentice-Hall, 1962); Paul Arthur Schilpp, ed., "The Library of Living Philosophers," *The Philosophy of John Dewey* (Evanston and Chicago: Northwestern University, 1939); Morton

White, *The Origin of Dewey's Instrumentalism* (New York: Columbia University Press, 1943); Arthur Wirth, *John Dewey as Educator* (New York: John Wiley & Sons, 1966).
Selected Works about pragmatic naturalism: A. J. Ayer, *The Origins of Pragmatism* (San Francisco: Freeman, Cooper and Company, 1968); John L. Childs, *American Pragmatism and Education* (New York: Henry Holt and Company, 1956); Edward C. Moore, *American Pragmatism: Peirce, James, and Dewey* (New York: Columbia University Press, 1961); Charles Morris, *The Pragmatic Movement in American Philosophy* (New York: George Braziller, 1970); Darnell Rucker, *The Chicago Pragmatists* (Minneapolis: University of Minnesota Press, 1968); Israel Scheffler, *Four Pragmatists: A Critical Introduction to Peirce, James, Mead, and Dewey* (New York: Humanities Press, 1974); Herbert W. Schneider, *A History of American Philosophy* (New York: Columbia University Press, 1946); H. S. Thayer, *Meaning and Action: A Critical History of Pragmatism* (Indianapolis: Bobbs-Merrill Company, 1968).

7. The reasons for Peirce's dismissal at Johns Hopkins University are not fully known; see Thomas S. Knight, *Charles Peirce* (New York: Washington Square Press, 1965), p. 15.

8. Philip P. Wiener, "The Evolution and Pragmaticism of Peirce," *Journal of the History of Ideas* 7 (June 1946): 321–50.

9. Charles Hartshorne and Paul Weiss, eds., *Collected Papers of Charles Sanders Peirce*, vols. 1–6, (1934–35; reprinted, Cambridge: Belknap Press of Harvard University Press, 1960).

10. Arthur W. Burks, ed., *Collected Papers of Charles Sanders Peirce*, vols. 7–8 (Cambridge: Harvard University Press, 1958).

11. Philip P. Weiner, ed., *Values in a Universe of Chance: Selected Writings of Charles S. Peirce, 1839–1914* (Garden City, N.Y.: Doubleday & Company, Anchor Books, 1958), p. ix.

12. James, *The Letters of William James*, edited by his son, Henry James, 2 vols. (Boston: Atlantic Monthly Press, 1920), 1:10.

13. Ralph Barton Perry, *The Thought and Character of William James: Briefer Version* (1948; New York: Harper and Row, Harper Torchbooks, 1964), p. 2.

14. Mead, *The Philosophy of the Act*, edited with an Introduction by Charles W. Morris, in collaboration with John M. Brewster, Albert M. Dunham, and David L. Miller; biographical notes by Henry C. H. Mead (Chicago: University of Chicago Press, 1938), p. lxxv.

15. Ibid., p. lxxvi.
16. Mead, *The Philosophy of the Present*, edited with an Introduction by Arthur E. Murphy, and prefatory remarks by John Dewey (La Salle, Ill.: Open Court Publishing Company, 1932).
17. Ibid., p. xl.
18. Dewey, "From Absolutism to Experimentalism," in George P. Adams and Wm. Pepperell Montague, eds., *Contemporary American Philosophy: Personal Statements* (London: George Allen & Unwin, 1930), 2:13.
19. The three editions of Dewey's *Psychology* have been collated and edited by the Center for Dewey Studies, Jo Ann Boydston, general editor, Southern Illinois University. Dewey, *Psychology*, vol. 2 of *The Early Works of John Dewey, 1882–1898* (Carbondale and Edwardsville: Southern Illinois University Press, 1968).
20. James, *Letters of William James*, 2:201–2; see letter to Mrs. Henry Whitman. See also, Darnell Rucker, *The Chicago Pragmatists (Minneapolis: University of Minnesota Press, 1968).
21. Boydston, ed., *The Early Works of John Dewey, 1882–1898*, 2:v.
22. C. Wright Mills, *Sociology and Pragmatism: The Higher Learning in America*, edited with an Introduction by Irving Louis Horowitz (New York: Paine-Whitman Publishers, 1964), p. 285. Mills refers to P. F. Douglas and J. B. Abbott.
23. Paul Arthur Schilpp, ed., *The Philosophy of John Dewey*, "The Library of Living Philosophers," 2d ed., rev. (New York: Tudor Publishing Company, 1951), p. 137.
24. Ibid., pp. 527–28.
25. James, *The Writings of William James: A Comprehensive Edition*, edited with an Introduction by John J. McDermott (New York: Modern Library, 1968), p. 429. When possible, subsequent references to this work will be made.
26. For recent works which show the phenomenological aspects in Mead and James, see: James M. Edie, "Notes on the Philosophical Anthropology of William James," in *An Invitation to Phenomenology: Studies in the Philosophy of Experience*, edited with an Introduction by James M. Edie (Chicago: Quadrangle Books, 1965), pp. 110–32; Maurice Natanson, *The Social Dynamics of George Herbert Mead* (Washington: Public Affairs Press, 1956); Bruce Wilshire, *William James and Phenomenology: A Study of the "Principles of Psychol-*

ogy" (Bloomington: Indiana University Press, 1968); John Wild, *The Radical Empiricism of William James* (Garden City, N.Y.: Doubleday & Company, 1968).

27. See note 6 above.
28. The John Dewey Society for the Study of Education and Culture was formed in February 1935. The society has sponsored a series of Yearbooks, Studies in Educational Theory, the Annual John Dewey Lecture, and the journal *Educational Theory*. The Charles S. Peirce Society was formed in 1946 with Paul Weiss as its first president. A journal is published in connection with the Society, *Transactions of the Charles S. Peirce Society*.
29. Amelie Rorty, ed., *Pragmatic Philosophy: An Anthology* (Garden City, N.Y.: Doubleday & Company, 1966), p. vi. Rorty says about this anthology: "I have also included some articles, such as those by Quine, Reichenbach, Carnap, and Putnam, which represent fairly radical adaptations and developments of some pragmatic theses by philosophers who would not consider themselves as falling primarily within the pragmatic tradition, but who nevertheless discuss the contemporary relevance and utility of the work of Peirce, James, and Dewey."

PART I: NATURE AND HUMAN LIFE

1. Peirce, *Collected Papers*, 1:402–3. The first number refers to the volume, and the numbers following refer to paragraphs, not pages.
2. James, *Talks to Teachers on Psychology* (1899; reprint ed., New York: W. W. Norton & Company, 1958), p. 33.
3. Dewey, *The Influence of Darwin on Philosophy and Other Essays* (1910; reprint ed., New York: Peter Smith, 1951), p. 19.
4. Dewey, *A Common Faith* (New Haven: Yale University Press, 1934), p. 15.
5. Ibid., p. 16.
6. Ibid.
7. Dewey, *The Quest for Certainty* (London: George Allen & Unwin, 1930), chaps. 1, 2.
8. James, "What Pragmatism Means," in *The Writings of William James*, p. 387.

9. Mead, *The Philosophy of the Act*, p. 641.
10. James, *The Varieties of Religious Experience* (1902; reprint ed., New York: Modern Library, 1936), p. 14.
11. Felix Kaufmann, "John Dewey's Theory of Inquiry," *Journal of Philosophy* 56 (1959): 826–36.
12. James, "The Continuity of Experience," in *The Writings of William James*, p. 293.
13. Dewey, *Experience and Nature*, chap. 1.
14. Richard J. Bernstein, "John Dewey's Metaphysics of Experience," *Journal of Philosophy* 58 (1961): 5–14; see also Gail Kennedy, "Comment on Professor Bernstein's Paper, 'John Dewey's Metaphysics of Experience,' " ibid., pp. 14–21.
15. Elizabeth Ramsden Eames and S. Morris Eames, "The Leading Principles of Pragmatic Naturalism," *Personalist* 43 (July 1962): 322–37.
16. Dewey, *Experience and Nature*, pp. 298–99.
17. Ibid., pp. 304–5.
18. Schilpp, ed., *The Philosophy of John Dewey*, p. 535.
19. Dewey, *Logic: The Theory of Inquiry*, pp. 23–24.
20. Eugene Freeman, *The Categories of Peirce* (Chicago: Open Court Publishing Company, 1934), pp. 57–58.
21. Murray G. Murphey, *The Development of Peirce's Philosophy* (Cambridge: Harvard University Press, 1961), p. 3.
22. James, *Essays in Radical Empiricism* (New York: Longmans, Green and Company, 1912), pp. 93–94.
23. James, "The Continuity of Experience," in *The Writings of William James*, p. 294.
24. Mead, *The Philosophy of the Present*, p. 68.
25. Mead, *Mind, Self, and Society from the Standpoint of a Social Behaviorist*; edited with an Introduction by Charles W. Morris (Chicago: University of Chicago Press, 1934), p. 130.
26. Mead, *The Philosophy of the Act*, p. 647.
27. James, "The Types of Philosophical Thinking," in *The Writings of William James*, p. 494.
28. Dewey, "The Vanishing Subject in the Psychology of James," *Journal of Philosophy* 37 (1940): 589–99.
29. Dewey, *Art as Experience* (New York: Minton, Balch & Company, 1934), p. 58.
30. Dewey, "The Reflex Arc Concept in Psychology," (1896); reprinted in *The Early Works of John Dewey, 1882–1898*, 5:96–109.
31. Dewey, *Logic: The Theory of Inquiry*, p. 30.

32. Dewey, *Human Nature and Conduct* (1922; reprint ed., New York: Modern Library, 1930), pp. 195–96.
33. Ibid., p. 196.
34. Mead, "A Behavioristic Account of the Significant Symbol," in *George Herbert Mead: Selected Writings*, edited with an Introduction by Andrew J. Reck (Indianapolis: Bobbs-Merrill Company, 1964), p. 244.
35. Ibid.
36. Mead, *Mind, Self, and Society*, pp. 177–78.

PART 2: KNOWLEDGE

1. Peirce, *Collected Papers*, 5:372.
2. Ibid., par. 379.
3. Ibid., par. 382.
4. Dewey, *Logic: The Theory of Inquiry*, p. 106.
5. Mead, *The Philosophy of the Act*, p. 82.
6. Dewey, *Logic: The Theory of Inquiry*, pp. 101–19.
7. Dewey, *How We Think* (Boston: D. C. Heath & Company, 1910), pp. 68–69.
8. Dewey, *How We Think*, rev. ed. (Boston: D. C. Heath & Company, 1933), pp. 102–18.
9. Mead, *The Philosophy of the Act*, pp. 79–91.
10. Peirce, *Collected Papers*, 5.376.
11. Dewey, *Logic: The Theory of Inquiry*, p 106.
12. Charles Morris, *Signs, Language, and Behavior* (New York: Prentice-Hall, 1946), p. 3.
13. Dewey, *Logic: The Theory of Inquiry*, p. 51.
14. Paul Weiss and Arthur W. Burks, "Peirce's Sixty-Six Signs," *Journal of Philosophy* 42 (1945): 383–88.
15. Peirce, *Collected Papers*, 2:228.
16. Mead, *Mind, Self, and Society*, pp. 42–45.
17. Ibid., pp. 45–46.
18. Peirce, *Collected Papers*, 5:388, 410.
19. Ibid., par. 390.
20. Ibid., par. 402.
21. James, "What Pragmatism Means," in *The Writings of William James*, pp. 377–78.
22. Ibid., p. 378.
23. Ibid., p. 380.

24. Dewey, *The Quest for Certainty*, p. 261.
25. Dewey, *Experience and Nature*, p. 90.
26. Peirce, *Collected Papers*, 6:189–209.
27. Dewey, *Logic: The Theory of Inquiry*, chap. 22.
28. Mead, *Mind, Self, and Society*, p. 126.
29. Dewey, *Logic: The Theory of Inquiry*, p. 47.
30. James, "What Pragmatism Means," in *The Writings of William James*, p. 379.
31. Peirce, *Collected Papers*, 5:402 n.
32. A. J. Ayer, *The Origins of Pragmatism* (San Francisco: Freeman, Cooper and Company, 1968), p. 5.
33. Knight, *Charles Peirce*, p. 14.
34. Peirce, *Collected Papers*, 5:172.
35. Ibid., par. 171.
36. Ibid.
37. Ibid., 1:562.
38. Ibid., par. 363.
39. Ibid., 5:169.
40. See May Brodbeck, "The New Rationalism: Dewey's Theory of Induction," *Journal of Philosophy* 46 (1949): 780–91; Paul Welsh, "Some Metaphysical Assumptions in Dewey's Philosophy," *Journal of Philosophy* 51 (1954): 861–67; see also the reply to Welsh by Elizabeth R. Eames, "Quality and Relation as Metaphysical Assumptions in the Philosophy of John Dewey," *Journal of Philosophy* 55 (1958): 166–69.
41. Dewey, *Logic: The Theory of Inquiry*, pp. 433–36.
42. Ibid., p. 124.
43. James, "Pragmatism's Conception of Truth," in *The Writings of William James*, p. 429.
44. James, "The Function of Cognition," in *The Writings of William James*, p. 149.
45. James, *The Meaning of Truth* (1909; reprint ed., Cambridge: Harvard University Press, 1975), p. 4.
46. James, "What Pragmatism Means," in *The Writings of William James*, p. 383.
47. James, *The Meaning of Truth*, p. 4.
48. James, "What Pragmatism Means," in *The Writings of William James*, p. 377.
49. Ibid., p. 388
50. Dewey, *Logic: The Theory of Inquiry*, p. 7.
51. Ibid., p. 8.
52. Ibid., p. 7.

53. Peirce, *Collected Papers*, 5:407.

54. Ibid., par. 565.

55. Mead, "A Pragmatic Theory of Truth," in *George Herbert Mead: Selected Writings*, p. 338.

56. Ibid., p. 338.

57. Ibid.

PART 3: VALUE

1. Stephen C. Pepper, "A Brief History of General Theory of Value," in *A History of Philosophical Systems*, ed. Vergilius Ferm (New York: Philosophical Library, 1950), pp. 493–503.

2. Dewey, "The Field of Value," in *Value: A Cooperative Inquiry*, ed. Ray Lepley (New York: Columbia University Press, 1949), p. 64.

3. Ibid., pp. 64–65.

4. Dewey, *The Quest for Certainty*, p. 243.

5. Dewey, *Theory of Valuation*, International Encyclopedia of Unified Science, vol. 2, no. 4 (Chicago: University of Chicago Press, 1939), p. 7.

6. Lepley, ed., *Value: A Cooperative Inquiry*, p. 6.

7. Dewey, *The Quest for Certainty*, pp. 245–46.

8. Dewey, *Experience and Nature*, p. 398.

9. Dewey, *Theory of Valuation*, p. 22.

10. Ray Lepley, ed., *The Language of Value* (New York: Columbia University Press, 1957).

11. James, "The Dilemma of Determinism," in *The Writings of William James*, p. 590.

12. Ibid., p. 598.

13. James, "The Moral Philosopher and the Moral Life," in *The Writings of William James*, p. 611.

14. James, "The Moral Equivalent of War," in *The Writings of William James*, pp. 660–61.

15. James, "The Moral Philosopher and the Moral Life," in *The Writings of William James*, p. 628.

16. Mead, "The Philosophical Basis of Ethics," in *George Herbert Mead: Selected Writings*, pp. 82–93.

17. Mead, "Scientific Method and the Moral Sciences," in *George Herbert Mead: Selected Writings*, pp. 248–49.

18. Dewey, *Theory of the Moral Life*, ed. Arnold Isenberg (New

York: Holt, Rinehart and Winston, 1960), pp. 8–10; reprinted from Dewey and James H. Tufts, *Ethics*, rev. ed. (New York: Henry Holt and Company, 1932).

19. Dewey, *Human Nature and Conduct*, p. 62.
20. Dewey, *Theory of the Moral Life*, pp. 11–12.
21. Dewey, *Human Nature and Conduct*, pp. 199–209.
22. Dewey and Tufts, *Ethics* (New York: Henry Holt and Company, 1908), pp. 364–68. See also, *Theory of the Moral Life*, pp. 55–56.
23. Kant, *Fundamental Principles of the Metaphysic of Morals*, trans. Thomas K. Abbot, ed. Marvin Fox (New York: Liberal Arts Press, 1949), p. 47.
24. Dewey, *Theory of the Moral Life*, pp. 77–88.
25. Ibid., p. 74.
26. Ibid., pp. 74–75.
27. Dewey, *Human Nature and Conduct*, pp. 238–47.
28. Dewey, *The Public and Its Problems* (New York: Henry Holt and Company, 1927), p. 6.
29. James, "On a Certain Blindness in Human Beings," in *The Writings of William James*, pp. 629–45.
30. James, *Varieties of Religious Experience*, p. 10.
31. Mead, *Philosophy of the Act*, p. 506.
32. Sidney Hook, *John Dewey: An Intellectual Portrait* (New York: John Day Company, 1939), p. 226.
33. Jerome Nathanson, *John Dewey: The Reconstruction of the Democratic Life* (New York: Charles Scribner's Sons, 1951). "The philosophy of John Dewey is the philosophy of democracy," p. 2.
34. Dewey, *The Public and Its Problems*, pp. 75–109.
35. Ibid., p. 90.
36. Ibid., pp. 50–51.
37. Ibid., pp. 12–13.
38. Dewey, "Democracy and Educational Administration," *School and Society* 45, no. 1162 (13 April 1937): 450.
39. Ibid., p. 459.
40. Dewey, *The Public and Its Problems*, pp. 150–55.
41. Ibid., p. 146.
42. Ibid., p. 203; see also, "Education and Social Change," *Social Frontier* 3, no. 20, p. 233; and *Freedom and Culture* (New York: G. P. Putnam's Sons, 1939), p. 128.
43. Reinhold Niebuhr, *Moral Man and Immoral Society* (New York: Charles Scribner's Sons, 1932), pp. xiii–xv.

44. Dewey, *Experience and Education* (New York: Macmillan Company, 1933), pp. 25–26.
45. Dewey, *Reconstruction in Philosophy* (New York: Henry Holt and Company, 1920), pp. 197–98.
46. Dewey, *The Public and Its Problems*, pp. 202–3.
47. Peirce, *Collected Papers*, 5:112.
48. James, "The Place of Affectional Facts in a World of Pure Experience," in *The Writings of William James*, p. 272.
49. Dewey, *Art as Experience*, p. 3.
50. Ibid., p. 15.
51. Mead, *Movements of Thought in the Nineteenth Century*, edited with an Introduction by Merritt H. Moore (Chicago: University of Chicago Press, 1936), p. 396.
52. Mead, *The Philosophy of the Act*, p. 455.
53. Dewey, *Art as Experience*, p. 77.
54. Mead, *The Philosophy of the Act*, p. 59.
55. Dewey, *Individualism: Old and New* (New York: Minton, Balch & Company, 1930), pp. 40–41.
56. Mead, *The Philosophy of the Act*, p. 458.
57. James, "Pragmatism and Religion," in *The Writings of William James*, p. 472.
58. James, "An Overview," in *The Writings of William James*, p. 803.
59. Peirce, *Collected Papers*, 6:500.
60. Ibid., par. 489.
61. Mead, *The Philosophy of the Act*, pp. 466–74.
62. Ibid., p. 478.
63. Ibid., p. 474.
64. James, *Varieties of Religious Experience*, pp. 31–32.
65. Dewey, *A Common Faith*, p. 2.
66. Ibid., p. 43.
67. Ibid., pp. 50–51.
68. Corliss Lamont, "New Light on Dewey's *Common Faith*," *Journal of Philosophy* 58 (1961): 21–28.

PART 4: EDUCATION

1. Dewey, *Democracy and Education* (New York: Macmillan Company, 1916), p. 384.
2. Dewey, "My Pedagogic Creed," *School Journal* 44 (1897): 77–80.

Reprinted in *The Early Works of John Dewey, 1882–1898*, V:84–95.

3. Dewey, *The School and Society*, rev. ed. (Chicago: University of Chicago Press, 1915). *The Child and the Curriculum* (Chicago: University of Chicago Press, 1902). Both works reprinted in one volume (Chicago: University of Chicago Press, Phoenix Books, 1956).

4. Dewey, *Lectures in the Philosophy of Education: 1899*, edited with an Introduction by Reginald D. Archambault (New York: Random House, 1966).

5. Dewey, *Experience and Education* (New York: Macmillan Company, 1938).

6. James, "Talks to Teachers on Psychology" first appeared in the *Atlantic Monthly* 83 (1898): 155–62, 320–29, 510–17, 617–26. These lectures were combined with others and published as *Talks to Teachers on Psychology and to Students on Some of Life's Ideals* (New York: Henry Holt & Company, 1898; also published, London: Longmans, Green & Co.; reprinted New York: W. W. Norton & Company, 1958).

7. Mead's most significant articles on education are: "The Relation of Play to Education," *University of Chicago Record* 1, no. 8 (22 May 1896): 141–45; "The Teaching of Science in College," *Science* 24 (1906): 390–97; "The Psychology of Social Consciousness Implied in Instruction," *Science* 31 (1910): 688–93.

8. Dewey, *The School and Society*, p. 11.

9. Dewey, "A Policy of Industrial Education," *New Republic* 1 (19 December 1914); reprinted in *Manual Training and Vocational Education* 16, no. 7 (March 1915): 393–97. Dewey wrote many articles on industrial education; for an exhaustive listing see Milton Halsey Thomas, *John Dewey: A Centennial Bibliography* (Chicago: University of Chicago Press, 1962).

10. Dewey, "A Policy of Industrial Education."

11. Rucker, *The Chicago Pragmatists*, p. 11 n.

12. Dewey, *Lectures in the Philosophy of Education: 1899*, p. 73.

13. Dewey, *Moral Principles in Education* (Boston: Houghton Mifflin Company, 1909), pp. 2–3.

14. Dewey, *Reconstruction in Philosophy*, p. 163; see also *Human Nature and Conduct*, pp. 189–98.

15. Dewey, *Democracy and Education* (1916; New York: Free Press, 1966), pp. 357–58.

16. Ibid., p. 360.

17. Ibid., p. 359.
18. Dewey, *Moral Principles in Education*, p. 11.
19. Dewey, *Theory of the Moral Life*, p. 98.
20. Dewey, *Art as Experience*, p. 18.
21. Dewey, "Art in Education," in *A Cyclopedia of Education*, ed. Paul Monroe (New York: Macmillan Company, 1911), 1:223.
22. Dewey, "The Aesthetic Element in Education," National Educational Association. *Journal of Proceedings and Addresses of the Thirty-Sixth Annual Meeting Held in Milwaukee, Wis., July 6–9, 1897* (Chicago: University of Chicago Press), p. 329.
23. Dewey, "Art in Education," p. 224.
24. Ibid., p. 224.
25. Ibid., pp. 224–25.
26. See, for instance, Jacques Maritain, *Education at the Crossroads* (New Haven: Yale University Press, 1943), pp. 12–14.
27. Dewey, *Democracy and Education* (Free Press), p. 52.
28. Ibid., p. 53.
29. Dewey, *How We Think*, p. 219.
30. Dewey, *Human Nature and Conduct*, p. 21.
31. Dewey, *Experience and Nature*, p. 412.
32. James, *Talks to Teachers on Psychology*, pp. 23–24.
33. Ibid., p. 27.
34. Dewey, "The Relation of Theory to Practice in Education," *Third Yearbook of the National Society for the Scientific Study of Education*, pt. 1 (Chicago: University of Chicago Press, 1904), p. 19.
35. James, *Talks to Teachers on Psychology*, p. 24.
36. Mead, "The Psychology of Social Consciousness Implied in Instruction," in *George Herbert Mead: Selected Writings*, p. 115.
37. Ibid., pp. 116–117.
38. Dewey, *Experience and Education*, pp. 23–52.
39. Mead, "The Relation of Play to Education," p. 141.
40. Ibid., p. 143.
41. Dewey, *Democracy and Education*, pp. 41–42.
42. Dewey, *Human Nature and Conduct*, pp. 95–105.
43. Dewey, *Democracy and Education*, p. 23.
44. Dewey, *Human Nature and Conduct*, p. 20.
45. Dewey, *The Child and the Curriculum*, p. 11.
46. Dewey, "Mediocrity and Individuality," *New Republic* (December 6, 1922); reprinted in *Characters and Events* (New York: Henry Holt and Company, 1929), 2:479.
47. Ibid., p. 482.

Index

DATE DUE

DEMCO 38-297